# Conquering
# Heart attack
# & Stroke

# Conquering
# Heart attack
# & Stroke

## Your 10 step self-defence plan

Published by Reader's Digest Association Ltd
London • New York • Sydney • Montreal

# medical experts

**WRITER**
Sheena Meredith MB BS

**CONSULTANT**
Dr Graham Jackson FRCP FESC FACC
Consultant Cardiologist, Guys & St Thomas Hospital

**WITH THANKS** to the British Heart Foundation,
The Stroke Association and Diabetes UK for their help and advice.

# about this book

If you're reading this page you've already taken your first step towards protecting yourself and your family from a heart attack or stroke. You'll soon discover that *Conquering heart attack & stroke – Your 10 step self-defence plan*, is clear and practical, giving you all the information you need to understand how problems arise, to assess your own or a loved one's vulnerability and to formulate a comprehensive strategy to fight back.

What's more, the advice in this book will help you to incorporate heart and brain-protecting habits into everyday life in easily manageable steps. You'll learn how ingredients like a hearty breakfast, laughter, sunshine, dark chocolate, friendship and red wine are all part of the recipe for a long, healthy life. You'll be able to decide which tactics best suit you and, because the self-defence plan is easy to adopt and enjoyable to maintain, you'll be motivated to persevere, so that your strategy evolves into long-term protection.

# how to use this book

If you're a 'grazer' when it comes to reading, you'll find that each chapter in the book is self-contained, so that you can dip in to find information fast on any topic of particular concern, be it the symptoms of a stroke or the best way to lose weight, assessing your own risk factors or choosing heart-friendly foods.

Though each chapter can be read individually, together they build into a coherent step-by-step plan that you can easily tailor to your own risks and needs. Chapter 1 will enable you to understand just what you're dealing with: the body-wide nature of the damage to arteries (the tiny tubes that carry blood around the body) that ultimately underpins most heart attacks and strokes, and the multiple factors that can affect your risk.

In chapter 2 you'll find out what happens during the course of a heart attack or a stroke and, most crucially, what actions to take. These events don't necessarily appear in the way they're portrayed on television or in films, and it's surprising how many people simply don't recognise what's happening right away, delaying vital treatment for themselves or their loved ones.

Next, we suggest that you do the comprehensive self-assessment in chapter 3. This will enable you to discover the factors that may influence your individual risk, so that you are aware which of these you need to take action against. Then in chapter 4 you'll be able to develop your own personalised plan to deal with your risks.

The subsequent chapters deal with specific areas of risk – your diet, your weight, your activity levels, your environment, and psychological factors. You'll know from your self-assessment which of these are most relevant for you, so you may want to concentrate on these first. But do read all the chapters, because together they will undoubtedly help you to build a unique and personal survival kit to defend yourself against both heart attacks and strokes. Then in the last chapter you'll learn how to keep your plan going to give you long-term protection for the rest of your life.

# Contents

**NOTE TO READERS**
While the creators of this work have made every effort to be as accurate and up to date as possible, medical and pharmacological knowledge is constantly changing. Readers are recommended to consult a qualified medical specialist for individual advice. The writers, researchers, editors and publishers of this work cannot be held liable for any errors and omissions, or actions that may be taken as a consequence of information contained within this work.

# introduction

While many people are aware of the dangers of heart attacks and strokes, relatively few realise that most of these events are, in essence, avoidable. Indeed, although both conditions now rank among the leading causes of death in most countries, at least 80 per cent of premature deaths linked to heart disease and strokes could be prevented by adopting simple measures, such as eating healthily, taking regular physical activity and avoiding the use of tobacco, according to the World Health Organisation. And as many as 90 per cent of first heart attacks could be avoided by making similar lifestyle changes, according to the landmark Interheart study involving 15,000 people from 52 countries. In *Conquering heart attack & stroke – Your 10 step self-defence plan* you'll discover simple ways to achieve these aims, and many more tactics that could dramatically reduce your personal risk.

Heart attacks and strokes are usually due to underlying cardiovascular disease, a condition featuring body-wide damage to the delicate lining of arteries, the tubes that carry oxygen and nutrient-rich blood to all the organs, tissues and cells in your body. You'll learn how the simple lifestyle changes you make to protect against heart attacks and strokes can dramatically cut your risk of many other conditions, too.

The advice in this book will help you to conquer linked problems such as obesity, high blood pressure, peripheral vascular disease and diabetes, and could also help you to reduce your risk of seemingly unrelated conditions such as arthritis, depression, osteoporosis and even cancer. It will help you to preserve your teeth, eyesight and hearing into old age, maintain strength, mobility and independence, and give you increased energy and joy in living.

## DEFENCE AGAINST 'DISEASES OF CIVILISATION'

That's because the same risk factors that can cause strokes and heart attacks are believed to underlie a host of other conditions. In fact, scientists are increasingly pinning a whole range of so-called 'diseases of civilisation' on, well, yes, our 'civilised' lifestyle – urbanised, stressed, sedentary, and over-fed but under-nourished.

By targeting the root causes, the strategies described here offer you personal protection against these modern enemies. Not only will following the plan enhance the rest of your life, it will probably prolong it. Studies show that people who adopt these tactics are less likely to die prematurely from heart disease, stroke or from any cause. Cardiovascular disease is among the most deadly of the 'diseases of civilisation'. Read on, and you'll be able to understand the threat, learn how to respond to an attack, and know just what you need to do to build up effective physical and mental defences. You'll understand the damaging role that Western diets, inactivity, stress and related factors play in the development of these disorders. And you'll see that this is potentially good news, because such lifestyle elements are within everyone's power to change.

## YOUR HEALTH, YOUR CHOICES

This is a book that encourages you to take positive action, rather than being a passive bystander to your own health, and to believe that heart disease and stroke can be beaten. It gives you all the information, tools and advice you need to combat cardiovascular disease in a coherent strategy that will enable you to take charge of your own health and to enjoy the benefits. Some goals may seem a challenge – but there are plenty of tips, tricks and some surprising suggestions to help you to stay with the plan and meet your goals.

Perhaps you've been told by your GP that you have high blood pressure or high cholesterol and are at increased risk. Possibly you are aware that your lifestyle is less than healthy and are already feeling the effects. Perhaps a friend, parent or sibling has been affected, or you may even have already suffered an attack.

Whatever your reasons for reading this book, and whatever your current health status, you'll find that it is a highly effective field manual of all the essential information you need to recognise warning signs, know when to act and what to do, assess your own risk, and minimise future threat. You'll also discover inspiring stories about people who have overcome cardiovascular conditions, or spotted the symptoms and rescued a loved one, or applied their skills to save a life. You'll gain understanding of the tactics you need to help yourself, as well as what medical input is required, and when, and how the latest screening tests, drug treatments and surgical techniques can help.

## CLEARING THE FOG OF MEDIA MESSAGES

The media constantly bombards us with messages about health. Television, newspapers, the internet – they're all crammed with medical stories, statistics and advice. The trouble is, when it comes to cardiovascular disease, many of them are gloomy, pessimistic or negative. We're all too fat, our favourite foods are potentially toxic, diseases such as diabetes are rocketing, heart attacks kill you, strokes result in permanent disablement, you should avoid everything you like, stop smoking, eat more fibre, take more exercise … It's often so off-putting that it's no wonder that many people simply tune out.

## WHY THIS PLAN REALLY WORKS

*Conquering heart attack & stroke – Your 10 step self-defence plan* has a different approach because the starting point is you. While the risk of succumbing to a heart attack or a stroke is a serious concern, and the thought of these threats is genuinely frightening, the aim of this book is to explain and provide information and solutions that will allay your fears. It may seem at times that the outcome of serious medical events is out of our hands, but the sort of knowledge you'll find here can help you to take control of your own destiny.

You'll also discover that protecting your health doesn't have to require Herculean effort, constant self-denial and a punishing routine of intimidating intensive cardiovascular workouts. This book doesn't plug some faddy diet, exercise craze or the latest wonder supplement. Instead, the advice spans the broad range of what today's medical experts now know about cardiovascular disease, and all the information is underpinned by authoritative medical facts and scientific studies. As well as explaining all the vital details that your doctor would tell you, if only he or she had all day to sit and chat about it, here you'll find information and advice that even your doctor may not be aware of. And you'll learn about the miracle tools that specialists can use to protect you, and how modern medicine can make a dramatic difference to your survival chances if you are threatened by stroke or heart attack.

## FAR FROM INEVITABLE

The book's clear message is that cardiovascular disease is not an inevitable consequence of getting older. In fact, it's eminently preventable, if you are aware of the key facts and risks underlying most cardiovascular disease. Even though most people don't think much about these dangers until they get to a certain age, it's never too late to make positive changes.

Of course, there are certain risk factors that you cannot alter – your gender, genes and family history, for example. But, as you'll learn, there is so much that you can do to counteract these. And while some damage may have been done by past bad habits, research reveals that much of this may be undone by taking appropriate action now, whatever your age or current state of health. So here you'll find the low-down on tried and tested ways to halt the progress of cardiovascular disease, combat the underlying causes, cut risk factors and boost your protection.

How do you achieve all this? You probably know that good nutrition, an active lifestyle and avoiding smoking are crucial. The book doesn't preach. You won't be encouraged to live on brown rice and lettuce leaves, pound the treadmill in the gym for hours each week (unless you want to) and drink nothing but water.

## ENJOYING LIFE IS THE KEY

Instead, you'll discover how healthy living can be a joy. You'll find out why a glass of red wine with dinner (at least one English hospital actually prescribes it to heart patients) and a square of luscious dark chocolate to follow can be a valid part of your defence plan. You'll learn about the heart-protecting effects of having fun, and why it is important to burn calories doing activities that you enjoy, whether it's singing, gardening or scuba diving. And how about the health benefits of watching a comedy film, chatting with friends or relaxing in the sunshine?

The message of *Conquering heart attack & stroke – Your 10 step self-defence plan* is that, whatever your risk (and almost everyone has some potential risk) you can reduce it and take charge of your health in a way that suits you. It's about making the most of everything modern medicine can offer while fighting these potential killers on your own terms. It's about enjoying life while empowering yourself to beat the threat of stroke and heart attack, recognising that the best person to protect you against disease, disability and premature death from these conditions is you. And, finally, the advice in this book doesn't simply aim to help you avoid these conditions, prevent disability and prolong life, but also to ensure that all those extra years you stand to gain are as healthy and happy as they can possibly be.

Sheena Meredith MB BS

# self-defence plan STEP 1

HEART ATTACK AND STROKE CAN AFFECT ALMOST ANYONE – BUT THE GOOD NEWS IS THAT MOST OF THE CAUSES ARE PREVENTABLE. STEP 1 SETS OUT THE BATTLEGROUND – THE BUILD-UP OF CONDITIONS THAT CAN PUT YOU AT RISK – AND REVEALS HOW A LITTLE KNOWLEDGE AND A FEW SIMPLE STRATEGIES ARE THE MOST POWERFUL DEFENCE.

# Know what
## you're up against

Every year hundreds of thousands of British people suffer a heart attack or a stroke. Such events may seem to occur without warning but are, in fact, almost always the result of underlying disorders and – as you'll discover – are far from inevitable if these conditions are prevented or treated in time.

Cardiovascular disease is the medical name for problems affecting the heart and blood vessels, which can so severely disrupt blood flow that a life-threatening heart attack or stroke occurs. Blood circulates constantly throughout the body, carrying to thousands of billions of cells the oxygen and the nutrients they need to survive. At the centre of this vast and wonderful delivery system is the heart, a powerful pump that drives blood along a network of 60,000 miles (100,000km) of blood vessels. Even when you are resting, it takes just over a minute for all 5 litres (nearly 9 pints) of your blood to be pumped around your body.

But what happens if something obstructs the flow? Just as a vehicle accident on a busy motorway may quickly lead to a serious pile-up, the consequences can be dangerous. The 10 steps described in this book will help you to not only counteract most of the risks but also to improve your general health and boost your chances of a long, active and happy life.

## LIFESTYLE CHANGES MAKE A DIFFERENCE

A wide range of factors contribute to the development of cardiovascular disease. Some, such as smoking, high blood pressure, lack of exercise and obesity, are well known. You may also be aware that stress can contribute to the dangers of heart attacks and stroke, that people with diabetes are more at risk of heart disease, or that high cholesterol levels in the blood can 'fur up' or 'harden' arteries, narrowing them and making both heart attacks and strokes more likely.

## FRESH CHALLENGES

There are other, more surprising conditions associated with cardiovascular disease that medical studies have uncovered in recent years. Excess abdominal fat, for example, has been shown to be an important risk factor, while snoring and gum disease may also be linked. This book offers a wealth of advice on how to assess and deal with these associated conditions, as well as a host of tips to inspire you to make the long-lasting changes that will protect you throughout your life.

## TACTICAL ADVANTAGE

If you are not actually ill, you may find it hard to believe that you are at risk. And research has shown that the younger you are, the less likely you are to accept that you could suffer a heart attack or stroke. Doctors in Israel proved this point when they examined the medical records of 41,000 young people. They found that more than one in ten knew that they had a family history of cardiovascular disease, yet these people were no more likely to take exercise or to avoid smoking than others with no genetic risk. What's more, they were more likely to be obese and to have treatable conditions such as high blood pressure or high blood sugar.

Reading the information in this book will give you a vital tactical advantage. You will realise how much you can do to help yourself – even if you have a family history of cardiovascular problems. Then, as you spot risks that might affect you personally, such as high blood pressure, you will learn how you can adapt your everyday life to reduce them.

## YOU ARE NOT ALONE

Just about everyone is vulnerable in some way – which is why cardiovascular disease is so potentially dangerous. But most of us can take some action to reduce that risk. For, as scientists understand more and

troubleshooting Q&A

### My uncle had a heart attack in his fifties. Am I at risk too?

Having a family history of heart disease does statistically increase your risk of developing a problem yourself and the closer the relative, the higher the risk. Tell your GP, and arrange to get your cholesterol and blood pressure checked regularly. And read on. You can't change your family history, but, as you'll discover, healthy lifestyle measures can substantially reduce your risk.

# an amazing transport system

**Y**our blood travels thousands of miles around your body carrying the oxygen and nutrients that you need to survive. The heart plays a central role, pumping out the oxygen-rich blood it receives from the lungs into arteries, which deliver it to thousands of billions of cells, and simultaneously pumping blood back through veins to the lungs to receive a fresh load of oxygen. The clearer your arteries, the more efficient the system.

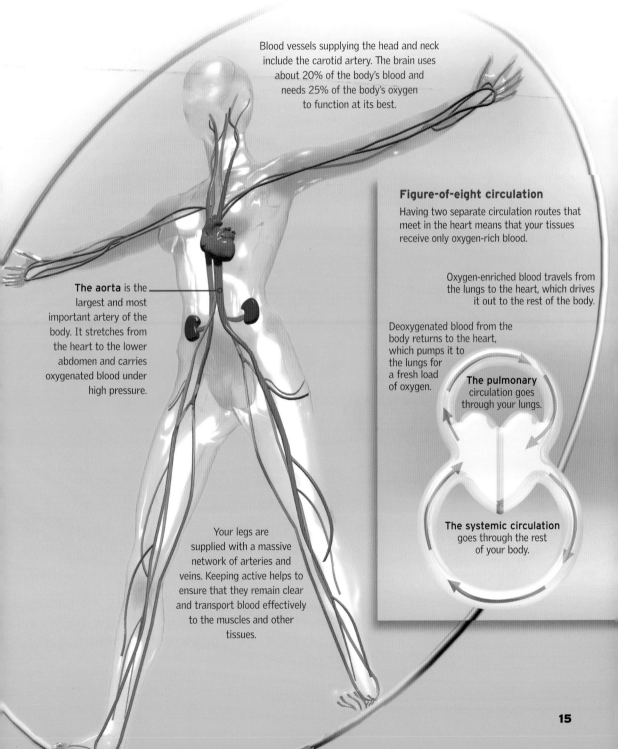

Blood vessels supplying the head and neck include the carotid artery. The brain uses about 20% of the body's blood and needs 25% of the body's oxygen to function at its best.

### Figure-of-eight circulation

Having two separate circulation routes that meet in the heart means that your tissues receive only oxygen-rich blood.

Oxygen-enriched blood travels from the lungs to the heart, which drives it out to the rest of the body.

Deoxygenated blood from the body returns to the heart, which pumps it to the lungs for a fresh load of oxygen.

**The pulmonary** circulation goes through your lungs.

**The systemic circulation** goes through the rest of your body.

**The aorta** is the largest and most important artery of the body. It stretches from the heart to the lower abdomen and carries oxygenated blood under high pressure.

Your legs are supplied with a massive network of arteries and veins. Keeping active helps to ensure that they remain clear and transport blood effectively to the muscles and other tissues.

more about how cardiovascular disease develops, one thing has become crystal clear: the way you live plays an important role. This book will give you the tools not only to reduce your risk but also to reverse some of the damage that may already have occurred inside your arteries.

## IT'S ALL ABOUT LIFESTYLE

Medical research indicates that lifestyle plays a huge role in determining an individual's likelihood of developing heart disease and there are many small adjustments that can dramatically improve your cardiovascular health. And this doesn't mean giving up all the little pleasures that make life worthwhile; defending yourself against heart attack and stroke need not be about self-denial.

You will discover how sensuous pleasures, such as consuming red wine or dark chocolate, having a massage or laughing with friends, can actually aid you in the fight. *Conquering heart attack & stroke* will show you how to incorporate these pleasurable defence strategies into everyday living. As a bonus, they'll also improve your general health.

# what causes the problem?

To reduce your risk of suffering from a heart attack or a stroke, it's worth trying to understand how and why cardiovascular disease occurs. It starts in a small way, with tiny changes in the walls of arteries that set off a process by which fats called lipids – together with cholesterol, calcium and other substances in the blood – are sucked into the arterial lining.

Gradually these fatty deposits build up and cause a narrowing of the inside of the arteries, which in turn restricts blood flow. At the same time, the deposits may harden, making the walls of the arteries thicker and less flexible, so that they are less able to expand and contract to regulate blood flow. That means that when you run, for example, your arteries are unable to widen to allow more oxygen-rich blood to flow to the muscles. You may find that you get out of breath quickly or start to experience chest pains.

The medical term for this is atherosclerosis – although it is frequently described as 'furring up' or 'hardening' of the arteries – and the substance that adheres to the arterial walls is called plaque. A build-up of plaque

# nine everyday changes that could save your life

**N**o matter where you live, and no matter what your age or gender, the findings of a landmark medical study published in 2004 hold an important message for everyone: a great deal of cardiovascular disease is preventable because most of its causes are linked to the way we live.

Known as the Interheart study, this worldwide examination of risk factors for heart disease provides compelling evidence that the daily lifestyle choices made by individuals can improve the health of their arteries and reduce their risk of heart attack and stroke. More than 15,000 men and women from 52 countries took part in the study. All had one thing in common: they had experienced a first heart attack. Participants were questioned about the details of their lifestyle, their medical and family history and their personal circumstances. They were given a physical examination, blood samples were taken, and they had their waist and hip circumferences measured. The results were then compared with those from healthy people living in the same communities.

When scientists analysed the mountain of data generated by the study, they came up with a startling finding: just nine factors accounted for 90 per cent of all first-time heart attacks. The study made it clear that, while rates of cardiovascular disease vary from country to country, in almost every geographic region, men and women of all ages and ethnic backgrounds are vulnerable for the same nine reasons.

On the basis of such research, the UK Department of Health insists that death from coronary artery disease – which claims one in three lives in Britain – is largely preventable. The message from Interheart is clear: change your lifestyle and live longer.

## the interheart 9

Each one of the nine risk factors identified by the Interheart study suggest that cardiovascular disease is far from inevitable. Each one is linked to unhealthy lifestyle choices, which can – with a few everyday changes – be modified to reduce your risk of both heart attack and stroke.

**1** Abnormal blood fats

**2** Smoking

**3** High blood pressure

**4** Diabetes

**5** Stress

**6** Obesity, especially abdominal obesity

**7** Eating too few fruits and vegetables

**8** A lack of daily exercise

**9** Excess alcohol intake

# the cholesterol story

**Y**ou hear a lot about cholesterol and it does play a significant role in the health of your heart and circulatory system. Cholesterol in the blood takes the form of small packages called lipoproteins, made up of lipids (fats) and protein. There are two kinds in your bloodstream – 'bad' LDL ('low-density lipoprotein) cholesterol and 'good' HDL (high-density lipoprotein) cholesterol. Too much LDL – often the result of eating a diet high in saturated fats – increases the risk of

atherosclerosis, the narrowing of the arteries that can lead to heart attacks and strokes. But HDL carries LDL cholesterol back to the liver for reprocessing and actually protects the heart.

If you have a high level of LDL cholesterol in your blood, the low-density lipoproteins can begin to adhere to the artery walls. This build-up contributes to the formation of plaque, which makes arteries narrower so blood cannot easily pass through to supply oxygen and nutrients. The sticky plaque attracts more plaque and a vicious circle begins.

inside the coronary arteries that supply blood to the muscle of the heart is a cardiovascular condition known as coronary artery disease. The narrowed arteries cannot supply sufficient oxygen-rich blood to the heart muscle to cope with periods of higher demand, such as during exercise.

## CHEST CRAMPS

One common symptom of coronary artery disease is pain or discomfort in the chest, known as angina. It can be brought on by physical activity, cold weather, intense emotions – such as anger – or even a heavy meal. Angina indicates that, at times of increased demand, your heart is desperately craving a better blood supply.

The symptoms are not unlike a muscle cramp after undertaking exercise, though the sensation of heaviness or tightness in your chest may spread to your arms, neck, jaw, back or stomach. The discomfort usually subsides within minutes, and will not cause any permanent damage to your heart. But it is an important wake-up call. You should consult your GP and consider how your diet and lifestyle might be affecting your health.

If the pain suddenly gets worse or occurs when you haven't exerted yourself and is not relieved by rest or medication, seek urgent medical help. Doctors call this 'unstable angina' and it can be caused by a small blood clot partially blocking a coronary artery. Unstable angina is very dangerous and indicates a much higher risk of a full-blown heart attack.

# a heart crisis

The most common cause of a heart attack is a blood clot that completely blocks a coronary artery, cutting off blood supply to the heart.

Scientists now know that so-called 'soft' plaque can be the dangerous trigger. Hard plaque contains more calcium and can grow relatively large, narrowing arteries, restricting blood flow and causing chest pain or high blood pressure. By contrast, 'soft' plaque, which causes less narrowing but is loaded with fatty deposits, can easily rupture without warning.

A rupture causes the lipids (blood fats) and other debris to spill out from the artery wall and form a clot which could block vital blood flow to an area of the heart muscle. The rupture of soft plaque is thought to be responsible for about 85 per cent of all heart attacks. Patches of soft plaque are also more difficult to detect as standard tests, such as CT scans, tend to measure calcium deposits, a sign of hard plaque.

## OTHER CAUSES

While clots are the most common cause, a heart attack can also occur if an artery goes into spasm, temporarily stopping the flow of blood. Atherosclerosis (narrowing of the arteries) can cause such a spasm – or it can be a reaction to drugs such as amphetamines or cocaine, viral infection, or smoking (particularly in women who also take the contraceptive pill), and even stress.

### PEOPLE WITH HEART DISEASE SHOULD TAKE LIFE EASY

**W**hether you suffer from angina or have had a heart attack or heart surgery, regular exercise is the best way to strengthen your heart muscle. Exercise helps to control blood pressure, cholesterol, weight gain and diabetes, and that usually means less medication. Crucially, exercise will reduce your risk of a further attack.

When the explorer Sir Ranulph Fiennes had a massive heart attack in 2003, he was rushed to hospital for double-bypass surgery. A few weeks later, while convalescing, he found that simply walking a few steps uphill made him breathless. He kept at it. From walking he progressed to jogging. Just four months later, Fiennes ran seven marathons on seven continents in seven days to raise money for the British Heart Foundation. In May 2009, aged 65, he conquered Mount Everest – the oldest Briton ever to reach the summit.

That's extraordinary, but anyone with heart disease can work some exercise into their lives. The best approach is to start on a modest scale and build it up gradually. In Step 7 you learn how.

Less common causes of heart attacks include:

● Clots or other 'debris' that travel from elsewhere in the body to lodge inside a coronary artery, a process known as coronary embolism.

● Clots that result from trauma, following an accident, or conditions in which blood thickens and more readily forms a clot, including, rarely, use of the contraceptive pill in women.

● Congenital abnormalities of the coronary arteries, present since birth.

● Certain rare conditions, such as thrombocytosis, where the 'stickiness' of the blood is increased, which can impede its flow and cause clots to form.

## WEAKENING THE WALLS

Atherosclerosis can cause other problems, too. The plaque build-up may weaken arterial walls, causing a swelling called an aneurysm. The intense pressure of blood flowing through the artery can cause the arterial wall to balloon out and, in extreme cases, to burst.

Family history raises the risk of aneurysm, as does smoking and high blood pressure. The most common site for an aneurysm is the aorta, the large artery, which carries blood down from the heart to the rest of the body. Without urgent treatment, a ruptured abdominal aortic aneurysm could be fatal.

Blocked arteries in other parts of the body may cause pain and a variety of other damaging effects. They can even result in disorders as serious as gangrene, when tissue dies because it is starved of blood.

## CHILDHOOD CONCERNS

These problems are not only affecting older people. In recent studies, signs of the fatty streaks on the inside of artery walls have been seen in youngsters, too – a development that worries scientists and health professionals. In a study of 294 adolescents at the Institute of Child Health in London, researchers noted blood vessel changes in teenagers as young as 13. Their artery walls were already losing elasticity.

**SECRET**weapon

### PULSE CHECK

For good reason, aneurysms are likened by some experts to ticking time-bombs: you get very little warning before a blood vessel bursts. However, there is one telling symptom of an abdominal aortic aneurysm (AAA) – the most common type – according to Jonothan Earnshaw, consultant vascular surgeon at the Gloucestershire Royal Hospital. Watch out for a pulsating sensation in the abdominal area, says Earnshaw. This is frequently accompanied by low back pain.

Older men are particularly at risk of AAA, so in 2009 the NHS launched a screening programme, in the form of a simple ultrasound scan, for every man over 65. But don't wait to be called. All men or women over 55 with a close relative who has had this type of aneurysm should ask their GP to arrange a scan. It could be life-saving.

The risk factors in children are the same as they are for adults – abnormal blood fats, high blood pressure, obesity and diabetes. In fact, the evidence that atherosclerosis can begin early in life is so powerful that GPs are being urged to take an active role in its prevention, by encouraging children who are overweight to modify their diet and to take more exercise. The Food Standards Agency (the UK's food watchdog) also recommends that children should be given semi-skimmed rather than full-fat milk from the age of two – to help to reduce their likelihood of developing cardiovascular problems in the future.

**A POWERFUL NUTRIENT**

Vitamin C helps our bodies to grow and to repair themselves. It is also an antioxidant, reducing the effect of harmful molecules called free radicals, which damage artery walls. In a small study, researchers at Boston University Medical Center found that vitamin C supplements can widen the arteries of patients with coronary artery disease. Two hours after patients had taken just one 2g vitamin C supplement, their arteries had expanded, while no change was seen in those who took a placebo (dummy medication). This suggests that vitamin C may even reverse some of the arterial damage caused by atherosclerosis.

## THE FOOD SOLUTION

Stopping the flow of harmful fats circulating in your bloodstream will help to keep your arteries clear and plaque-free, whatever your age. That means adjusting your diet in such a way that you avoid saturated fats and reduce your LDL cholesterol levels (see page 18). The most effective dietary changes you can make are explained in Step 5.

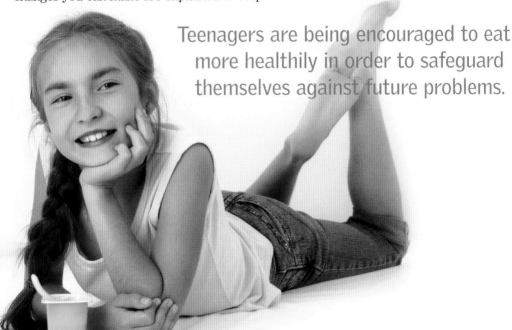

Teenagers are being encouraged to eat more healthily in order to safeguard themselves against future problems.

Continued on p24 ▶

# your body: **under attack**

**W**hen you think of inflammation, you may visualise a hot, red, tender area of skin – a site where your immune system is mounting a heated and healing defence against attack, as happens when a cut becomes infected. In much the same way, our immune system is programmed to react against what it sees as microbial invaders in our arteries. Scientists are discovering more about the key role played by this internal 'inflammation' in the artery-damaging process called atherosclerosis.

Medical researchers no longer believe that high blood cholesterol is the only culprit in atherosclerosis – the process whereby fat-laden plaque is deposited on arterial linings. Most experts now acknowledge that the whole process of arterial damage is set off and sustained by inflammation.

What happens is that white blood cells – the frontline troops in our body's immune system – are attracted by the sludge-like plaque deposits inside artery walls. They bombard these deposits with chemicals, which in turn helps to create more plaque, and to prompt plaque to rupture, causing the formation of blood clots and leading to heart attack. At high levels, inflammation can double or even quadruple the risk of heart attack.

The theory of this inflammation 'cascade' fits well with research showing that many of the traditional risk factors linked to heart attacks and strokes, such as high blood cholesterol levels, high blood pressure, diabetes and obesity, are factors which also provoke inflammation.

## INFLAMMATION DETECTORS

Doctors hope to use this new understanding of how inflammation underlies atherosclerosis in order to predict the risk of heart attack and stroke much earlier than was possible in the past. Several chemicals found in the bloodstream act as 'markers' of inflammation in the body. One of these, known as CRP (C-reactive protein), increases when inflammation is present and can be valuable in monitoring disease activity. Increased CRP levels have also been linked with other cardiovascular risk factors, such as

**RED**alert

**FAT AND UNFIT?**

**O**besity increases the risk of inflammation, according to a study of 452 men published in the *British Journal of Sports Medicine*. The study found that white-blood-cell counts were lowest in men who were physically fit and highest in those who were most overweight. On average, the higher a man's proportion of body fat, the higher his white-cell count, supporting evidence that fat cells actually produce inflammatory chemicals. The researchers also noted that being fit seemed to counteract the effect of extra fat, suggesting that physical fitness plays a large role in combating inflammation.

smoking, high cholesterol and abdominal obesity. On the other hand, eating plenty of fish and having higher levels of vitamin C have been linked with lower CRP levels. (The role of key protective foods is discussed in Step 5.)

## SENSITIVE BLOOD TEST

Recently, a new way of measuring inflammation related more specifically to the risk of heart disease has been developed, known as a high-sensitivity CRP test, or hsCRP. Research has shown that hsCRP levels are elevated years in advance of an individual's first heart attack or ischaemic stroke, and raised levels are highly predictive of recurrent heart attacks and strokes, diabetes and death from cardiovascular disease. Cardiologists already use hsCRP as part of a combined test – which also measures levels of cholesterol and the blood fats known as triglycerides – to give the clearest profile yet of cardiovascular risk. At present, however, the test is not widely available in the UK.

Keeping fit greatly reduces your risk of the type of inflammation that sparks off arterial damage.

# stroke is a **brain attack**

Atherosclerosis can affect all arteries in the body, so it is not only your heart that could suffer damage. When plaque builds up on the carotid arteries supplying blood to the brain, narrowing the vessels and restricting blood flow, it is known as cerebrovascular disease. While there is no brain equivalent of angina – you won't get a headache, for instance – the blood flow to your brain is generally lowered and less oxygen and fewer nutrients may get through to critical areas.

This is thought to be one of the reasons why older people may complain that they can't think clearly – they become more forgetful, for example, and have trouble concentrating and processing ideas as fast as they once could. Significantly, this is especially true of people who have been diagnosed with high blood pressure or cardiovascular disease.

## WHAT TYPE OF STROKE?

Strokes are rather more complicated than heart attacks. The majority of them, called ischaemic strokes, are caused by a clot blocking a blood vessel narrowed by atherosclerosis. The clot may have formed following a rupture of plaque, as happens in the most common form of heart attack (see page 19), or it may have travelled from the heart, from one of the arteries in the neck or elsewhere in the body. Clots that move through the bloodstream in this way are known as emboli, and when they lodge in the brain the event is called a cerebral embolism.

However, around one in five strokes is due to bleeding in the brain, following the tearing of an artery wall. This is known as a haemorrhagic stroke, and is particularly likely to occur in an individual with high blood pressure. The effects of a haemorrhagic stroke are often more severe than those of ischaemic stroke, and the treatment of the two types of stroke is very different, as explained on page 54.

# **identifying** the triggers

Both heart attacks and strokes are generally the result of atherosclerosis that has built up over decades, but the culmination of this process in a sudden attack is often preceded by an event known as a trigger.

Triggers have one thing in common: they prompt the nervous system to flood the body with stress hormones, putting strain on the heart and blood vessels. A trigger factor can result in a sudden surge in blood pressure or make the heart beat faster – occasionally beyond the point at

## I use the contraceptive pill. Does this make me more at risk?

Probably not much, if at all. Very early types of contraceptive pill contained high doses of oestrogen that could increase the risk of blood clots, and some studies suggested that older women who took the pill in its early days had a slightly increased risk of cardiovascular disease – but only while taking it. The hormone doses now used in the pill are much lower, and don't seem to increase the risk of heart attack in young women with no other risk factors (such as smoking, diabetes or high blood pressure). And although the Pill does increase the chance of having a stroke, the risk is tiny – about 1 in 24,000 per year among women taking the Pill who don't smoke and have normal blood pressure. That's less than the risk of being killed in a road accident.

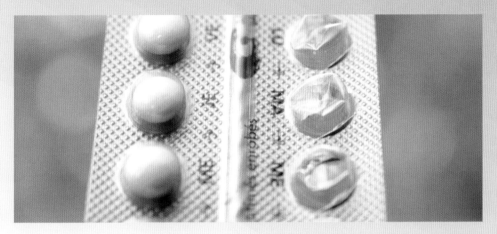

which it is able to cope with the extra workload. Some triggers narrow blood vessels, prompt clots to form or increase damage to the lining of arterial walls. Others may lead to a tear in a blood vessel or an erratic heart rhythm that may cause the heart to stop altogether.

Later in this book you will discover more about risk elements and the steps you can take to halt, and even reverse, the process of atherosclerosis. You will also learn about a whole range of factors that can trigger a heart attack or a stroke – ranging from a powerful emotion, such as anger, to a fat-laden meal or a bitterly cold day.

**RED**alert

### MINI-STROKES

A transient ischaemic attack (TIA), or mini-stroke, occurs if an artery supplying part of the brain becomes temporarily blocked, shutting off the blood supply. Any effects – such as slurred speech or a drooping facial muscle – are usually over in minutes, leaving no apparent damage, but may last as long as 24 hours.

However short-lived, a TIA should never be ignored. Without treatment, there is a one in four chance that someone who has had a mini-stroke will suffer a full-blown stroke within weeks. Even if symptoms appear to go away, it is important to seek urgent medical help.

To picture the effects of high blood pressure, think of a river forced into a narrow gorge: your blood hurtles against the walls of narrowing arteries, damaging the inner lining.

# silent enemy

**H**igh blood pressure is the main risk factor for stroke and a major risk factor for heart disease. If you have high blood pressure, you are three times more likely to develop heart disease or stroke, and twice as likely to die from one of the conditions, as people with lower levels.

Blood pressure is the force of blood flowing through your arteries and pushing against their vessel walls. You need some pressure to keep blood moving, but if the pressure is too high, the effect of blood pounding through the vessels thickens and hardens the arterial muscles, damaging the arteries' inner lining. Blood cells and fat deposits gather at the damaged areas, forming plaque. The consequence is a rapid acceleration in the furring of the arteries.

## Know your numbers

When did you last get your blood pressure checked? If you can't remember, make an appointment at your GP practice today. One in three people with high blood pressure don't know they have it – there are no obvious symptoms. Every day some 350 preventable strokes or heart attacks occur as a result of uncontrolled high blood pressure, so thousands of lives a year could be saved if more people were aware of the problem and had treatment to bring their blood pressure levels down.

When your blood pressure is measured, two readings are taken, expressed as an upper and a lower number. The upper number denotes systolic blood pressure, or the force on the artery walls when your heart is contracting to pump out blood. The lower number is the diastolic pressure, or the force when the heart is at rest between beats.

- A healthy reading is 120/80 or less (systolic pressure/diastolic pressure).
- A consistent reading of 140/90 or higher is diagnosed as high blood pressure, whatever your age, and requires treatment.

Blood pressure is measured in millimetres of mercury (mmHg). If your blood pressure is on the high side, a reduction of just 10mmHg in systolic pressure and 5mmHg in diastolic pressure will cut your risk of stroke by 38 per cent, with a 16 per cent risk reduction of heart disease.

# working out your
## personal risk

The nine risk factors identified by the worldwide Interheart study (see page 17) demonstrate that lifestyle is a major influence on cardiovascular health – and, by extension, that there are many things we can do to promote our own wellbeing – but they don't represent the full picture.

While lifestyle adjustments may have a beneficial effect on such factors as high blood pressure, high cholesterol, gum disease and obesity, there are a few things you cannot control, such as your age, your gender and whether you have a family history of cardiovascular problems. And the study doesn't mention your emotional state, which can play a role, too. Stress, loneliness, a lack of outside interests, pessimism and anger are all negative factors that – together with other risks – may make you more vulnerable. Then there are also environmental factors such as air pollution, extremes of cold or heat, excessive noise and toxic chemicals.

REDalert

**WORLD CUP WARNING**

Calm down! Getting distraught while watching your favourite football team lose a crucial match could trigger a heart attack. On the three days after the England team lost to Argentina in a penalty shoot out during the 1998 World Cup, hospital admissions for heart attacks soared by 25 per cent. An earlier study in the Netherlands revealed a 50 per cent increase in deaths from both heart attacks and strokes on the day the Dutch team was eliminated from the European football championship. There is one small consolation for female football fans – it was only the men who succumbed.

## POSITIVE INTERVENTION

As doctors become better at identifying those patients most at risk from heart disease and stroke, they will be better able to pinpoint the most effective preventive treatments. For example, they may give statins (cholesterol-lowering drugs which also lower inflammation) to those with a raised level of the inflammation-detecting protein CRP (see pages 22–23), irrespective of their blood cholesterol level. Since about half of all strokes and heart attacks occur in people with a normal blood cholesterol level, this is potentially very important. And, in one review involving 2,557 people monitored for an average of eight years, people with raised CRP levels ran twice the risk of a heart attack or stroke even after taking account of other known risk factors.

Increased understanding of the inflammation 'cascade' caused by the presence of plaque in the arteries (see page 22) also offers the prospect of better preventive treatment. Such treatment would be specifically

## GET MOVING

Appropriate exercise can do much to prevent, counteract or reverse the internal changes that underlie cardiovascular disease. Indeed, physical activity can have such beneficial effects on circulatory problems associated with diabetes and high blood pressure that, in some cases, it is possible for people who take up an exercise programme to reduce their medication or even to stop taking tablets altogether.

Exercise may help to ward off strokes as well. A study looking at the benefits of exercise in people aged 50 to 77 who were suffering from depression demonstrated that, after 16 weeks of exercise, participants displayed sharper memories and better planning and organisational skills – a result of the improved flow of oxygen-rich blood to the brain. The results suggest that exercise might be able to offset some of the decline in mental acuity linked to the ageing process.

Statins are often prescribed for people at high risk of heart disease to reduce 'harmful' LDL cholesterol levels.

aimed at blocking this chain of events before it starts or interrupting its progress. For example, many people at high risk of developing cardiovascular disease are prescribed statins to reduce their level of LDL cholesterol. But statins are also anti-inflammatory, and research now shows that they can reduce the additional cardiovascular risk linked with raised CRP levels.

## taking the tests

If you are experiencing symptoms such as chest pain or breathlessness that suggest a heart risk, your doctor may refer you for assessment by a specialist. The exploratory tests that could be offered include:

- **Electrocardiogram** (ECG) – a recording of the electrical activity of your heart. This may be done while you are lying down or, if you get symptoms predominantly after exertion, while you exercise on a treadmill. Sometimes you will be fitted with wires to monitor the electrical activity of your heart during a 24-hour period.

- **Magnetic Resonance Imaging** (MRI) – a scan that uses a very powerful magnet to create cross-section images of internal body tissues, so that doctors can see the physical structure of the heart. You will be asked to lie very still on the machine couch which slides into the tunnel-like scanner and you may be offered headphones or ear plugs as the scanner is operating because, although painless, it is very noisy.
- **Radionuclide scans** – various tests in which tiny amounts of radioactive substances are injected into your bloodstream. When these reach the heart, they can be detected by a special camera, producing images of your coronary arteries or showing how well your heart is pumping. For one of these tests, myocardial perfusion imaging (MPI), an isotope injection is given after the patient has been pedalling on an exercise bike or treadmill; a scan is then performed to show the blood flow in the heart muscle.
- **Computed Tomography** (CT) – a special type of X-ray that produces detailed pictures of cross-sections of the body. Sometimes it is used to assess how much calcium has been deposited in your coronary arteries, a measure of hard plaque, which is made up of calcium and collagen.
- **Angiography** – X-ray pictures taken after the injection of a special dye to reveal the coronary arteries.

If exploratory tests reveal that you have severe coronary artery disease, your doctor may recommend surgical treatment to reduce the risk of a heart attack. For example, it may be possible to open up the coronary arteries (angioplasty) or to bypass them altogether (coronary artery bypass graft surgery). You can find out more about these treatments in Step 2.

····· Continued on p32 ▶

**SECRET**weapon

### DENTAL HYGIENE

**G**um disease has been linked with an increased risk of cardiovascular disease. Regular tooth-brushing and flossing will keep your gums healthy, and you should visit your dentist regularly for check-ups; it is especially important to see your dentist if you have any bleeding from the gums. Using mouthwash daily also helps to kill off the bacteria that cause inflamed gums and can help to prevent the build-up of dental plaque, which leads to gum problems. See Step 8 for more details.

# hidden dangers of diabetes

The number of people diagnosed with diabetes – a risk factor for cardiovascular disease – is growing at an unprecedented rate. Experts link the increase to obesity.

Between 1997 and 2003, there was a 74 per cent growth in the recorded number of new cases of diabetes, and by 2005 more than 4 per cent of the population was classed as having diabetes – almost double the 1995 figure. In addition, more than half a million people may have the condition and not know it. The bad news is that people with diabetes are up to eight times more likely than non-diabetics to die from cardiovascular disease.

There are two main types of diabetes mellitus: Type 1, which typically develops in childhood, and Type 2, which is by far the most common and largely responsible for the current explosion of diabetes cases. Both involve the action of insulin, a hormone produced by the pancreas, which promotes the uptake of glucose (sugar) – the body's main source of energy – into cells; any upset in this function can lead to abnormally high levels of glucose in the blood, which causes problems and defects in various parts of the body.

While Type 1 is caused by a shortage or lack of the hormone and requires life-long insulin treatment, Type 2, which tends to develop later in life (but is being seen at ever younger ages), occurs either because the body isn't making sufficient insulin or because cells have become resistant to the effects of insulin (insulin resistance), so the body can't metabolise glucose properly (glucose intolerance). As a result, a dangerous vicious circle develops – blood glucose levels rise, the body produces more insulin to lower them, but because the cells aren't responding properly, glucose continues to build up in the blood and the demand for insulin increases.

## RED alert !

### TUMMY FAT DANGER

Abdominal fat releases lipids that are carried in the blood to the liver, where they may accumulate as a type of fat called triglycerides. Raised blood levels of triglycerides are linked with an increased risk of cardiovascular disease. In the liver, these fats can also disrupt the organ's key role in processing glucose (sugar) and insulin. Research has shown that the flow of lipids to the liver is greatest overnight, and that this increases the risk of insulin resistance, partly explaining why people with large amounts of abdominal fat are at an increased risk of diabetes.

## A CLUSTER OF RISK FACTORS

If you already have insulin-resistance and glucose intolerance, studies show that you are likely to develop Type 2 diabetes within ten years until you take some remedial action. While some of the risk may be inherited, weight gain and an inactive lifestyle intensify the problem.

Medical experts call the cluster of risk factors for both diabetes and cardiovascular problems 'metabolic syndrome'. The key features that they have identified include insulin resistance and glucose intolerance but also abdominal obesity, high blood pressure, blood fat abnormalities and higher than normal

Research suggests that
losing just 5 to 7 per cent of your body weight
can cut your risk of developing diabetes by 60 per cent.

levels of blood glucose. The condition is also linked to inflammation (see page 22) and a tendency for the blood to clot too readily. Studying the syndrome has helped doctors to understand how these conditions together cause underlying changes that contribute to cardiovascular disease, and ultimately to your risk of heart attacks and strokes.

## inside information

In one US study of people in their sixties or older who had metabolic syndrome, the majority of those who followed a specific diabetes prevention programme, which included dietary and exercise recommendations, regained normal blood glucose levels and reduced their risk factors for heart disease. On average, they lowered their chance of developing diabetes by 70 per cent. By contrast, other people in the study who only took medication specifically designed to reduce the chance of their developing diabetes, cut their risk by just 31 per cent.

## REDUCING THE RISK

While it is difficult to measure insulin levels directly, your doctor can use two simple glucose tests to assess whether you are glucose intolerant (and therefore likely to be insulin resistant). If the result of either test is abnormal, your doctor may well advise you to adopt the sort of lifestyle changes recommended in this book – by, for example, cutting your intake of calories and saturated (animal) fats – for instance by substituting lean chicken and fish for red meats and eating more fruit and vegetables. Boosting the amount of physical activity you undertake – an ideal level is 30-40 minutes brisk walking at least five days a week – also increases the sensitivity of muscle cells to insulin, helping them to metabolise glucose. Research suggests that losing just 5 to 7 per cent of your body weight can cut your risk of developing diabetes by 60 per cent.

# emerging evidence

**C**ardiovascular disease is not a clear-cut problem. It is caused by a web of factors, so scientific researchers are always searching for links to help them to discover precisely how and why it develops. All the following elements are thought to be significant:

- **Fat cells** – these normally act as an energy store, pumping out 'fuel' in the form of fatty acids when the body calls for it. But fat tissue also produces hormones that regulate body weight and, if you are overweight, it releases inflammatory chemicals too, which are thought to promote some of the complications linked with obesity, such as insulin resistance, diabetes, heart disease and arthritis.
- **Fibrinogen** – this protein produced by the liver is important in blood clotting. Raised fibrinogen levels are linked with inflammation and are found in people with insulin resistance and those who have suffered coronary artery disease, heart attack or stroke. It has been suggested that, as well as acting as a marker of risk, fibrinogen may contribute to the development of atherosclerosis.
- **Apolipoprotein B** – this protein, known as apo(B), plays a key role in the production of cholesterol and its transport around the body. It bonds with LDL ('bad') cholesterol in the bloodstream. Raised apo(B) levels are associated with inflammation, and research shows that apo(B) is a better predictor of cardiovascular risk and of how well an individual will respond to cholesterol-lowering drugs than tests that simply measure cholesterol levels.
- **Homocysteine** – high levels of this blood protein have been linked to increased risk of high blood pressure and heart disease. Homocysteine is believed to damage cells that line the coronary arteries. While homocysteine levels can be reduced by taking folate, a vitamin found in raw fruit and vegetables, and 'antioxidant' vitamins, experts are still not sure if doing so directly reduces cardiovascular risk.

# fighting back

Doctors now realise that cardiovascular disease is far more complicated than had once been thought, and that there is a multitude of interlinked elements that may affect an individual's risk. Far too often, cardiovascular disease is diagnosed only after someone has experienced a heart attack or a stroke. The plain fact is that you may have atherosclerosis and not know it. That is why it is so important to be aware of the risk factors and to take action before a dramatic event occurs.

## DRAWING UP A STRATEGY

Your first line of defence against heart attack and stroke is to identify your own personal risk factors and to develop a strategy to counteract them. The next step is to carry the strategy through. As you will discover,

It's important to recognise your personal risk factors. Then you can draw up a practical plan to overcome and eliminate them – one by one.

making some small but crucial changes is not particularly difficult. Later steps in this book describe the easiest and simplest ways to influence those risks for the better and to fit your control strategy into your daily routine, with accompanying tips to make the whole process more fun.

## START NOW – TODAY

Look back – right now – at those nine factors identified by the Interheart study (page 17), and make a note of how many of them apply, or might apply, to you. What could you do at this very moment to start to reduce your risk and to begin the push towards healthier arteries? Give up the next cigarette? Eat a piece of fruit? Go for a brisk walk?

One of the central messages of this book is that change is easiest – and most effective – if you make it in small stages. Think of it as a journey to a place you would really like to visit. You can't arrive instantly: travelling

## HAPPINESS

It's no joke, say scientists. Laughter and feel-good emotions can help to protect us from heart disease. Researchers at the University of Maryland School of Medicine found that, when we chuckle, the tissue that forms the inner lining of our blood vessels expands – a healthy response which increases blood flow. By contrast, mental stress caused blood vessels to constrict.

Listening to enjoyable music also increases blood flow to the arteries. Researchers believe that, when we experience pleasure, our brains release beneficial endorphins that directly affect our vascular system.

takes time. But each step you make will bring you a little closer to your destination. You will find out that each stage of the voyage can be a joy in itself, and the things you learn on the way will stay with you for ever.

## SETTING GOALS

This book provides a great deal of advice and a wealth of practical tips for making vital lifestyle changes that can diminish your risk of diabetes, cardiovascular disease, heart attack and stroke. But everyone needs to start by setting goals. For instance, if you are overweight, here are some goals you might consider:

- Reduce your intake of calories, especially the amount of saturated fat you eat, by substituting lean chicken and fish for red meats, and choosing colourful and nutritious vegetables (see Step 5).
- Lose 5 to 7 per cent of your body weight – if you weigh around 14st (90kg) now, that's about 11lb (5kg).
- Increase your physical activity by, for example, walking to the shops. An ideal level of exercise is a brisk 30 minute walk on five days each week.

## inside information
# the polypill

What if a single tablet taken daily could slash the incidence of cardiovascular disease? That was the idea of two London University professors of preventive medicine, Nicholas Wald and Malcolm Law, back in 2003. Their pill would combine a statin with blood-pressure-lowering drugs, aspirin and folate to simultaneously reduce four cardiovascular risk factors: 'bad' LDL cholesterol, blood pressure, homocysteine and platelet function (involved in blood clotting). The idea generated controversy, but now trials of just such a tablet have started in six countries. Dubbed the Red Heart Pill, it incorporates aspirin, a statin and two blood-pressure drugs. Early results from a trial in India, involving more than 2,000 people and reported in *The Lancet* in March 2009, were promising. So perhaps the widespread use of a polypill could indeed, in the original words of Wald and Law, 'have a greater impact on the prevention of disease in the Western world than any other single intervention'.

## TAKING ACTION

The more you understand about atherosclerosis – from the point when plaque gets deposited in your arteries to the complex conditions that underlie cardiovascular disease – the better your chances of finding ways to prevent, halt or even reverse it. As already indicated, the damage can frequently be averted by adjusting your lifestyle in relatively small and easy ways that can make a huge difference to your health.

Knowing what you are up against and accepting that these risks can potentially affect all of us is the first crucial step. In Step 2 we will show you how to recognise an emergency and, as importantly, explain the most effective action you can take to save your life or the lives of others.

Later on, you will discover a host of ways to assess your own vulnerability to cardiovascular disease, in order to create your own personalised plan of progressive lifestyle changes to lower your risk of heart attack and stroke. By making the right lifestyle choices, you may never have to face the threat of either event.

MYTHS ✗

### POTATOES COUNT AS VEGETABLES

No they don't – at least, not in terms of the 'five a day' portions of fruit and veg that are recommended as a daily minimum target to protect against cancer, heart disease and stroke. Potatoes may be both delicious and healthy (if not fried), but in nutritional terms they are starchy carbohydrates, like rice or bread.

But canned or frozen vegetables, including baked beans and canned tomatoes, do count – something that three-quarters of parents didn't know when surveyed by the Department of Health. Dried fruits also count and pure fruit juice can count as one portion – but only one.

People seem confused – and this may help to explain why only 58 per cent of Britons manage to eat five portions of fruit and vegetables per day, according to a survey by the Food Standards Agency. For advice on how to introduce more fruit and vegetables into your diet see Step 5.

Frozen vegetables do count as one of your 'five a day'.

# self-defence plan
## STEP
# 2

HOWEVER MUCH YOU KNOW ABOUT RISK FACTORS, AN ACTUAL HEART ATTACK OR STROKE IS A SHOCKING WAKE-UP CALL. IN BOTH CASES, TIME IS OF THE ESSENCE, SO BE ALERT FOR DANGER SIGNS AND LEARN WHAT YOU CAN DO QUICKLY TO SAVE YOUR OWN LIFE OR THE LIVES OF OTHERS.

# Recognise
## the danger signs

**T**his step opens with a challenge. You may think you know what happens when someone has a heart attack or stroke – but do you really? Just consider: every 2 minutes someone in this country suffers a heart attack; and every 5 minutes someone has a stroke. What if it was someone close to you? Would you know what to do?

A recent survey by the British Heart Foundation revealed that many people don't recognise the signs of a heart attack and, as a result, may put their own or their loved ones' lives at risk by not taking the correct urgent action. The same is true of strokes; swift treatment can not only save a life but also prevent long-term disability.

The following pages outline vital information that could help you to control a crisis and make the right decisions in an emergency. You'll learn all about the danger signals and find out what you could do instantly that might make all the difference. You'll begin to understand why early medical intervention is essential. And you'll discover some of the modern medical miracles – from clot-busting drugs to intricate surgery – that can minimise the damage that a heart attack or stroke may cause.

## BLOCKED BLOOD SUPPLY

As explained in Step 1, the underlying causes of most strokes and heart attacks are similar and the ensuing damage usually results from an interruption of the blood supply to a vital organ. When the blood supply is cut off, cells starved of oxygen and vital nutrients start to die.

If this occurs in the heart, the muscle cells supplied by the blocked artery can no longer function, and if blood supply is not restored quickly, parts of the muscle may die, leaving the heart permanently weakened. Sometimes, the heart's rhythm becomes irregular and the heart may even stop which, unless someone can get it pumping again, is fatal within minutes.

Strokes are largely preventable but your risk is a little higher if a grandparent, parent or sibling has had one.

# the myths about
## heart attacks and strokes

**The statements below are common fallacies. Discover why.**

- **If you don't have chest pain, you can't be having a heart attack False.** In a heart attack, blood supply to the heart muscle is interrupted and heart muscle cells start to die, which may cause chest pain – but not necessarily; about one in three people admitted to hospital with a heart attack does not have severe chest pain.
- **A heart attack gives you sudden, intense pain** In some people it does – as in the classic 'TV heart attack', where actors clutch their chest in agony. But most real heart attacks build up more slowly, with milder pain or discomfort.
- **If you're worried you may be having a heart attack or stroke, you should call your GP False.** Call an ambulance immediately.
- **Heart attacks are rare in women False.** In fact, a woman is four times more likely to die from a heart attack than from breast cancer; after the menopause, heart attacks kill more women than men.
- **Strokes cannot be prevented False.** Strokes are largely preventable. Stopping smoking, reducing high blood pressure, losing excess weight, taking regular exercise – all drastically reduce risk. A landmark 2009 study involving more than 20,000 adults revealed that people who either smoked, drank excessively, were inactive or ate few or no fruits or vegetables were more than twice as likely to suffer a stroke.
- **There's no effective treatment for a stroke False.** That's why doctors tell you to get to hospital as soon as possible. For the most common type of stroke, caused by a blood clot, treatment with clot-busting drugs within 4½ hours (the sooner, the better) can significantly reduce the chance of death or permanent disability.
- **Strokes only affect old people** On the contrary, more than a quarter of strokes occur in people under the age of 65. Even children can be affected, though this is very rare.
- **Strokes do not run in the family False.** Your risk of a stroke rises if a parent, grandparent or sibling has had a stroke, especially if they had high blood pressure.
- **Stroke recovery is not possible after the first few weeks False.** While the most significant improvements occur in the early weeks, recovery can continue for months, even years, particularly if care and rehabilitation begin early.

Similarly, if cells in your brain are deprived of their blood supply, they too become damaged and your brain may no longer be able to issue instructions to other parts of your body. Whatever function is controlled by those damaged brain cells – movement or speech, for example – is suddenly impaired. If blood flow is not rapidly restored and brain cells in one area start to die off, the damage may be permanent.

# don't delay

Why do so many people who have heart attacks fail to realise what they are experiencing? One reason is that symptoms can be confusing. A patient may say, 'I just didn't feel ill.' Some people cannot believe that a heart attack could happen to them, particularly if they are fit and active. So they delay seeking medical help. As many as one in three heart attack patients dies before reaching hospital – yet these are often lives that might have been saved if the patient, or those around him or her, had recognised the warning signs. Immediate action increases your chances of survival dramatically. You will discover all the most common symptoms, and some less common ones, for both heart attack and stroke in the following pages.

## troubleshooting Q&A

### I get angina. How could I tell if I was having a heart attack?

Most pain caused by angina is alleviated by rest. So, if you experience chest pain that either starts when you are sitting down or doesn't get better when you stop what you are doing, think heart attack. Similarly, if the pain is more severe than usual, or if it continues for more than 20 minutes or after you've taken your medication, you should call an ambulance; other symptoms may include nausea and sweating.

## TIME IS BRAIN

If someone appears to have had a stroke, rapid hospital admission is important so that doctors can run tests to find out how serious the damage is and what has caused it. They can then select the right emergency treatment in order to prevent permanent disability.

Sometimes stroke symptoms occur temporarily, disappearing after a few minutes or hours. This is called a TIA (transient ischaemic attack, or mini-stroke) and also requires urgent medical attention. A TIA, which is caused by a temporary reduction in the blood supply to part of the brain, is an important warning; without treatment, it is estimated that one in four people who've had a TIA could suffer a full-blown stroke within a month.

Anyone who has experienced a TIA and is deemed to be at high risk of having a full stroke should be assessed within 24 hours of the onset of symptoms by a specialist, who will recommend the best course of action.

## HELP AT HAND

If you live alone and believe you may be at risk of a heart attack or stroke, ask your local authority about a community alarm system. Or contact Age Concern and find out about their personal alarm service – you can get a portable 'panic button' to wear that alerts family, neighbours or emergency services if you have a problem and cannot reach a telephone. See their website http://www.aidcall.co.uk/personalcare/ for further details.

# cardiac crisis

A heart attack may be caused either by ruptured plaque (see page 19) leading to a clot in a coronary artery or by another event that cuts off vital blood supplies to heart muscle. The medical term for a heart attack is 'myocardial infarction', often shortened to MI, which indicates that some cells in the heart muscle (myocardium) have died because of lack of blood supply (an infarction). In the worst case, the heart stops beating altogether and goes into cardiac arrest. But, with rapid treatment, damage to the heart muscle can be halted and, if blood flow is restored in time, a full recovery is possible. Otherwise, a part of the heart muscle will be permanently damaged, leaving an area of scar tissue. If the scar tissue is extensive, you may experience long-term breathlessness.

REDalert !

### YOU MAY NOT HAVE CHEST PAIN

People experience heart attacks in different ways. In one major study of 400,000 people over four years, published in the *Journal of the American Medical Association*, one in three patients admitted to hospital with what was later confirmed to be a heart attack had no chest pain at all. Women and diabetics were among those least likely to have typical symptoms, more than half of whom had no chest pain. According to Dr Ghada Mikhail, a consultant cardiologist, women are more likely to suffer unusual fatigue, shortness of breath, back pain or abdominal pain.

## EFFECTIVE TREATMENT

Sometimes a heart attack can disturb the flow of electrical impulses that normally generate your heartbeat to set

# taking action – heart attack

It is not always easy to tell whether someone is having a heart attack. But intervention could save the life of someone close to you. It is often up to those around the victim to spot the signs and take urgent action. If you are unsure, don't hesitate. Call 999 and make it clear it's a suspected heart attack. Ambulance staff would far rather attend to tell you it's not, than be called out too late.

## WHEN SECONDS COUNT

Research has shown that treatment started within an hour of the onset of symptoms reduces the risk of a death and lessens damage to the heart. The British Heart Foundation estimates that people who receive medical help within this time-frame are three times more likely to survive a heart attack. That is why it's important to recognise the symptoms, and why, if you suspect that someone is having a heart attack, you should call an ambulance within 5 minutes.

## COMMON SYMPTOMS MAY INCLUDE:

- Central chest pain
- Dull, aching discomfort, or heaviness, in the chest – often mistaken for indigestion
- Pain spreading to the arms, neck or jaw
- Nausea, feeling sick
- Feeling of impending doom
- Sweating, feeling cold and clammy to the touch
- Shortness of breath

## LESS COMMON SYMPTOMS MAY INCLUDE:

- A sensation of squeezing, or pressure around the chest
- Feeling generally unwell along with chest pain
- Pain in the chest that spreads to the back or abdomen
- Dizziness, feeling faint, or light-headed, along with chest pain
- (In women) pain in the back, jaw or abdomen, or unusual fatigue

## SYMPTOMS CAN DECEIVE

Symptoms of a heart attack vary from one person to another and may be less obvious in women than in men. Diabetics are more likely to have a 'silent' attack, without chest pain; instead they may suffer shortness of breath, nausea, faintness or loss of consciousness.

# early morning alarm

**Y**ou might think that heart attacks and strokes would tend to strike when you're tired at the end of the day. In fact both occur most frequently in the early hours of daylight. Heart attacks are 40 per cent more common between 6am and noon than at other times of day, and more than 45 per cent of strokes occur during these hours. Similarly, sudden cardiac deaths are 29 per cent more common in the morning, and serious rhythm disturbances, heart failure deaths and ruptured aortic aneurysms follow a similar pattern.

There are numerous reasons why the first few hours after waking are so hazardous. Stress hormones such as adrenaline and cortisol, as well as the male hormone testosterone, peak in the early morning in preparation for the day, and cause an increase in heart rate and blood pressure. Relative dehydration overnight and an increase in platelet 'stickiness' make blood clots more likely, and medication effects may be wearing off since a bedtime dose.

So it makes sense to get up gradually and allow time for a leisurely start to the day. Have a long, relaxing stretch and preferably a warm-up before you start moving about. Avoid sudden bouts of exertion first thing, especially if you are not particularly fit, and especially in very cold weather (another trigger for heart attacks and stroke).

## Stretch and get up slowly in the morning.

It's also important to stay as calm as possible and not to get upset about problems at work or the frustrations of commuting. Study the de-stressing techniques in Step 9. Check with your doctor that any medications you take will last the night, and make sure to time your last doses of the day accordingly.

## troubleshooting Q&A

### I have high blood pressure and I like to run in the morning. Am I increasing my risk of a heart attack?

No, not if you are used to exercising regularly. It is sudden unaccustomed exertion that poses the greatest hazard to health. And that fact appears to hold true even if you already have heart disease. According to an American study of patients who had had a heart attack and later took part in a cardiac rehabilitation programme, there was no significant difference in the rate of complications whether the patients exercised at 7.30 in the morning or 3 o'clock in the afternoon. The patients always followed a stretching and warm-up routine before taking exercise, with a cool-down period afterwards – following a golden rule for anyone who exercises (see Step 7).

off the sequence of regular heart muscle contractions that drives blood around your body. If this happens, you may develop heart-rhythm abnormalities, known as arrhythmias.

Arrhythmias are most common in the first 3 to 6 hours following an attack. Some are mild, but they may cause palpitations, dizziness, chest pain, shortness of breath or fatigue. Others can be life-threatening. If you are in hospital, arrhythmias can be detected and treated – another reason for seeking prompt emergency assistance. If damage to the heart muscle is extensive, heart failure may follow. Your heart cannot pump strongly enough to propel blood around your body and you are likely to experience breathlessness that may be severe as fluid accumulates in your lungs.

Heart failure can usually be diagnosed quickly from the symptoms, a physical examination and various tests. It can also be treated effectively in hospital with drugs that lower blood pressure, prevent further heart muscle damage, and reduce the heart's workload. However, severe cases may need surgery to bypass the blocked coronary artery and restore blood flow.

## ASPIRIN

Chewing one 300mg standard aspirin tablet in those crucial moments before an ambulance arrives can help to minimise the damage caused by a heart attack.

Aspirin works by reducing the 'stickiness' of the platelets that are an important part of the body's blood-clotting mechanism, and so may stop a dangerous clot from progressing. But aspirin should not be taken for a suspected stroke in case it is haemorrhagic (caused by a bleed), which aspirin could exacerbate.

- Don't take aspirin if you are allergic to it, or if you are taking warfarin or other anti-clotting drugs.
- If you are with someone who is having a heart attack, check that the person is not allergic to aspirin, then ask where you can find some.
- If you are on your own, take aspirin only if there are some readily to hand. Do not search the house – you need to stay still.
- Take one aspirin tablet and chew it slowly; don't swallow it. This is a faster way to get the drug into your bloodstream.

Aspirin works by reducing the 'stickiness' of the platelets that are an important part of the body's blood-clotting mechanism

Don't hesitate to call the emergency services if you or anyone around you may be experiencing a heart attack or stroke.

# what happens during a stroke?

There are two main types of stroke and each requires quite different treatment, so doctors have to pinpoint the type as soon as possible. The first and most common type is an ischaemic stroke, which is rather like a heart attack: a blood clot blocks one of the arteries supplying the brain, cutting the blood supply to brain cells that control functions such as speech or movement. The other type, known as a haemorrhagic stroke, occurs when an artery wall leaks, causing bleeding into the brain. In both cases the result is similar: the patient's brain cells are unable to perform their usual control functions and could die, leading to permanent disability, unless intervention is swift.

## INSIDE YOUR BRAIN

Changes to the connections between brain cells begin to occur within 3 minutes of the onset of stroke symptoms, according to animal research carried out by scientists in Canada. But, with prompt treatment to restore blood flow, 94 per cent of these connections can be repaired.

That is why it is so crucial for a stroke victim to get to hospital quickly. The sooner you are assessed and treated, the better your chances of a full recovery.

# taking action – stroke

**I**f you think that you or someone near you may be having a stroke, call 999. Ask for an ambulance and make it clear to the emergency operator that the person may have suffered a stroke. More importantly, tell the paramedics when the ambulance arrives. They will then take you to the nearest hospital with a stroke unit, avoiding life-threatening delays.

## ACT FAST

The effects of a stroke can be felt in almost any part of the body. Yet someone who has just suffered one will probably be extremely confused and not realise what is happening or be able to act quickly. It is often up to family, friends or carers to recognise a stroke and to get help fast.

## NO WARNING

Symptoms of a stroke come on suddenly. Since people who are experiencing a stroke frequently rely on those around them to spot what's happening, the Department of Health is urging everyone to learn the **FAST** test, which assesses the three most common symptoms:

**F**acial weakness – can the person smile? (Check also for a drooping mouth or eye)

**A**rm weakness – can the person raise both arms?

**S**peech problems – can the person speak clearly and understand what you say?

If the answer to one or more of these questions is NO, it's
**T**ime to call 999.

## OTHER POSSIBLE SYMPTOMS INCLUDE:

- Confusion or difficulty understanding
- Weakness, paralysis or numbness on one side of the body
- Double or blurred vision, loss of vision in half of the visual field
- Difficulty walking, loss of balance and coordination
- A sudden excruciatingly severe headache

Owain Wyn-Jones

# A FAST response

Owain Wyn-Jones will be for ever grateful that someone very close to him knew about the FAST test. Because Laraine Adams - then his girlfriend, now his wife - spotted the telltale signs of a stroke, he reached hospital in 40 minutes, well within the $4\frac{1}{2}$ hours during which clot-busting treatment is most effective.

'We'd been at our friends' house for dinner the night before,' says Laraine, 'and had drunk quite a lot of wine. When Owain got up the next day, he said he felt as if he was still drunk. He stumbled a bit and had a headache. As we sat having a cup of tea, he leaned over and put his head on my shoulder. When he sat up, I noticed his face had fallen on one side.'

Luckily, they'd seen a FAST campaign advert on television. 'I remembered it because we'd thought it was so shocking.' She immediately asked Owain to lift up both arms. 'He couldn't lift his left one. And he couldn't stand up, because his left leg gave way under him when he tried.'

She worried that if she took him to A & E, they might think it was just a hangover. Also, Owain was only 30. 'I thought it was a stroke, but it was very hard to believe.' So she quickly telephoned NHS Direct, and talked to a nurse.

'There is a very short window in which a stroke can be treated, so acting quickly is imperative.'

'Once the nurse heard his symptoms, she  sent an emergency response unit to us. Owain was taken to North Staffordshire Hospital, which has a specialist stroke unit.' He was treated with a clot-busting drug and stayed in hospital for four days.

Owain had no apparent risk factors, but stress, says Laraine, may have played a part. 'He was worried about his business and was working very long hours.'

Since then he has been forced to take things much easier. And he looks great, she adds, but still has problems with memory and concentration. As a result of their experience, the couple feel strongly that everyone should be aware of stroke symptoms.

'If you suspect it, don't feel you may be wasting doctors' time,' urges Laraine. 'There is a very short window in which a stroke can be treated, so acting quickly is imperative.'

# while you wait for help

Remind yourself that most people survive a heart attack or a stroke. Once you have called 999, you can improve the odds of recovery by knowing exactly what to do before the paramedics arrive. Crucially, the patient must stay still and calm to minimise the pressure on the cardiovascular system and reduce the amount of oxygen the body requires.

## IF YOU ARE ALONE

- Leave the front door on the latch so it can be opened from outside.
- Stay calm.
- Sit or lie down.
- Have the phone ready, next to you.
- Do not eat or drink anything other than small sips of water.
- Call a neighbour or family member to wait with you if possible.

## WHAT YOU CAN DO TO ASSIST

- Don't leave the person alone.
- Help him or her to sit or lie down to be comfortable.
- Check the time; this information may be helpful to the ambulance crew.
- Offer reassurance that the ambulance is on its way.
- Don't give food or drink other than water (except when the patient has medication to take in case of an attack – in which case, give it at once).
- Call the person's GP; information about past medical history may be helpful to the ambulance crew and hospital doctors.
- If possible, gather all the patient's current medication so that this can be sent to the hospital with the patient.
- If you know about basic first aid, do an ABC check – on Airways, Breathing and Circulation.
- If the patient vomits, turn the head to one side to reduce choking risk.
- Watch out for signs of cardiac arrest, where the heart stops beating altogether. The person will stop breathing and will not have a pulse. Be prepared to start resuscitation.
- If the person is unconscious, place in the recovery position (**see page 48**), but continue to watch breathing to see if resuscitation is needed.

**SECRET**weapon

### A STROKE UNIT

If you suspect that you or someone close to you may be having a stroke or mini-stroke, it is important to try to get to a hospital with a specialist stroke unit. Such units include a multi-disciplinary team of doctors, nurses and therapists skilled in the field of stroke medicine, which can greatly improve recovery prospects.

Just like heart attacks, strokes must be treated as medical emergencies. A stroke unit can provide rapid and early diagnosis, vital to saving lives. If tests show that your stroke is due to a blood clot, a drug given within 4½ hours of the onset of symptoms greatly improves your chance of a full recovery, and the earlier it is given the better.

# recovery position

**I**f someone is unconscious but breathing, he or she should be put into the recovery position to keep the airway open and ensure there is no risk of choking. If the victim is lying flat, bend the arm nearest to you upwards, so the forearm is at right angles to the upper arm, then lay the other arm across the chest. Support the head and gently roll the person towards you onto the side, with the head resting on the arm that was across the chest. Bend the upper leg to prevent the victim from rolling too far. Check the pulse and breathing regularly until medical help arrives.

# life-saving skills

If someone collapses with a heart attack or a cardiac arrest, their chances of survival more than double if a bystander performs cardiopulmonary resuscitation (CPR) to keep the heart beating. If the heart stops during an attack, the patient may lose consciousness, and will die within minutes if blood flow to the brain and other vital organs is not restored. CPR buys time. When the ambulance arrives, paramedics may be able to restart the heart with an electric shock, a process known as defibrillation.

Conventional CPR involves two elements – chest compressions to keep blood pumping through the heart, combined with mouth-to-mouth breathing to maintain a flow of air into the lungs, though compression-only CPR is rapidly gaining favour – especially for those untrained in CPR.

## MAKING IT EASIER TO HELP

Fewer than one in three people who experience cardiac arrest in a public place is helped by a bystander. Why is this? Some people are not sure what to do, but many may be deterred by the mouth-to-mouth element. And, in fact, recent research suggests that mouth-to-mouth respiration may not be as essential as once thought. There is also evidence that the pause in compressions required to carry out artificial respiration may reduce the patient's chances of recovering his or her heartbeat.

# compression-only CPR

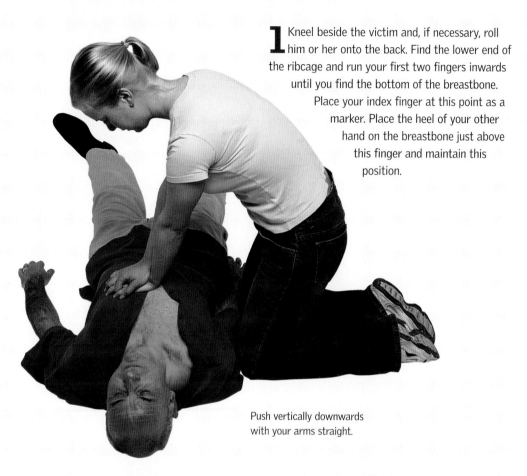

**1** Kneel beside the victim and, if necessary, roll him or her onto the back. Find the lower end of the ribcage and run your first two fingers inwards until you find the bottom of the breastbone. Place your index finger at this point as a marker. Place the heel of your other hand on the breastbone just above this finger and maintain this position.

Push vertically downwards with your arms straight.

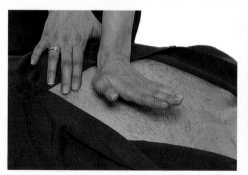

**2** Move your other hand on top of the first and interlace the fingers of both hands. Lean forwards, with your shoulders over the patient. Keeping your arms straight, push down, aiming to press the lower breastbone down by about a third of the depth of the chest. Release the pressure without removing your hands. If you are unwilling or unable to give mouth-to-mouth ventilation, the Resuscitation Council (UK) now recommends uninterrupted chest compressions at a rate of 100 per minute – but points out that this is only effective for about 5 minutes.

# the Bee Gees

**D**on't know how fast to perform chest compressions? Make sure that you're familiar with the 1977 Bee Gees hit 'Staying Alive'. It has 103 beats per minute, close enough to the 100 per minute ideal rhythm for chest compressions in cardiopulmonary resuscitation (CPR). Researchers played the song to 15 doctors and medical students learning CPR on dummies, and told them to time their chest compressions to the beat. Five weeks later they were tested without the music, but asked simply to recall the 'Staying Alive' rhythm while performing compressions. They achieved impressive average compression rates of 109 to 113 beats per minute. Many people hesitate to undertake CPR because they're not sure of the rhythm, but performing CPR properly can treble the survival rate after a heart attack – so 'Staying Alive' could help someone to do just that.

When doctors in Tokyo studied 4,068 people who were not in hospital when they suffered a cardiac arrest, they noted the number who had received CPR from bystanders, including compression-only CPR. After assessing the degree of brain damage among survivors 30 days later, they reported that more than twice as many had 'a favourable neurological outcome' when resuscitation had been attempted.

## UNEXPECTED RESULTS

What really surprised them was that among those who had stopped breathing and for whom resuscitation had begun within 4 minutes of their heart attack, compression-only resuscitation produced a better outcome than full CPR, more than doubling the number who survived without brain damage. Adding mouth-to-mouth respiration showed no benefit in any of the patient groups studied.

The UK Resuscitation Council agrees that, for people untrained in Basic Life Support, it may be preferable to give chest compressions rather than to attempt full CPR.

## DEFENCE tactics

### TRAINING

**R**esuscitation is easy – if you know how to do it. So why not find out? One highly successful venture, Heartstart UK, a British Heart Foundation (BHF) initiative, has 3,300 schemes across the country and has already taught 1.9 million people how to perform cardiopulmonary resuscitation (CPR) as part of an emergency life support (ELS) course, which teaches techniques that could keep someone alive until emergency help arrives.

The Heartstart UK groups offer free ELS training – typically a 2 hour hands-on session – for local groups, schools and companies.

Learning CPR is especially useful if you live with someone at risk from cardiovascular disease.

See the British Heart Foundation website http://www.bhf.org.uk and the Resources section, page 240, for further information on Heartstart UK and other first-aid courses.

Keith Lawrenz

# Saving a life

When Keith Lawrenz, a 43 year-old American, collapsed in the street in the West End of London, he had good fortune on his side. For nearby worked Peter Marchant, a St John Ambulance volunteer trained to attend emergency calls received by the ambulance service and give care until the ambulance arrives.

'I was at work and the local milkman came running in and told me that a man had collapsed round the corner,' Peter recalls. When he got there, Keith had been put into the recovery position by two first-aiders. 'But I noticed that his lips were blue and he was gasping with agonal breathing.' (Irregular 'agonal' gasps can occur during a cardiac arrest.)

Keith's heart had stopped so Peter immediately rolled him onto his back and began CPR. While he performed chest compressions, he called out to one of the first-aiders to give mouth-to-mouth and the other to check that an ambulance was on its way. When it arrived 5 minutes later Peter was asked to continue the compressions while the paramedics tried to restart Keith's heart with a defibrillator and drugs. A second ambulance crew arrived and took over CPR while they repeated their attempts. After the second shock, Keith's heart re-started.

> 'I noticed that his lips were blue and he was gasping with agonal breathing.' Keith's heart had stopped.

He was rushed to hospital and Peter didn't expect to hear any more. But the next day he was told that Keith and his wife, who had flown over from the USA, were trying to contact him.

When Peter went to see him in hospital, Keith thanked him warmly and said, 'Everyone keeps calling me the miracle around here, but you're a part of that.'

In recognition of his dramatic intervention, Peter was given the Voluntary Ambulance Service of the Year Award. Keith's heart had stopped for 24 minutes. He went on to make a full recovery: without Peter's resuscitation efforts he might well have died.

'I was absolutely elated to find out that he was OK,' Peter says, 'my training ensured that I was able to keep him alive.'

## YOUR BLOOD

When diagnosing a possible heart attack in a patient who may have symptoms such as chest pains, medical staff are aware that speed is of the essence. First they will take an ECG (electrocardiogram) to record the heart's electrical impulses and to detect an irregular rhythm or other abnormalities that indicate a heart attack. But if the ECG is inconclusive, blood tests are performed because these will reveal if the heart muscle has sustained any damage. Such blood tests are usually taken within 2 to 3 hours and then repeated up to 12 hours after a suspected attack.

What they measure is the level of an enzyme called troponin, which is released into the bloodstream if the heart muscle is damaged or dying. The second blood test is routine to confirm the results. If the tests are positive, doctors will determine the best treatment. If negative, the patient is usually sent home.

# how hospitals save lives

When treating a heart attack or stroke, doctors have three urgent aims: to save life, to ease pain, and to keep the heart muscle or brain from permanent harm. If an ambulance has been called the attending crew will assess the patient en route for the hospital and feed back as much information as they can so that treatment can begin immediately.

# heart treatment

If you are rushed to hospital with a suspected heart attack, the first actions of the medical staff will be to attach you to a cardiac monitor and an intravenous drip. You will then be given oxygen and pain-relief medication while an electrocardiogram (ECG) test is performed to trace the electrical activity of your heart. Staff will also take a sample of your blood, which will be tested for the presence of enzymes released from

# life-saving heart surgery

## ANGIOPLASTY

If you reach hospital within 3 to 4 hours, doctors may try to open up your coronary arteries mechanically – this is known as coronary angioplasty and is the preferred option if time permits. A thin tube with a balloon at the tip is threaded up from your groin and into your coronary artery. A small amount of dye is injected so that the site of the blockage can be seen using an X-ray video (a test called a coronary angiogram) and the balloon is inflated to widen the artery. The tube is then withdrawn, although a small metal coil known as a stent is usually left in place in the artery to keep it open and to prevent further blockages. Some stents even release drugs to help keep the artery clear.

## BYPASS SURGERY

Angioplasty is successful in opening up about 90 per cent of clogged arteries. It rapidly relieves pain and can reduce damage to the heart muscle. However, for some conditions, this procedure is not suitable. If your main coronary artery is blocked, or if you have multiple blockages or a complicating condition such as diabetes, doctors may decide to perform an immediate coronary artery bypass graft (CABG) instead.

CABG entails open heart surgery, a major procedure. A healthy blood vessel taken from elsewhere in the body is linked to the two ends of your coronary artery either side of a blockage, to provide an alternative, clear passage for blood to flow to your heart muscle. Often, two or three coronary arteries are bypassed during the same operation.

damaged heart muscle. And all this will take place within minutes of your arrival in the emergency room. Doctors may start treatment while waiting for the results of the blood tests. You may be given aspirin or put on a heparin drip – both have blood-thinning, anti-clotting properties.

If doctors suspect that your symptoms are due to spasm of a coronary artery (see page 19), they may inject a drug to try to relieve this. If your heart rhythm is abnormal, you may be given medication or electric shocks, or a temporary pacemaker may be implanted under your skin to control your heartbeat.

## HEALING DRUGS

If angioplasty (see panel above) cannot be performed promptly, the patient will often be given a thrombolytic drug, which acts to dissolve the clot blocking the coronary artery and restore blood flow to the heart.

Thrombolytic drugs work by attacking fibrin, the substance in your blood that keeps a clot together. The sooner the drugs are given, the more likely they are to prevent permanent damage to your heart muscle. They are most effective when administered within the first 3 to 4 hours (preferably within the first hour) following the onset of symptoms. However, they will give satisfactory results up to 6 hours and still have some benefit up to 12 hours after symptoms have first appeared.

## SPECIAL DELIVERY

Thrombolytic or clot-busting drugs have revolutionised the treatment of heart attacks. These drugs are effective in opening up the coronary arteries in about half of all patients, reducing damage and improving the chances of long-term survival.

In some areas of the country, ambulance paramedics responding to suspected heart-attack calls now carry thrombolytic drugs with them, so that they can be administered straight away (after an ECG test has been carried out, to confirm the heart attack). When the patient arrives in hospital, doctors will monitor his or her condition carefully since clot-busting drugs can promote bleeding.

## SECRETweapon

### TELEMEDICINE

Until recently, when Dr Tony Rudd, consultant stroke physician at St Thomas' Hospital in London, received an urgent call in the early hours, he would get on his motorbike and ride to the hospital's A&E department to assess an emergency admission. It took him half an hour – time that a stroke patient could ill afford to lose.

Now, when he receives an emergency call, Tony logs on to his laptop inside his living room, linking up to a camera in A&E. It lets him examine an emergency patient remotely, while a highly trained nurse acts as his eyes and ears. The doctor can focus on particular parts of the patient's body as required – the camera is sensitive enough for him to examine the pupils in his patient's eyes, for example. He can talk to his patients and hear their answers. He can explain everything to friends or family who are present and supervise the staff in the A&E department giving the treatment.

The presence of a mobile camera on the stroke unit at weekends means that he can do a ward round without leaving his house.

# stroke treatment

If you were to suffer a stroke, the emergency services will usually take you to the nearest hospital with a specialist stroke unit or a specialised stroke team as immediate expert assessment and treatment is important to ensure the best possible outcome.

On arrival, you would have your blood pressure measured and an ECG to check for abnormal heart rhythms. Blood samples are taken to test for diabetes, high cholesterol or blood clotting problems and other conditions.

The doctors' first priority is to identify the type of stroke – whether it was triggered by a clot or a bleed; if, for instance, the stroke was triggered by a bleed, it would be extremely dangerous to administer an anti-clotting drug.

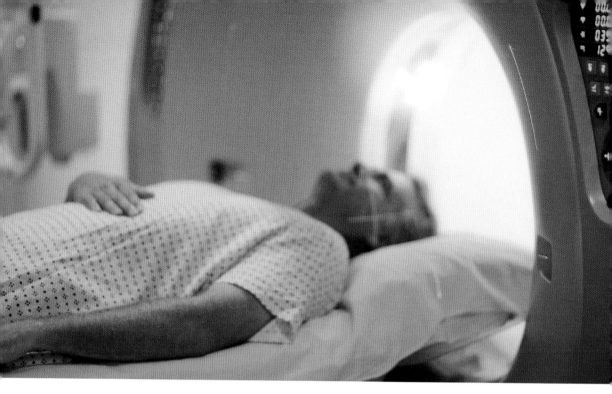

## ... immediate expert assessment and treatment is important to ensure the best possible outcome.

One or more of the following diagnostic tests may be used to identify the type of stroke – ischaemic (caused by a blood clot) or haemorrhagic (caused by a bleed):

- Computed tomography (CT) scan – a scan based on multiple X-rays, which is used to produce a 3D picture that can confirm the diagnosis of a stroke and demonstrate whether it has been caused by a bleed in the brain.
- Magnetic resonance imaging (MRI) scan – a scan that creates pictures generated by a magnetic field, used to identify the precise location of the stroke and help medical staff to decide on further therapy.
- Cerebral angiogram – a special X-ray taken after the injection of a dye into the arteries supplying the brain. It provides a detailed map of the blood flow to the brain, revealing where there is a blockage or a bleed within the brain's blood supply.

## RESUPPLYING THE BRAIN

If a stroke is found to have been caused by a blood clot, aspirin is given and thrombolytic drugs may be started by injection to dissolve the clot. This can significantly reduce the risk of long-term disability, provided treatment is given within 4½ hours of the onset of symptoms. Up to

6 hours after a stroke, a clot-busting drug can be delivered via a catheter directly to the site of the blockage or the clot can be broken up mechanically. Again this treatment reduces the risk of permanent disability, but is not yet routinely available in the UK.

If after a non-disabling ischaemic stroke or a TIA, tests identify a substantial blockage in the carotid artery, doctors may suggest an operation to open up the artery in order to reduce the risk of another stroke. You may also need medication to reduce blood pressure and blood clotting, and to lower cholesterol.

## TREATING A BLEED

In patients who reach hospital after a haemorrhagic stroke, the original bleed has usually stopped. To reduce the risk of further bleeding, doctors monitor blood pressure carefully and prescribe medication to keep it under control. If doctors think that your stroke is related to taking aspirin or an anti-clotting drug such as warfarin, you may be given a drug to reverse its effects. Occasionally in the case of a bleed, surgery may be suggested to drain the blood from your brain, though this isn't suitable for everyone. Open surgery or keyhole surgery may also be advised to seal a cerebral aneurysm if this is what has caused the bleed.

Recovery can continue for months, even years. The brain is a remarkable organ. Some studies have shown improvements up to 14 years later.

# the road to recovery

When the patient's condition has been stabilised, the process of recovery begins. For most people, it takes time to adjust. Your heart may be going through changes as part of the healing process, and doctors will want to monitor you closely to make sure that you do not develop signs of heart failure or heart rhythm abnormalities. You may be referred for tests to assess if further treatment could reduce your risk of another attack.

## BRAIN REPAIR

Some recovery from the physical symptoms of stroke may happen while you are still in hospital, but it is a process that can continue for months, even years. The brain is a remarkable organ. After a stroke, recovery occurs partly as a result of brain cells which were temporarily damaged starting to function again, and partly as a result of other parts of the brain unaffected by the stroke taking over the functions of the damaged area. Some studies have shown improvements in neural function up to 14 years later. During the recovery period, you'll receive help from a range of key health professionals, both in hospital and at home, whose input will be crucial to your successful rehabilitation.

## GOING HOME

When you're discharged from hospital, you will be prescribed with medication that you will probably have to take for the foreseeable future to protect against further attacks. Both heart and stroke patients may require blood pressure-lowering drugs, aspirin and other anti-platelet drugs that prevent blood clots from occurring in the future, as well as cholesterol-lowering drugs. Others may also require drugs for conditions such as diabetes and abnormal heart rhythms. It is important to follow your doctors' instructions and take all medications exactly as prescribed.

## READY FOR REHAB

People who have had a heart attack or a stroke should be offered the chance to enrol in a local cardiac or stroke rehabilitation programme. Some areas of the country are better served than others in this respect, and it's a good idea to enlist the help of your GP (see box, page 58). The programmes usually last for around three months and are designed to speed up recovery and help you to return to a normal routine. They are usually offered in a hospital outpatient unit, in a community setting such as a GP practice or sports centre, or at the patient's own home.

Research indicates that a cardiac rehabilitation programme after a heart attack can improve five-year survival rates by about 26 per cent. Therapists can help people to make adjustments to their lifestyle – such as

**SECRET**weapon

### OPTIMISM

There is powerful evidence to suggest that, if your general outlook is optimistic, you have a lower risk of heart attack, stroke and death from cardiovascular disease than someone who is constantly negative about life. And if you have already had a heart attack and yet remain positive about the future, you are three times less likely to suffer a second attack than those with a more pessimistic response.

In one study that followed the fortunes of 122 men who had had a heart attack, 21 of the 25 dyed-in-the-wool 'pessimists' had died eight years after the attack, compared with just six out of 25 confirmed 'optimists'.

Another study of 309 patients who had undergone coronary artery bypass graft surgery showed that optimistic patients were only half as likely as pessimistic ones to be rehospitalised with complications including infection, angina, a repeat heart attack or the need for further surgery.

## SEE YOUR GP

Enlist the help of your GP in your fight back against cardiovascular disease. Your GP is in overall charge of your medical care when you come out of hospital and it's important to see him or her for regular follow-up checks. Tell your doctor if you're experiencing any new symptoms or having problems with side-effects of medication.

Think of your local GP practice as a vital resource. Your doctor can help you to find a local rehabilitation programme that suits you (some centres ask for a GP referral). He or she can tell you about fitness schemes run by the council, or at nearby leisure centres. Depending on your needs, your GP can also put you in touch with community health services or social services and can arrange for a community or district nurse to make regular visits. (See Resources, page 240.)

giving up smoking, adopting a healthier diet, losing weight and getting fit – and can also help patients to deal with the anxiety and depression that are common after a heart attack.

Rehabilitation is crucial for stroke patients, too. Many people make a full recovery, but others have some lasting impairment and may need help with day-to-day living. A rehabilitation team may include physiotherapists, speech therapists and occupational therapists, who help people to regain function or cope with problems that can affect walking, talking, dressing or writing.

## FIGHTING BACK TO FITNESS

An essential part of rehabilitation is to help you to reduce your risk of having a heart attack or a stroke in the future. Remaining positive is part of that process. So remember:

- If you survive a heart attack, there is an 18 per cent chance that you could have a second one within three years or, viewed positively, a 72 per cent chance that you won't.
- Similarly, if you survive a stroke, you have a 25 per cent chance of suffering another within 5 years or a 75 per cent chance that you won't.

There are countless ways in which lifestyle changes can cut your cardiovascular risk. Here are a few things to consider:

- Having a stressful job more than doubles your risk of another heart attack within two years of the first one.
- Stopping smoking after a heart attack reduces your risk of a further attack by 32 per cent.
- Controlling high blood pressure is of paramount importance. According to the Stroke Association, many strokes in men and women could be avoided if blood pressure was kept under control.
- Increasing your level of physical activity after a heart attack reduces your risk of having another one by 78 per cent.

- Moderate exercise and eating five portions of fruit and vegetables a day can reduce stroke risk in men and women by around a quarter.
- Men and women who have one or two glasses of red or white wine per day more than halve their risk of a second heart attack compared with teetotallers. But there is no benefit in exceeding the recommended limits – 14 units a week for women, 21 for men. Excess alcohol intake is a well-established risk factor for both heart attack and stroke.

A moderate consumption of wine may halve your risk of a second heart attack – friends help, too ...

## A FRIENDLY CHAT

Don't forget to involve your friends and family in your rehabilitation. Their emotional support can be invaluable at a time when you may be feeling anxious or depressed. There is evidence that it may also lower your risk of having another attack. A study of 600 patients at Manchester Royal Infirmary found that people who had a close friend, partner or relative in whom they could confide after a heart attack halved their risk of another attack during the following 12 months compared with those without such a strong bond.

Consider joining a Heart Support group. Set up by patients for patients, these groups also give families the chance to meet and talk to people who have been through the same experience as them. Groups meet socially, arrange to take weekend walks together, and learn to enjoy life again during the period of recuperation. Members of the Stroke Association's Family and Carer Support team make home visits, too, and can give practical advice – or just sit and chat. (To find out more, see Resources, page 240.)

## GETTING ACTIVE

Taking up exercise after you have had a heart attack or a stroke is one of the most important factors in your recovery. But the prospect can be rather daunting. Remember that exercise will be recommended only if your doctors judge that you are sufficiently fit.

Before starting an exercise programme, heart patients are sometimes asked to undergo an echocardiogram (a test that allows medical staff to visualise the heart by bouncing sound waves off it) to assess their heart function and a treadmill test to check that that their heart can cope with a moderate exercise routine without problems.

Doctors advocate regular exercise as the best way to strengthen your heart after an attack. Two types in particular are recommended: aerobic exercise – such as walking, jogging, cycling or swimming – and careful resistance (strength) training.

## LOOKING TO THE LONG TERM

As discussed in Step 1, atherosclerosis is a disease affecting the whole body. Treating the immediate effects of a heart attack or stroke will not get rid of atherosclerosis, and long-term medication can control the problems it causes only to a limited

The vital thing is to keep active and take regular exercise, so your heart gets used to a gentle workout.

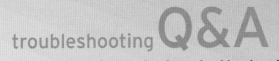

## If I've experienced a heart attack, should I avoid having sex?

After you have been given the all-clear to engage in moderate exercise – which your doctors will probably recommend anyway – then having sex is as safe as, say, running up the stairs: both activities will increase your heart rate to around 130 beats per minute (your heart rate at rest is around 70 beats per minute). Fewer than one per cent of heart attacks are caused by intercourse, and the risk is no greater for someone with a history of heart attack or angina than for anyone else.

Most people are able to start having sex again within two to three weeks of having a heart attack. But check with your doctor first if you are still getting chest pains or if you have very high blood pressure or heart rhythm disturbances (which may be signalled by palpitations). Physically fit people are able to enjoy sex with no increased risk.

The vital thing is to keep active and to take regular exercise, so your heart gets used to a gentle workout. The more you exercise, the safer sex becomes.

extent. That is why most people who have had heart attacks are advised by their doctors to make alterations to their lifestyle that will reduce the risk of further attacks.

Many of the lifestyle changes that doctors suggest for people at risk of or recovering from a heart attack or a stroke reflect the advice outlined in this book: stop smoking, eat healthily, increase your activity levels, lose pounds if you are carrying too much weight, avoid stress. You will learn more about all these things.

So, even if you have already had a heart attack or stroke, or if you have been given a timely warning in the form of worsening angina or a mini-stroke, absorbing the advice provided in the following steps will help to boost your recovery and lessen your future risk.

## YOUR UNIQUE SURVIVAL KIT

You know how to recognise the vital symptoms of heart disease and stroke and how you can take action to protect yourself and those close to you. Even more importantly, you have learned that swift action makes a difference and can saves lives.

Now that you understand the risks, it is time to consider how to make the changes that will give you lifelong protection against cardiovascular disease. Step 3 will give you the tools to examine your current lifestyle in detail, with the aim of identifying ways in which you may be damaging your own health. You can then work out your own risk profile and start to make a range of small adjustments that could have a major and positive impact on your health in the years to come.

# self-defence plan

## STEP 3

MOST OF US COULD DO SOME SIMPLE THINGS TO IMPROVE THE HEALTH OF OUR HEART AND ARTERIES. NOW IS THE TIME TO FIND OUT IF THE WAY YOU LIVE IS AFFECTING YOUR RISK OF FUTURE PROBLEMS AND IDENTIFY KEY AREAS WHERE SMALL CHANGES CAN MAKE ALL THE DIFFERENCE.

# Assess
## your risk

The following pages present a series of questionnaires that will help you to assess what effect your lifestyle choices may be having on your health. Once you understand your risk profile, you'll be in a better position to decide which elements of your daily life may need to be modified to give you the best protection against heart disease and stroke.

## HOW DOCTORS CALCULATE RISK

As preventive medicine gains ever more prominence in the health service, GPs are taking a more proactive role in patient care. For example, if you are aged over 40, your GP may invite you to have a 'heart health check' to determine your risk of developing cardiovascular disease in the future.

The scoring system generally employed by GPs to assess a patient's risk takes account of age, gender, systolic blood pressure (the higher figure, see page 26), blood cholesterol levels, and whether a patient smokes. As far as cholesterol is concerned, what matters is the ratio between the total cholesterol and the 'good' HDL cholesterol (see page 18); the higher the proportion of HDL the better. A computer program is used to analyse the data that has been collected and to estimate the likelihood of a patient experiencing a heart attack or a stroke within the next ten years.

## THE BIG PICTURE

When deciding if drug treatment or a referral to a cardiologist should be advised, a GP will also note whether the patient already has signs of cardiovascular disease – especially angina – or peripheral arterial disease, or a family history of heart attack or stroke.

The doctor will look at linked problems such as diabetes or obesity and measure a patient's weight and height. The result gained from these measurements is called body mass index, or BMI; if you would like to calculate your own BMI, follow the method described on page 66. The formula that doctors use to estimate risk is complicated, but there are online calculators where you can feed in your own figures and work out your risk (for example, http://hp2010.nhlbihin.net/atpiii/calculator.asp and http://qr2.dyndns.org/ ). You will need to know your blood pressure and cholesterol levels (both total cholesterol and HDL cholesterol) but, as

both are important health indicators, it is well worth asking your GP to check them, especially if you are aged over 40.

## CAUGHT IN THE WEB

Risk factors tend to be interlinked, and can exacerbate each other, so the more risk factors you have, the higher your overall level of risk. In fact, cardiovascular risk resembles an intricate spider's web. Obesity, high blood pressure and diabetes all increase your risk. And, obesity combined with a high intake of salt or excessive alcohol consumption also raises the risk of high blood pressure. A poor diet can contribute to obesity, diabetes, high blood pressure and high cholesterol – all of which feed into your overall risk, as well. Stress increases risk both directly and by increasing blood pressure. The older a person is, the more susceptible he or she is to raised blood pressure caused by stress at work. And so on.

## ... smoking increases your risk dramatically

Habits play a role too, especially smoking, which is specifically highlighted in the risk-prediction charts used by medical staff.

● If you are a man under 50 who is also a non-smoker with normal blood pressure and cholesterol levels, your chance of getting cardiovascular disease within the next ten years is low (less than 10 per cent). Change just one element – add a smoking habit, for example – and your risk of heart attack or stroke rises to between 10 and 20 per cent.

● If you are a woman aged between 50 and 59, smoking increases your risk dramatically – pushing it as high as 30 per cent if you also have high blood pressure and a high level of 'bad' LDL cholesterol in your blood (see page 18).

# troubleshooting Q&A

## I'm 67, fit and active, and I eat healthily. Am I still at risk?

Many older people who have a healthy lifestyle remain free of cardiovascular disease – particularly those who are not exposed to the bad diet, sedentary occupations and high levels of stress typical of 'civilised' Western societies. But generally in the UK, as in other Western and Westernised cultures, the risk of developing cardiovascular disease does increase with age, since over the years we reap the consequences of more and more exposure to various factors detrimental to health such as environmental pollution. So, the older you are, the more you need to take account of any personal added risk factors that you uncover as you work through this chapter.

## DEALING WITH THE HAZARDS OF MODERN LIFE

None of us can protect ourselves against all risk – but there are steps we can take to avoid obvious hazards. For example, minimising consumption of junk food and eating plenty of fruit and vegetables will have a beneficial effect on blood cholesterol levels and help to regulate blood pressure. What you eat and drink plays a huge role in your wellbeing and in Steps 5 and 6, you'll discover more about the simple dietary rules that make all the difference – replacing animal fats with healthier oils whenever possible, for instance, and keeping your calorie intake under control.

Walking in the countryside or in your local park will improve your fitness and benefit your heart and lungs. (Air pollution is another enemy of cardiovascular health, as is stressful, excessive noise or the sleep disturbance that comes with both noise and light pollution.) See Step 8 for ten everyday hazards – including plastics that have been linked to cardiovascular disease – and discover how to combat or avoid them.

## HEALTHY BALANCE

Reducing stress at work and ensuring that, however deskbound you are, you incorporate some activity into your day will also boost your chances of avoiding heart attacks and strokes. In Step 7, as well as fitness routines, you'll discover 'deskercises' to counteract the potential harm that a sedentary day can wreak on your body systems. In Step 9, you'll find out the best ways to tackle stress and learn sleep-promoting strategies and general tactics to enhance your sense of wellbeing even under pressure.

Few can avoid all the detrimental aspects of modern life. The goal is to achieve a healthy balance. By understanding that for most activities and circumstances there is a risk:benefit ratio, you can decide which are acceptable, which are avoidable and which you can compensate for.

# estimating your risk

The information and questionnaires on the following pages are designed to help you to assess how well you are protecting your heart and arteries in various aspects of your life.

As you work through the sets of questions, you may find it helpful to use a notebook or diary to jot down your scores and your risk assessment, so you can look back and monitor your progress in the coming months as you gradually reduce your risk in different areas. Be honest in your answers – and read on. Step 4 supplies solutions to any problem areas.

# your vital statistics
## WHAT'S YOUR BMI?

Numerous medical studies confirm that being overweight and carrying too much fat, especially abdominal fat, increases the risk of having a heart attack or a stroke. One of the best ways of discovering whether you are overweight for your height is to work out your body mass index, or BMI, a standard formula for measuring body fat (see below), which is a much better measure than weight alone because it takes account of height.

# how lean are you?

Calculating your body mass index (BMI) is the best way to assess whether you are overweight for your height. Follow this formula:

## CALCULATE YOUR BMI

**1** Note down your weight in kilograms (1kg = 2.2lb) _____

**2** Note down your height in metres (1m = 39.37in), then square it _____ x _____ = _____

**3** Divide your weight by your height squared _____ ÷ _____ = body mass index _____

A BMI of between 18.5 and 25 is considered healthy. If your BMI is in the 26–30 range, you are classed as overweight. If your BMI is in the 31–40 range, you are obese; if 41 or over, you are severely obese. Note: Muscle weighs more than fat, so people who are very muscular will have a high BMI without the associated health risks.

## WATCH YOUR WAIST

Your waist size is also key because it reveals how much fat you have around your abdomen. Find a tape measure and note down your waist circumference. For people of European origin, waist size should not exceed 94cm (37in) for men or 80cm (32in) for women. The figures are slightly lower for people of South Asian, Chinese, Japanese, African and South American origins, who have a higher risk of cardiovascular disease.

Even if your BMI is within the healthy range, you may still be at higher risk of developing long-term problems if you carry too much weight in your abdominal area. To find out if you fall into this category, you can calculate your waist-to-hip ratio (WHR). Start by measuring your waist at its narrowest point when your stomach is relaxed. Then measure your hips at their widest point. Now divide your waist measurement by your hip measurement to get your WHR.

Women should have a waist-to-hip of no more than 0.80; for men it should be no more than 0.90. For more information about the importance of these numbers and what to do if they are too high, see Step 6.

**RED**alert

### YOUR WAISTLINE

Losing abdominal fat can dramatically lower your risk of having a stroke or a mini-stroke. When scientists in Germany studied 379 people who had had a stroke or mini-stroke, and then compared them with 758 people in the same age and sex groups, they found that measures of abdominal fat were strongly associated with the risk of an attack.

Men with a waist circumference greater than 102cm (40in) and women whose waists measured more than 89cm (35in) had a four-fold increased risk of stroke compared with those with normal waist sizes. Similarly, people with the highest waist-to-hip ratio (over 0.97 for men or 0.84 for women) had almost eight times the risk of stroke compared with those with the lowest waist-to-hip ratio (less than 0.92 for men or 0.78 for women).

## TAKE YOUR PULSE

You can assess your general level of fitness simply by measuring your pulse rate while you are at rest. In one study of nearly 130,000 post-menopausal women who had no history of heart problems, those with the lowest resting pulse rate (fewer than 62 beats a minute) were significantly less likely to have a heart attack or die of coronary artery disease within the following eight years than those with the highest rate (more than 76 beats a minute). A similar association between pulse rate and cardiovascular risk has been demonstrated in studies involving men.

To check your resting pulse rate, make sure that you can see a clock or watch with a second hand. Then feel on the inside of your wrist about two fingers' breadth above the base of your thumb, or in the hollow on one

You can get a good idea of your general fitness level simply by measuring your pulse rate when at rest.

side of your windpipe, just under your jawbone, at the level of your Adam's apple (see photograph). While looking at the second hand of the clock or watch, count the number of heart beats you can feel in 15 seconds. Multiply the figure you arrive at by four to get the number of heart beats per minute – your pulse rate.

Check your pulse rate when you are still and calm – an ideal time is just after you wake up, as long as you haven't just been seriously startled by a loud alarm clock. As a guide, the average adult resting pulse rate is about 75 beats a minute for a woman and 70 for a man. Note down your current rate in your diary – as you get fitter, it should decrease.

## OTHER POINTS TO NOTE

As mentioned earlier, smoking sends your cardiovascular risk spiralling. The risk posed by smoking increases with age and subsides only after five years have elapsed since the smoker kicked the habit. So, if you do smoke, you need to recognise smoking as a serious risk factor and, for the sake of your heart and brain, you would be wise to take steps to give up. See Step 8 for some sound quitting strategies.

Surprisingly perhaps, scientific studies have also established a significant link between gum disease and the risk of experiencing a heart attack or a stroke. So be alert for red, swollen or bleeding gums; gums that bleed when you brush your teeth represent an early sign of gum disease. You have a greater risk of gum disease if you smoke, grind your teeth or are under stress. Good dental care will benefit your general health, so ensure that you have regular check-ups.

Robert Cutter

# A lucky escape

Robert Cutter, who runs a civil engineering business, was working on some machinery in a quarry when he experienced unusual, cramp-like pains across his chest. 'I felt really unwell and my face was hot and sweaty,' he says, 'but I didn't have a clue what was going on. The pains got so bad that I went home and finally managed to get upstairs - but then dropped to the floor. I phoned my sister, who dialled 999.'

When the ambulance arrived 20 minutes later, an ECG (electrocardiogram) confirmed that Robert had had a heart attack. It was more than an hour since the onset of his symptoms, and the nearest hospital was 45 minutes away. But Robert was lucky: the ambulance crew had just started to carry the clot-busting drug tenecteplase, and he was the first person in the new scheme to receive the drug out of hospital.

The effect was remarkable. 'As soon as they gave me the drug I was completely OK,' says Robert.

Amazingly, he suffered no damage to his heart and went home a few days later. A later test revealed that one of his coronary arteries was kinked - probably a condition he was born with - and a device called a stent was inserted to hold the artery open.

'Now I'm careful to eat the right things, more fish, greens and salads. Eating is crucial - what you eat is what you are.'

But Robert also acknowledges that before the attack, his blood pressure had been a little high. He didn't relax or exercise very much, and his diet was unhealthy.

'Now I'm careful to eat the right things, more fish, greens and salads. Eating is crucial - what you eat is what you are. And I was smoking a bit before - but I've stopped that now, I avoid cigarettes like the plague.'

Since adopting his new regime, his general health has improved. 'I go walking and cycling now too. I still have a busy lifestyle running my own business. It is stressful but I enjoy it and I try not to worry so much.'

# your body's fuel

**A**n unhealthy diet can increase your risk of heart attacks and strokes. So it is important to keep an eye on what you eat and drink. Answer the questions below and record your score. When you get to the end, add up all the figures to find out whether your drinks, snacks and meals help to protect you – 'low' – have a 'moderate' but not especially helpful effect, or could be raising your cardiovascular risk – 'increased'.

## Which would you prefer as a quick snack?

| | |
|---|---|
| An apple, a banana or a handful of grapes | 15 |
| Carrot sticks with a dip | 10 |
| A handful of nuts – salted | 5 |
| – natural | 10 |
| Crisps, a biscuit or a slice of cake | 0 |

## How many portions of oily fish do you eat per week?

(salmon, trout and mackerel are examples of oily fish)

| | |
|---|---|
| 0 | 0 |
| 1 | 10 |
| 2–4 | 15 |

Women who are or plan to become pregnant are advised not to have more than two portions of oily fish per week because high concentrations of mercury from ocean pollution may be present in the body fats of some oily fish, representing a potential danger, through the mother, to the health of an unborn child.

## How many times a week do you eat ready-meals or takeaways?

| | |
|---|---|
| 0 | 15 |
| 1 | 5 |
| More than 1 | 0 |

## How many portions of the following do you have in an average week?

(sausages, pies, burgers, pasties, kebabs, fatty meats, e.g. streaky bacon)

| | |
|---|---|
| 0 | 15 |
| 1 | 5 |
| More than one | 0 |

## On average, how often do you eat cakes, pastries, biscuits or crisps?

| | |
|---|---|
| Most days | 0 |
| 2–3 times a week | 5 |
| Once a week or less | 15 |

## What kind of fat do you tend to cook with?

| | |
|---|---|
| Butter, lard or dripping | 0 |
| Vegetable oils | 5 |
| Olive oil | 15 |

## Which of these cooking methods do you use most often?

| | |
|---|---|
| Deep frying | 0 |
| Pan frying | 5 |
| Grilling, poaching, baking or steaming | 15 |

## Which is closest to your usual breakfast?

| | |
|---|---|
| Nothing: I never eat before mid-morning | 0 |
| A coffee and pastry on the way to work | 0 |
| The full fry-up: bacon, eggs, sausages and fried bread | 0 |
| Wholemeal toast and marmalade | 5 |
| Muesli/high-fibre cereal such as Weetabix, with fresh fruit | 10 |
| Porridge or fruit with low-fat yoghurt | 15 |

## Do you check labels for saturated, hydrogenated and trans fats (the 'bad' ones) and act on what you find?

| | |
|---|---|
| Yes, always | 15 |
| Sometimes | 5 |
| Never | 0 |

## Do you check labels for salt content and act on what you find?

| | |
|---|---|
| Yes, usually | 10 |
| Sometimes | 5 |
| Never | 0 |

None of us should be eating more than 6g salt (2.4g sodium) a day, so avoid foods with more than 1.5g salt (0.6g sodium) per 100g and look in preference for those with 0.3g salt (0.1g sodium or less) per 100g.

## Which of these is the closest to your drinking pattern?

| | |
|---|---|
| Teetotal – no alcohol or less than one drink per month | 10 |
| Moderate drinking – 2–14 units a week for women<br>3–21 units a week for men | 15 |
| Excess drinking – more than 14 units a week for women<br>more than 21 units a week for men | 0 |
| Binge drinking – regularly consuming 6 or more units<br>in a single session | 0 |

A half a pint of beer or a standard pub measure (50ml) of fortified wine, such as sherry or port, is 1 unit. One small glass of wine (125ml) or a standard pub measure (25ml) of spirits = 1.5 units.

## Do you eat white rice, white pasta, white bread or sugary breakfast cereals:

| | |
|---|---|
| Daily | 0 |
| 3–4 times a week | 5 |
| Once or twice a week, or less often | 15 |

## ADD UP YOUR TOTAL SCORE

## YOUR RISK ASSESSMENT

| low | moderate | increased |
|---|---|---|
| 100 or more | 50–99 | 49 or less |

# your body's output

There is plenty of evidence that physical activity – or, rather, the lack of it – plays a considerable role in the development of cardiovascular disease. Getting fit may require quite a lot of effort since so many of today's jobs involve sitting for long periods of time. Evenings in front of the television don't help either. So how active is your lifestyle? For the benefit of your heart and arteries, should you be doing more?

### Which activities do you do regularly (at least once a week)?
- Go to the gym, run, cycle or play a sport                          15
- Enjoy a leisurely walk in the park                                  10
- Run up the stairs instead of taking the lift                        5
- Reach for the remote control                                        0

### If you work, how much activity do you get in the course of a working day?
- Walk to the photocopier or coffee machine a few times               0
- Make the effort to walk at least part of the way to work,
  or run upstairs a couple of times during the day                    5
- At least a third of my working time is spent moving around          10
- Manual work, constantly on the go                                   15

### On average, how many hours a day do you spend not sitting or lying down?
- 6 or more                                                           15
- 3–5                                                                 5
- Fewer than 3                                                        0

### Score 5 points for each hour's activity you do during an average week:
- Housework                                                           ---
- Gardening                                                           ---
- DIY                                                                 ---
- Walking the dog                                                     ---
- Cleaning the car                                                    ---

### On average, how much exercise do you get each week that makes you out of breath?
- At least 30 minutes, five days a week                               15
- Two hours or less in total                                          5
- None                                                                0

### How many hours a week do you spend watching television?
- 15 or more                                                          0
- 5–14                                                                5
- Fewer than 5                                                        15

### Can you climb two standard flights of stairs without getting out of breath?
- Yes, running                                                        15
- Yes, walking pace                                                   10
- No                                                                  0

Would people describe you as a fidget?
- Yes                                                                    10
- No                                                                     0

Your ideal day off would be spent doing which of the following?
- Lying in front of the television and raiding the fridge occasionally    0
- Relaxing with a good book and spending time with your family            5
- Taking a walk in the park and meeting friends for lunch                10
- Sailing, hill-climbing, fencing or a similar energetic activity        15

Would you run to catch a bus or train that was about to leave rather than wait for the next one?
- Yes                                                                    10
- No                                                                     0

## ADD UP YOUR TOTAL SCORE

## YOUR RISK ASSESSMENT

| low | moderate | increased |
|-----|----------|-----------|
| 60 or more | 36–59 | 35 or less |

# your work

**S**tress at work can affect your chances of developing cardiovascular disease. Answer yes or no to the following questions to assess your risk (skip this section if you are self-employed, unemployed or retired).

Do you regularly feel under pressure at work?
Do you feel your immediate boss is sometimes unfair?
Do you commute to work by public transport?
Do you regularly work longer than 45 hours per week?
Do you take work home more than once a month?
Do you answer work emails or phone calls away from the office?

## ADD UP THE NUMBER OF 'YES' ANSWERS

## YOUR RISK ASSESSMENT

| low | moderate | increased |
|-----|----------|-----------|
| 0–2 | 3–4 | 5–6 |

# your daily surroundings

**Y**our cardiovascular risk can be affected by a variety of factors in your environment, from the people with whom you share your home to the air you breathe. Answer yes or no to the following questions:

Do you live with someone who smokes?
Do you live within earshot of a main road?
Do you regularly walk or cycle in heavy traffic?
Is your home or workplace often noisy?
Does most of your food come in plastic packaging?
Most days do you only see the people you work with?

## ADD UP THE NUMBER OF 'YES' ANSWERS

## YOUR RISK ASSESSMENT

| low | moderate | increased |
|-----|----------|-----------|
| 0–2 | 3–4 | 5–6 |

# your nights

**How many hours of sleep do you usually get at night?**

| | |
|---|---|
| 5 or less | 0 |
| 6 to 8 | 15 |
| 9 or more | 0 |

**Which most closely describes your usual sleeping pattern:**

| | |
|---|---|
| I sleep soundly all night | 15 |
| I may wake once to go to the bathroom but fall asleep again easily | 15 |
| I have trouble falling asleep but sleep soundly the rest of the night | 5 |
| I tend to wake several times in the night and have difficulty getting back to sleep | 0 |
| I wake up early in the morning and it's pointless trying to sleep again | 0 |

**During the day do you regularly:**

| | |
|---|---|
| Wake up still feeling tired | 0 |
| Feel tired or sleepy most of the day | 0 |
| Tend to drop off unexpectedly when you sit quietly | 0 |
| Take a siesta | 10 |

**Do you snore?**

(Answer yes if your partner or your children say you do, even if you don't believe it.)

| | |
|---|---|
| Yes | 0 |
| No | 15 |

Do you sleep in the same room as a snorer?

- Yes                                                                          0
- No                                                                          10

## ADD UP YOUR TOTAL SCORE

## YOUR RISK ASSESSMENT

| low | moderate | increased |
|-----|----------|-----------|
| more than 35 | 16–34 | up to 15 |

# the people around you

**Which of these best describes your home life?**

- Stressful                                                                    0
- Dull                                                                         0
- Supportive                                                                  15
- Friendly chaos                                                             10

**If you have a principal relationship, would you describe it as mainly:**

- Happy and supportive                                                       15
- A bit of a compromise                                                       5
- Tense and argumentative                                                     0
- Wretched and unhappy                                                        0

**How many friends do you have in whom you can confide?**

- None                                                                         0
- 1–2                                                                          5
- 3–5                                                                         10
- More than 5                                                                15

**Are you friendly with at least one neighbour?**

- Yes                                                                         10
- No                                                                          0

**How many hugs did you share on an average day this week?**

- None                                                                         0
- 1–3                                                                          5
- 4 or more                                                                  15

## ADD UP YOUR TOTAL SCORE

## YOUR RISK ASSESSMENT

| low | moderate | increased |
|-----|----------|-----------|
| 40 or more | 16–39 | less than 15 |

# your inner life

The way you feel, your habits, attitudes and interests all play a role in your risk of experiencing cardiovascular disease. Discover how your interaction with life could be adding to – or protecting you from – the risk of heart attacks and strokes.

**Do money worries sometimes keep you awake at night?**
- Yes   0
- No   10

**Do you make sure you have some time to relax, if only for a few minutes, every day?**
- Yes   15
- No   0

**How would you describe your general health?**
- Pretty good   15
- Just a few niggling problems   10
- I have a number of health problems that interfere with my life   0

**Do you ever experience panic attacks, when you get anxious, feel shaky and your heart beats very fast?**
- Yes   0
- No   5

**Do you often feel lonely?**
- Yes   0
- No   10

**Do you often get irritable or uncontrollably angry?**
- Yes   0
- No   10

**Do you sometimes feel there's no point trying to make things better?**
- Yes   0
- No   10

**Do you have a hobby or interest that takes you out of the house, at least once a week?**
- Yes   15
- No   0

**Do you regularly pursue interests that stimulate your mind (such as doing crosswords, reading books, learning a language, playing chess)?**
- Yes   15
- No   0

**Would people describe you as having a good sense of humour?**
- Yes   15
- No   0

How do you feel the next five years are likely to turn out?

- I'm excited about them                                    15
- I know I'll cope with any problems                         10
- Thinking about the future makes me anxious                  0

## ADD UP YOUR TOTAL SCORE

## YOUR RISK ASSESSMENT

| low | moderate | increased |
| --- | --- | --- |
| 80 or more | 29–79 | less then 30 |

# your happiness

How often during the past week have you felt the following emotions?

- I felt hopeful about the future
- I was happy
- I enjoyed life
- I felt that I was just as good as other people

For each of the four items, score as follows:

0 = rarely or none of the time (less than 1 day during the week)

1 = some or a little of the time (1-2 days a week)

2 = occasionally or a moderate amount of the time (3-4 days a week)

3 = most or all of the time (5-7 days a week)

If you're not sure, try recording your feelings at bedtime each day next week.

## YOUR RISK ASSESSMENT

Add up your total score for all four items. The maximum possible is 12, a generally happy state of mind, and the minimum 0, not happy at all. The higher your score, the more protection you have against cardiovascular disease.

# turning point

So now you have put your life under the microscope and uncovered a rich seam of information – not only about your health but also about your personality, your feelings and your behaviour. The more frequently you scored moderate or high in the risk assessments, the more seriously you should take the need for action now to modify your risk. In Step 4, you will discover how to initiate changes that will help you to reach your goal of a healthy heart and healthy arteries.

# self-defence plan
## STEP 4

NOW YOU'VE LEARNT MORE ABOUT THE LINKS BETWEEN LIFESTYLE CHOICES AND GOOD HEALTH, YOU CAN USE THIS INSIGHT TO HELP YOU DEVISE A PRACTICAL APPROACH TO CUTTING THE RISK OF STROKE, HEART DISEASE AND OTHER RELATED CONDITIONS.

# Make your personal plan

If you have considered all the issues covered in Step 3, completed the questionnaires, and taken stock of the results, you should now be able to make a fair assessment of how your lifestyle might be affecting your risk of developing cardiovascular disease. You should also have discovered which category (or categories) of risk is most relevant to you – whether it's an expanding waistline, an unbalanced diet, a stressful job or regular loss of sleep.

Some of the information revealed in Step 3 may have surprised you. Did you know, for example, that gum disease is a risk factor for heart attacks? Or that housework and gardening can protect your arteries? Or that simply sitting for long periods or watching television for hours on end are risk factors for cardiovascular disease in their own right?

## FIGHTING BACK

Apart from your age and gender, you have the power to modify every single one of the risk factors identified in Step 3. You may need to enlist the help of your GP to combat some of them. Others you'll be able to tackle yourself as you develop your long-term strategic plan to protect against heart attacks and strokes and the atherosclerosis (artery damage) that usually causes them.

## THE POWER OF PLEASURE

What you'll also discover is the importance of emotional wellbeing and how happiness, underpinned by supportive relationships and stimulating interests, holds a vital key to good health. And you'll find out how you can reduce your cardiovascular risk by identifying the elements of your own life that bring you pleasure and enjoyment – be they hobbies that you're passionate about or special people who make you happy.

# think yourself well

**H**ow healthy you believe yourself to be may have a crucial bearing on your life expectancy. In one research study, a group of hotel cleaners – many of whom perceived themselves as inactive and unfit – were asked to listen to a presentation about the ways in which their daily cleaning routine provided them with an excellent physical workout. They were given information sheets showing how many calories they used while performing such tasks as vacuuming a staircase or cleaning a bathroom. A few weeks later, the workers had lost an average of 2lb (1kg) in weight, had reduced their blood pressure levels and had achieved some reduction in body mass index (BMI) and body fat – and yet none of them had changed their diet or exercise habits at all.

## ADDED HEALTH BENEFITS

Looking after the health of your arteries will benefit your general physical and mental health, and give you a good chance of avoiding other, linked conditions, such as peripheral arterial disease and diabetes. As you grow older, having healthier arteries will help to preserve your teeth, eyesight and hearing, and make it less likely that you will develop dementia.

Having healthier arteries will help to preserve your teeth, eyesight and hearing as you grow older.

## MOMENT OF TRUTH

While completing the lifestyle questionnaires in Step 3, you may have noted potential  health problems that you'd never considered before. Perhaps you were surprised when you measured your BMI (see page 66), or by the amount of abdominal fat you had acquired (see page 67). You may have noticed how breathless you tend to get while climbing stairs – and how little exercise you take. Were you aware how many cigarettes you were smoking? Or did you realise that you never seem to have time to unwind these days and feel edgy and tense?

These are some of the risk factors identified in the Interheart study described in Step 1 (see page 17). It's worth looking back and considering the nine factors that account for 90 per cent of all first-time heart attacks.

If you scored 'low' in most of the questionnaires, congratulations. Whether you knew it or not, you are doing most things right. But for most people there will be something to change and the following steps make that easy and enjoyable. The most encouraging aspect of all this advice is that you will feel better, younger and fitter if you make the critical tweaks.

# get a cardiovascular health check

Making an appointment with your GP is an excellent starting point as you begin to assess the practical ways to address any of the health risks you uncovered in Step 3. This is particularly important if you are over 40 and haven't had your blood pressure or cholesterol checked in the past couple

## Making an appointment with your GP is an excellent starting point to address any health risks you've uncovered.

of years. If you have several risk factors, you could ask your doctor to carry out a full check-up on the health of your heart, known medically as a cardiovascular risk assessment. Such advice applies if you are a heavy smoker, if your waist measurement (in a woman) exceeds 80cm (32in) or (in a man) 94cm (37in), if you have a family history of heart disease or stroke, or if for any other reason you are at a higher risk of developing heart disease.

## DISCUSS DIABETES

Overweight people who are concerned about developing metabolic syndrome or 'pre-diabetes' (see pages 30–31) should ask their GP to monitor their urine for sugar and, if necessary, to arrange blood tests to check their blood sugar levels.

'About half of those people who are diagnosed with Type 2 diabetes already exhibit signs of cardiovascular disease at the time of diagnosis,' says Simon O'Neill, a director of Diabetes UK. Taking action to overcome underlying problems such as obesity could help to reduce your risks of both problems.

## SECRET weapon

### GENETIC INFORMATION SERVICE

Coronary heart disease (CHD) tends to run in families, though your risk is greatly reduced if you are healthy and fit. Certain rare inherited heart conditions are more dangerous, however, as they develop in young people regardless of lifestyle, are often symptomless and can cause Sudden Arrhythmic Death Syndrome (SADS).

In April 2009, the British Heart Foundation launched the Genetic Information Service to advise families affected by SADS and to ensure that they can get speedy referral to a clinic for inherited cardiac conditions. The helpline number is 0300 456 8383 and the service is staffed by trained cardiac nurses who provide support and information on genetic clinics nationwide.

Patients referred to specialist clinics will be given an electrophysiological test (EPS) to detect any abnormal electrical activity within the heart. If suitable, they may receive radiofrequency ablation, a specialist procedure which – without drugs or surgery – can eliminate the problem.

## YOUR CALCIUM SCORE

One of the tools doctors may use to diagnose heart disease is an EBCT (electron beam computed tomography) scan. (Although not usually offered on the NHS, EBCT scans are widely available privately.) The scan can reveal information about soft tissues as well as bones, which means that it may be used to examine internal organs such as your heart. EBCT scans can identify and measure calcium deposits that are found in a build-up of hard plaque on artery walls. If you have no calcium, you can assume that your risk of having a heart attack is very low. However, most people develop some plaques containing calcium in their arteries as they age, so the older you are the less likely you are to have a zero score. A mid-range score indicates that serious measures are required to reduce cardiovascular risk. A high coronary calcium score means that you almost certainly have coronary heart disease.

## PROTECTIVE MEASURES

If your doctor tells you that you have a moderate or high risk of developing cardiovascular disease, he or she may recommend that you try to improve your diet, take more exercise, set a target for weight loss and cut down on stress. Advice on all these aspects of healthier living are covered in future steps in this book, as are plenty of tips for making changes to engrained habits simple and fun. If you smoke, you should tackle this as your top priority and, if necessary, enlist your GP's help to find the therapy or medication that will help you to quit. All of these measures will also help to lower your blood pressure.

If you are at high risk (that is, you have a 20 per cent or greater chance of developing the disease over the next ten years) you may be prescribed statins to reduce cholesterol levels and perhaps also drugs to reduce blood pressure or to treat diabetes. In this case, the measures outlined in *Conquering heart attack & stroke* will be an added bonus. The invaluable information in the rest of the book will enable you to keep your treatment on target, and it could help you to reduce your medication. You might eventually be able to stop taking the tablets altogether.

Smoking is such a major risk factor that you should make it your top priority to quit.

# your scores and your choices

The results you obtained from completing the questionnaires in Step 3 reveal which factors are contributing most strongly to your risk of having a heart attack or stroke. You need to focus attention on any instance where you scored 'moderate' or 'increased'. Make a list of the problem areas identified by the questionnaires and then follow the guide below to find practical advice and imaginative strategies for tackling them.

## your body individual risk factors:

- **Excess weight**
- **Abdominal fat**
- **Smoking**
- **High resting pulse rate**
- **Gum disease**

### WHERE TO FIND HELP

If you need to lose weight, Step 5 will help you to make a thorough reassessment of your diet as well as providing a multitude of tips on how to make the small changes that will yield large benefits for your weight.

Step 6 allows you to work out what's causing you to put on weight, and takes a long hard look at the dangers posed by processed food and junk food. It also describes tactics for resisting temptation and gives advice on where to go for expert professional help.

If you are carrying too much abdominal fat, you'll know that it's notoriously difficult to shift. Step 6 explains how a two-pronged attack of diet and exercise really does work – even if the enemy has gained a lot of ground – and includes a list of those foods that can actually protect you against putting on too much fat around your middle.

Step 7 is full of ideas for getting pleasure out of physical exertion, even if exercise is not your favourite thing. It also has tips for building up cardiovascular strength and stamina.

A high pulse rate when you are at rest tends to indicate a lack of fitness. Step 7 sets out strategies for getting active that can be incorporated with ease into everyday life, without the need to spend long sessions in the gym. It is worth noting that a trained athlete can have a pulse rate as low as 40 beats per minute, while the average resting heart rate for an adult is between 60 and 100 beats per minute.

If you are a smoker, you have probably tried at least once to break the habit. It's a difficult thing to do if you're living a fast-paced life. But did you know that, however much you smoke, reducing the number of cigarettes smoked by half reduces your risk by half? In Step 8 you will learn how to shore up your willpower by a combination of physical and psychological tactics. See the Resources section (page 240) for useful helplines. (Studies have shown that people who have support – medical, emotional or both – are much more likely to succeed in giving up.)

Gum disease increases your risk of experiencing heart disease or stroke. In Step 8 you will find out how to spot the early signs of gum disease and learn what you need to do to prevent it.

# your body's fuel individual risk factors:

- Not enough fruit or vegetables
- Too many saturated or trans fats
- Not enough oily fish
- Too many processed or junk foods
- Too many snacks
- Cooking unhealthily
- Too much salt
- Too much alcohol
- Too many refined carbohydrates

## WHERE TO FIND HELP

Your diet has a major impact on the condition of your arteries. Step 5 identifies the best foods for healthy arteries and those to avoid. Also explained is the latest research into why fruit and vegetables and certain types of fat provide potent protection against heart attack and stroke. Cutting down on sodium, or salt, is key in the battle against high blood pressure, but it's not just the salt we add to food that should concern us; anything from canned soup to biscuits can contain hidden salt.

# small change, big gain

If everyone in the UK simply replaced an unhealthy daily snack (a chocolate bar, a bag of crisps, a cake or a pastry) with a healthy one (such as a piece of fresh or dried fruit, raw vegetables such as carrots or celery, unsalted nuts or seeds), it could lead to the prevention of nearly 6,000 deaths from cardiovascular disease each year. Scientists at the University of Liverpool have calculated that each person would consume around 4.4g less saturated fat per day, leading to 2,400 fewer deaths from coronary artery disease and 425 fewer deaths from stroke. In addition, we would each take in around 500mg less salt a day, potentially saving a further 3,120 lives a year.

## your body's output individual risk factors:

- **Sedentary job and too much sitting in general**
- **Too much television**
- **Not enough exercise**
- **General lack of fitness**
- **Not enough walking**

### WHERE TO FIND HELP

Step 7 shows you how to enjoy getting into shape. Even if you are taking up exercise for the first time later in life, there are gentle activities to benefit your circulation, increase your muscular strength and help you to live longer. And you'll learn how everyday activities, including gardening and housework, burn calories and help you to keep fit.

---

**SECRET**weapon

### TAKE THE STAIRS

Even a change as simple as climbing up and down the stairs at work instead of using the lift could improve your chances of living longer, according to researchers in Switzerland. A team from the University of Geneva asked 69 university employees who each habitually took less than 2 hours' exercise a week to abandon the lift and to use the stairs. Over a period of 12 weeks the volunteers climbed or descended on average 23 flights of stairs a day (up from five a day before the study). Their lung capacity, blood pressure, waist measurements and cholesterol levels all improved, reducing their risk of premature death by about 15 per cent.

Tear yourself away from the box.

Ray Chadd

# How I changed my lifestyle

Turning 50 had a special but serious significance for Ray
Chadd. 'I felt perfectly fit and healthy but I couldn't help
remembering that my father had died suddenly of a heart attack
at the age of 56. That had been a terrible shock. I started
wondering if I might be vulnerable in my fifties, too.'

What especially concerned him, too, was that his youngest
daughter was only 3 years old. 'My wife wanted me to go for
a check-up. I never went to the doctor, I was never ill. But
she said something like "What would we do without you?" and
that was enough. I made an appointment at the surgery.'

The GP found that Ray's blood pressure was, indeed, on the
high side and advised him to be careful with his diet and cut
down on salt. He began to eat more fruit and vegetables, less
meat and fewer biscuits and cakes.'You may laugh, but plain
yoghurt mixed with fresh fruit became my favourite food. I
felt better and I had more energy, too. We started playing
tennis, which was fun and relaxing. That was good because it
was a stressful time. I was Head of English at a further
education college that was going through a lot of change.'

'Plain yoghurt mixed with chopped-up fresh fruit
became a favourite food. I felt better and I had
more energy too.'

Ray was also referred to a cardiologist and was told that
he had an irregular heart beat, too. 'That was an added reason
to keep my weight and blood pressure under control.'

Now 66 and semi-retired, Ray still has regular BP check-
ups but feels perfectly fit and has successfully avoided the
statins that many of his contemporaries have to take.

For that he thanks his lifestyle tweaks - a moderate diet,
plus regular exercise up and down the many stairs at his
home, and walking his son's dog on the North Downs. He was
also pleased to note a recent Dutch study, which concluded
that a little wine daily is even better protection against
heart attacks than being a teetotaller. 'I certainly enjoy red
wine,' says Ray,'but I only drink about half a glass a day.'

# your work individual factors:

- **Pressure at work**
- **Unfair boss**
- **Commuting**
- **Long hours**
- **Taking work home**
- **Work emails or phone calls away from the office**

## WHERE TO FIND HELP

If you are an office worker, you probably find that, even when you manage to escape from your desk, someone tries to reach you by mobile phone. Some days it seems impossible to distance yourself from work obligations. Step 9 outlines some stress management techniques and explains why it's so important to set yourself limits and learn to switch off from work.

# your daily surroundings
## individual risk factors:

- **Living with a smoker**
- **Living near a main road**
- **Exposure to heavy traffic**
- **Exposure to loud noise**
- **Dealing with domestic stress**
- **Living alone**

## WHERE TO FIND HELP

Smoking endangers not only your own health but the health of those around you. Step 8 offers effective strategies for breaking the habit. If there is another smoker in the family or among your group of friends, see if you can make a pact to quit together.

**SECRET**weapon

### EARPLUGS

Exposure to the din of modern life may increase an individual's risk of heart disease. Studies of car assembly workers in the USA suggests that continuous exposure to noise increases blood pressure, but that using ear defenders can largely prevent this. Conversely, by protecting your arteries you will also protect your hearing, since cardiovascular disease can clog the tiny arteries that feed the delicate hearing mechanisms of the inner ear. Whatever the source of noise in your life – aircraft, traffic, road drills or machinery – using a pair of earplugs is a cheap and easy way to take care of your hearing, and your heart.

Noise pollution can be particularly difficult to avoid if you live or work in an urban area or work around noisy machines. Step 8 includes advice on how to protect yourself from noise pollution and the toxic substances that lurk in your environment.

# your nights individual risk factors:

- Snoring
- Sleeping with a snorer
- Too little – or too much – sleep
- Disturbed sleep
- Daytime sleepiness

## WHERE TO FIND HELP

Sleep deprivation exerts a serious toll on our bodies. Simply stated, people who sleep better live longer, and in Step 9 you will find expert advice on how to sleep easy, as well as advice on how to deal with snoring.

# your inner life individual factors:

- Financial worries
- Insufficient relaxation
- Feeling unhealthy
- Panic attacks
- Loneliness
- Hopelessness or pessimism
- Lack of interests
- Inadequate mental stimulation
- Poor sense of humour

## WHERE TO FIND HELP

Most of us assume that external things are what make us happy. But Step 9 dispels this myth and explains that the key to a full and healthy life is finding the strategy that suits you.

# the people around you
## Individual risk factors:

- Stressful home life
- Non-stimulating home life
- Unsupportive relationship
- Lack of friends
- Isolation from neighbours

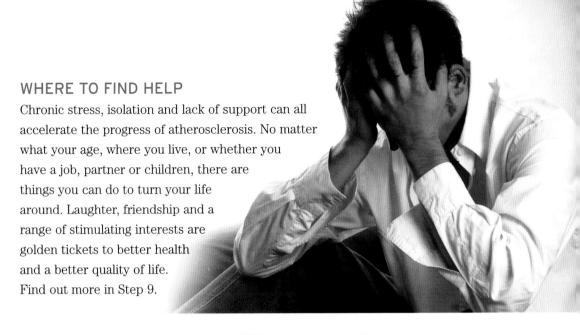

## WHERE TO FIND HELP

Chronic stress, isolation and lack of support can all accelerate the progress of atherosclerosis. No matter what your age, where you live, or whether you have a job, partner or children, there are things you can do to turn your life around. Laughter, friendship and a range of stimulating interests are golden tickets to better health and a better quality of life. Find out more in Step 9.

# it's time to **talk tactics**

Don't try to put right everything at once. If you suddenly decide that you must lose a stone in a fortnight, embark on a major exercise programme immediately and revolutionise your eating habits, you probably won't get far before you become discouraged and give up (especially if you also need to tackle other tough issues such as stopping smoking, dealing with a difficult boss, or deciding what to do about an unhappy relationship).

## THE KEY TO SUCCESS

To boost your confidence and maintain your motivation, start by making changes that are minor but sustainable. Here are some ideas for small changes that will make a big difference.

## FROM LITTLE ACORNS ...

- Make an appointment with your doctor or dentist.
- Buy olive oil instead of your usual cooking oil.
- Use the stairs instead of the lift at work.
- Swap one unhealthy snack today for a piece of fruit.
- Eat fish instead of meat for dinner tonight.
- Leave work on time one day this week.
- Take the salt cellar off the table.
- Give your partner a hug for no reason.
- Go for a half-hour stroll instead of watching television.
- Invite your neighbour over for coffee.

## SET 'SMART' GOALS

If you are determined to make your plan work and to maintain it, you will need to define and prioritise your goals. For example, based on what you learnt in Step 3, choose one element of your life associated with a high risk of cardiovascular disease, read the relevant information here and decide on the most important changes that you need to make. Set your targets, write them down, and give yourself a timeframe for achieving them.

For example, if you need to lose 1½ stones (9.5kg ) to achieve your ideal weight, it is clear that this will take several months. So set an interim goal, such as losing 5lb (2.2kg) by the end of next month. Similarly, if you acknowledge that your diet has many shortcomings, don't imagine that you can put everything right in a few days. Pick small, specific targets, such as forgoing a ready meal or takeaway once a week and making one or two home-cooked meals from scratch using healthy ingredients. Or take healthy snacks to work instead of buying chocolate bars and crisps from a vending machine or the local shop.

Make the process of changing to a healthier lifestyle as much fun as you can. For instance, for every 1kg (2lb) you lose, reward yourself in some way. Take a weekend's break, buy something special, look up old friends – and plan for a future that features a healthier, happier you.

Set an interim goal, don't imagine that you can put everything right in a few days.

### BE REALISTIC ...

One thing you will be aware of by now is that warding off heart attacks and strokes is not a short-term manoeuvre like a crash diet. If the many small changes you are contemplating are going to keep you protected for the rest of your life, you need to work them into your everyday routine, and you will then have the motivation to keep them going.

### ... AND PRAGMATIC

Another important element of the process is to decide what you can change. It's no good telling your boss that you refuse to work late ever again, but you can quietly look around for a new job, or retrain to enable you to move to a company that makes fewer demands on your personal life. Or you might decide to use some relaxing techniques to reduce stress related to overworking or a difficult work environment.

If you live next to a main road, you may not be in a position to move home, but you could buy earplugs to help you get a better night's sleep. Throughout this book you will find a wealth of advice to help you to fend off cardiovascular risks even though you my not be able to avoid them altogether.

## MAINTAIN MOMENTUM

Once you understand what's realistic, you can devise a timetable. You cannot alter the habits of a lifetime in a few weeks but you can start to make changes that will last, and build on them. You will find it useful to keep a running record in a notebook, so you can see your successes, or note what didn't work and try something else.

Take advantage of whatever support is available. Tell your friends that you are stopping smoking and ask for their help; cajole your partner or children to join you in getting involved in more physical activity; talk to your GP if you run into problems with your weight-loss regime. As your GP knows, by making these healthy changes now, you will be less likely to have dangerous fats attacking your arteries – and you will be less likely to need medication for high blood pressure or high cholesterol or even heart disease in the future.

### MUSIC

Learning to play a musical instrument could be good for your heart, say scientists at the University of Oxford and the University of Pavia in Italy. They studied breathing and circulation in 24 young people before and while the subjects listened to excerpts of music. Half were trained musicians who had been playing instruments such as the violin, piano, flute, clarinet or bass for several years. The rest had no musical training. The music ranged from slow classical music (Beethoven and Indian raga) to fast-paced rap (the Red Hot Chili Peppers). While the faster and more complex rhythms speeded up breathing and circulation, slower, more meditative tracks slowed breathing and heart rate in all participants. However, the effects were strongest on the musicians, who were more used to synchronising breathing with musical phrases. The scientists suggest that the relaxing and stress-reducing effects of music could be useful in preventing and treating heart disease and stroke.

## YOUR PLAN FOR LIFE

In the steps that follow you will discover the tactics and strategies, the important facts and expert advice, to help keep your cardiovascular system healthy. By targeting the root causes now, you will prolong your life. You have already begun taking charge in ways that work for you.

# self-defence plan

## STEP 5

DELICIOUS MEALS ADD TO THE ENJOYMENT OF LIFE AND THERE'S NO NEED TO FORGO THEM TO PROTECT YOUR HEART AND ARTERIES. HEALTHY DIETS OFTEN INCLUDE THE FRESHEST, TASTIEST AND MOST COLOURFUL NATURAL FOODS BECAUSE THESE ALL HELP TO BUILD UP RESISTANCE TO CARDIOVASCULAR PROBLEMS.

# Discover the pleasures of healthy eating

**Y**our eating habits have a crucial influence on your risk of cardiovascular disease. Obesity, high cholesterol and disturbed blood sugar in particular are among the food-related factors underlying heart attacks. But we are all given so much conflicting information about healthy eating that, for those people who want to improve their diet, it is difficult to know who to believe or how to start.

## HELPING YOU CHOOSE

Step 5 aims to cut through the general confusion about diets to provide clear, accessible advice based on the most authoritative research and expert opinion. You will find out about foods that can wreak havoc on your body, such as saturated fats, salt, refined carbohydrates and sugar. And you will learn about beneficial foods such as fruit and vegetables, fish, and even red wine, that help fight the causes of cardiovascular disease. This advice will help you to make informed choices and add more delicious ingredients to what you eat every day.

## MAGIC FOODS

Don't be put off by the thought that you need to change everything. There are enjoyable and simple ways to enhance your diet without self-sacrifice. Eating fresh, natural foods that are full of flavour will encourage you to develop a totally new eating pattern. Building up your dietary defences in stages will make change easier and help you to adopt eating habits that will benefit your long-term health. In fact, once you have followed this healthy eating plan for a month, you will never look back.

**I'm pretty fit, I'm not overweight and I play football three times a week. Surely I don't need to worry about what I eat?**

An active lifestyle is undoubtedly beneficial to health, but if you want to keep your body in peak condition in the years to come, you will need to give it the right sort of fuel. So, it really is in your own interests to find out about foods that will protect your heart and arteries, foods that will help to build and maintain your bones and muscles, and foods that will help to keep your weight down as you get older – and adapt your long-term diet accordingly.

# what's wrong
## with our diets?

People in the UK are getting fatter. Part of the reason is that many of us tend to make poor choices – eating processed foods that are high in sugar, refined carbohydrates, salt and unhealthy fats. These also tend to be laden with calories which, for anyone with an inactive lifestyle, are hard to burn off. This spells trouble for our health because it prompts the body to make too much 'bad' LDL cholesterol, which together with other factors, such as inflammation, leads to the formation of artery-clogging plaque.

During the past 50 years, more and more of us have come to depend heavily on convenience foods and takeaways. A scan of the food aisles in any supermarket will reveal how many common items are far from pure and natural. Most are either processed or artificially sweetened, flavoured or coloured, or laced with chemical preservatives to keep them from spoiling. And it is worth remembering that, when fresh raw wholefoods are canned, precooked or turned into instant ready meals, many essential vitamins, minerals and nutrients are lost.

## CLUES FROM THE PAST

Our bodies are not designed to thrive on processed food. Genetically, we are still hunter-gatherers – as we have been since the late Palaeolithic era, or Stone Age, some 40,000 years ago. Yet our diet is completely different from that of our ancestors who ate only natural foods obtained by hunting and foraging. More than 70 per cent of energy intake in modern Western diets comes from foods that were unknown in the Stone Age. These include refined carbohydrates such as those in white flour, white bread

Avoid refined
carbohydrates such as
white flour, white bread and
white rice, which have been heavily processed.

and white rice, which have been heavily processed, thereby removing many of their beneficial qualities. Since the modern diet is calorie-dense rather than nutrient-dense, many of us are eating more calories daily than we can use up in physical activity. As a result, we put on weight.

What's more, for most people, affordable food is much more readily available than it has ever been. So – unlike our distant ancestors, who struggled to obtain enough food to live on – we often need to limit our intake for our own good health.

'Throughout human evolution, access to food was the major challenge for survival,' explains Professor Stephen O'Rahilly, co-director of the Institute of Metabolic Science, Cambridge. 'People who had genetic variants that made them good at storing food as fat would be the most likely to survive and pass the trait on.'

This natural tendency rarely led to obesity, because it was balanced by the energy expended in obtaining food. Today we don't have to go out and catch our food. We don't even have to move; the supermarket will deliver it to our door. And what we choose to eat can make matters worse.

This mismatch between our lifestyle and that of our early forebears is a major factor in the current surge in obesity, hypertension, diabetes, stroke and heart disease. Historical and anthropological studies suggest that our ancestors were largely free of the degenerative cardiovascular diseases that beset many of us today; this also applies to societies in areas of the modern world that are not subject to Western nutritional influences.

## THE POWER OF NATURAL FOODS

So what are the benefits of a Stone Age diet? Our ancestors ate mainly game meats, fish, vegetables, berries, other fruit and nuts – broadly speaking, they either speared it or picked it. It was a diet rich in lean protein, monounsaturated and polyunsaturated fats, and especially

A high-fat, high-sugar diet not only encourages weight gain but is to some extent addictive.

omega-3 fatty acids (see page 105), fibre, vitamins, minerals and other beneficial plant chemicals. These natural foods contain elements that help to keep our cardiovascular system in good condition. In fact, when volunteers in a recent Swedish study followed a 'Stone Age diet' for three weeks, eating as our distant ancestors did, they reduced their average calorie intake by 36 per cent, raised protective antioxidant levels in their blood, reduced their systolic pressure (the first number in a blood pressure reading), and had a 72 per cent reduction in levels of a harmful clot-promoting factor in the blood. They also lost weight, slimmed their waistlines and reduced their body mass index (BMI). Other research has shown that a Stone Age diet not only lowers blood pressure but also improves insulin sensitivity and lowers levels of C-reactive protein, another risk marker for heart disease (see page 22).

**RED**alert **!**

**JUNK FOODS MAY HAVE
AN ADDICTIVE EFFECT**

A diet of junk food may change brain pathways that regulate food intake and programme us to eat more. Laboratory tests have shown that animals fed a high-fat, high-sugar diet promptly increase their consumption of this type of food. This strongly suggests that a high-fat, high-sugar diet not only encourages weight gain but is to some extent addictive, making it very difficult to lose weight unless the diet is changed.

## UNPROCESSED IS BEST

Following a healthy food plan means selecting whole, unprocessed foods and cutting down on foods that are pre-packaged, pre-prepared or highly refined, including sugar and white bread.

The Stone Age diet contains little or no grains or rice, but these are not 'bad' foods unless they are over-refined. Eating whole grains and brown rice is, in fact, beneficial because both contain plenty of fibre, which keeps the digestive system healthy and satisfies the appetite, so we need to eat less. Like fruit and vegetables, whole-grain wheat, maize and brown rice are good sources of insoluble fibre. Oats, oat bran and pulses provide soluble fibre, which contributes to heart health by binding to 'bad' LDL cholesterol and removing it as waste from the body.

# the key to
# low blood pressure

Cutting your salt intake is one of the most important changes you can make to keep your blood pressure at a healthy level. One of the benefits of natural rather than processed foods is that they contain little or no sodium chloride (table salt) – and it's the sodium that is potentially harmful.

Scientists had unexpected confirmation of the damaging effects of salt when they studied a fascinating tribe of South American Indians, the Yanomami, who live in the rainforests of Brazil and Venezuela. The tribe's diet contains little fat, no refined carbohydrates – and no salt. When they die as adults, the Yanomami show no evidence of the cardiovascular disease that is omnipresent in Western civilisations. The average adult blood pressure is lower than 100 systolic (the top number in a reading) and just over 60 diastolic (the second number) – an ideal, healthy level.

## WISE UP TO SALT

You don't have to travel to the Amazon to start cutting sodium, or salt, out of your diet. Reducing daily salt intake by just 0.75g (750mg) – roughly the amount contained in a 40g piece of Cheddar cheese – can reduce systolic pressure by 2 to 4 points and diastolic pressure by 1 to 2 points.

According to the Food Standards Agency, we should eat no more than 6g salt or 2.5g sodium daily (6g salt contains 2.5g sodium). Most of us take in much more than that. But it is not salt in cooking or even salt that we add to meals that's the prime culprit. The sodium in processed and pre-prepared foods, such as soups, bread, ready-meals and even biscuits, accounts for more than three-quarters of our average salt intake.

## CHECK FOOD LABELS

If you want to cut down on the amount of salt you consume, it is worth getting into the habit of reading the labels on food packaging before you put items into your shopping basket. Don't be fooled into thinking that

**RED**alert

### THE SNACKING HABIT

Many people munch between meals without a second thought. And studies suggest that when we reach for a snack we don't generally compensate by eating less later on, and that in general we take in more calories than we burn in physical activity. Most snack foods – such as cakes, crisps and biscuits, and sugary drinks, which are just snacks in liquid form – are much more energy-dense than natural unprocessed foods. In Step 6, you will discover how to snack healthily and how to break a bad snacking habit.

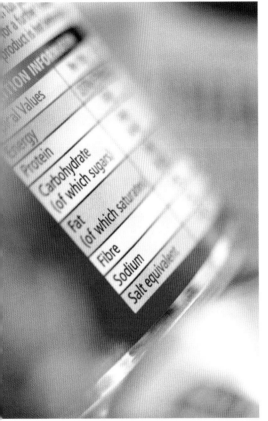

Get into the habit of reading the labels
on food packaging before you put items into
your shopping basket.

'reduced sodium' means 'low sodium'. It simply means that the product contains 25 per cent less than a comparable product. Anything with more than 1.5g salt or 0.6g sodium per 100g has a high salt content and it may be worth looking for a lower-salt variety. Low-salt foods have 0.3g salt (0.1g sodium) or less per 100g.

## POTASSIUM THE PROTECTOR

Eating foods that are rich in potassium, such as fruit and vegetables, has the opposite effect to that of salt, helping to lower your blood pressure and consequently reduce your risk of developing cardiovascular disease. Potassium helps to balance the effects of sodium in the body, so maintaining high levels of potassium has clear health benefits.

Scientists advise that it is the ratio of sodium to potassium in your body that's important. In one study of 2,974 people aged between 30 and 54 whose blood pressure readings were slightly under levels considered high, those with the highest sodium levels in their urine were 20 per cent more likely to suffer a heart attack or stroke over the following ten to 15 years than those with the lowest sodium levels. And those individuals with the highest sodium-to-potassium ratio – in other words, far higher levels of sodium than potassium – were 50 per cent more likely to experience a stroke, a heart attack or another form of cardiovascular disease than those with lower ratios.

## FIGHT BACK WITH FRUIT

Since potassium is largely derived from fruit and vegetables, increasing your intake will not only help to counteract the effects of too much salt but also provide you with nutrients known to have a protective effect against heart attack and stroke. Potassium-rich fruit and vegetables include avocados, bananas, grapes, dates, prunes, raisins, watermelons, leafy green vegetables, broccoli, Brussels sprouts, lentils and spinach.

# beneficial fats

Most of us know that we eat too much fat and that this increases our risk of obesity, itself a major risk factor for high blood pressure and diabetes. And as explained in Step 1, obesity boosts the risk of inflammation (see page 22), which scientists now know plays a key role in atherosclerosis, in the formation of plaque in our arteries and in triggering heart attacks. The solution is not to cut out all fats, however. Some fats are hugely beneficial – the omega-3s in salmon, for instance, and the monounsaturated fats in olive oil, nuts and avocados that lower cholesterol and have been shown to reduce inflammation in arteries. Our bodies need fats. Indeed, at least 25 per cent of our daily calorie intake should be made up of fats, provided that they are largely unsaturated.

## THE LOW-FAT MYTH

Since early studies had indicated that people who ate high-fat diets tended to have more heart attacks, medical experts used to think that following a low-fat diet would help to prevent cardiovascular disease. But more recent research has shown that this approach was flawed. In a 2006 study, the first long-term research of its kind, scientists who had followed 49,000 women for eight years were surprised to find that eating a low-fat diet did not protect against heart attack, stroke or any form of cardiovascular disease.

What had not been appreciated by the earlier experts was that only certain types of dietary fat increase the amount of artery-clogging cholesterol in the blood. And the low-fat myth persists. It is still the case that many people who want to lose weight cut back or even cut out all types of fats, including those in olive oil and nuts that help to lower cholesterol and to safeguard the heart in other ways.

**DEFENCE**tactics

### CUT DOWN ON SATURATED FATS

There are some simple ways to reduce the amount of saturated fat in your diet. Here are some top tips based on recommendations from the Food Standards Agency – which, if followed, could save 3,500 premature deaths each year:

- Grill foods, especially meat, rather than frying.
- Choose leaner cuts of meat.
- Remove the skin from poultry and trim fat from meat before cooking.
- Choose lower-fat hard cheese. Grate rather than slice hard cheeses, or use smaller amounts of stronger-flavoured varieties.
- Use low-fat spreads instead of butter or margarine.
- Before buying packaged foods, check the labels for the saturated-fat content.
- Cut down on your consumption of cakes, sweets, desserts and biscuits.
- Eat healthier snacks such as pieces of fresh or dried fruit.
- Switch from full-fat to semi-skimmed or skimmed milk.

Continued on p102 ▶

# Our body's own
# good and bad fats

**T**he two most important types of fat in your blood are cholesterol and triglycerides. Regular consumption of 'protective' foods will help to keep them at healthy levels.

## CHOLESTEROL – GOOD AND BAD

Your liver, intestines and even your skin create your body's own cholesterol. It binds to proteins and is transported around the body in complex molecules called lipoproteins. Amongst other functions, cholesterol helps to build cell membranes, insulate nerve fibres and make hormones, vitamin D and fat-digesting bile acids.

There are two types of cholesterol. The potentially harmful variety is characterised by low-density lipoproteins (LDLs). Its role is to carry fat from the liver to be used by body cells. LDLs are harmless until they come into contact with unstable molecules in the blood called free radicals, which damage the cholesterol in a process called oxidation. Oxidised LDLs are sucked into the inner linings of artery walls and contribute to the build-up of plaque and inflammation. Excess body fat in the abdominal area, a diet high in saturated fats and lack of activity can all prompt the liver to produce more LDLs.

## HEALTHY HDL

'Good' cholesterol is characterised by high-density lipoproteins (HDLs), which travel around the bloodstream mopping up LDLs and transporting them back to the liver for disposal. They may also act as antioxidants, stopping LDLs from causing damage in artery walls. The higher your level of HDL cholesterol, the closer you are to the 'natural' cholesterol balance enjoyed in early hunter–gatherer societies and the lower your risk of having blocked arteries that could prompt a heart attack or stroke.

**PROTECTIVE FOODS:** Unsaturated fats – from plants, fish and nuts – can lower LDL and raise HDL levels. Omega-3 fats from oily fish, such as salmon, and also from walnuts and rapeseed oil, are particularly good at raising HDL levels, as is soluble fibre, found in whole grains, brown rice, fruit, grapes and lentils.

## TRIGLYCERIDES

Triglycerides are fats that collect excess calories from the food we eat and speed them away to fat cells for storage. Then, when our bodies need extra energy between meals, stored calories are released. If you eat more calories than you are burning off through activity, your triglyceride levels will rise. Levels tend to be high in obese people and those with diabetes or metabolic syndrome, and are raised by consumption of fatty or sugary foods or excess alcohol. High levels of triglycerides are linked to an increased risk of cardiovascular disease, especially in women.

**PROTECTIVE FOODS:** Similarly, unsaturated fats (particularly monounsaturated from oils such as olive and rapeseed); fruit (especially citrus) and vegetables; whole grains; and omega-3 fatty acids in fish such as sardines, mackerel and herring.

## 'DO I NEED TO HAVE TESTS?'

Some people are more at risk of high cholesterol and high triglycerides than others, so being slim and eating healthily doesn't necessarily protect you. There are few physical clues or symptoms linked to the levels of these fats in your bloodstream, which is why it is important that people in any of the groups below should ask their GP for a cholesterol and triglyceride test:

- Anyone over 40.
- People with established cardiovascular disease, for example a history of angina, heart attack, stroke or peripheral vascular disease.
- People with a close family history (parents or siblings) of heart disease or stroke at a young age.
- Anyone – even children – with family members who have a hereditary cholesterol disorder called familial hypercholesterolaemia.
- People with risk factors for cardiovascular disease, such as diabetes, high blood pressure, smoking or obesity.

Cholesterol and triglycerides are measured in millimoles per litre (mmol/L). In the UK the average total cholesterol level is 5.7mmol/L, whereas the ideal level for someone without any other risk factors is 5mmol/L or less with an LDL level of 3mmol/L or less. In individuals with a risk factor such as diabetes or high blood pressure, the total cholesterol level should be 4mmol/L or less with an LDL level of 2mmol/L or less. A triglyceride check is usually done on the same blood sample as that given for a cholesterol test. A normal triglyceride reading is less than 1.7mmol/L. Over 2 is high and over 4.5 very high.

If the tests reveal high levels of harmful fats in your blood, your GP will advise you to change your diet, in particular to cut down on saturated fats, and to take more exercise. There is some simple advice on how to do this in the steps that follow. If your cholesterol levels remain high, you may be prescribed cholesterol-lowering statin drugs (which also reduce harmful inflammation).

# fats in meat, poultry and fish

A serving size is 75g (2¾oz) unless otherwise indicated.

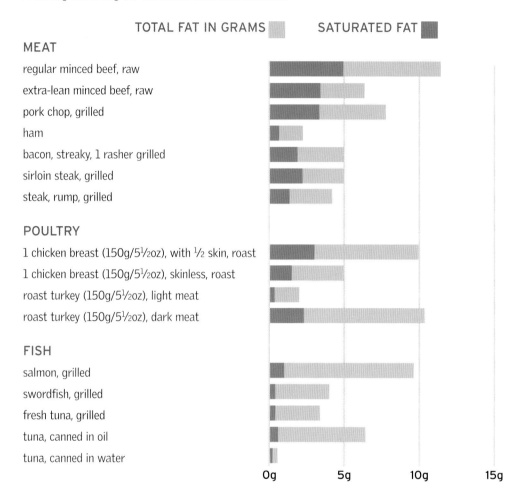

TOTAL FAT IN GRAMS    SATURATED FAT

**MEAT**
- regular minced beef, raw
- extra-lean minced beef, raw
- pork chop, grilled
- ham
- bacon, streaky, 1 rasher grilled
- sirloin steak, grilled
- steak, rump, grilled

**POULTRY**
- 1 chicken breast (150g/5½oz), with ½ skin, roast
- 1 chicken breast (150g/5½oz), skinless, roast
- roast turkey (150g/5½oz), light meat
- roast turkey (150g/5½oz), dark meat

**FISH**
- salmon, grilled
- swordfish, grilled
- fresh tuna, grilled
- tuna, canned in oil
- tuna, canned in water

0g    5g    10g    15g

# harmful fats

The type of fat that is particularly damaging to the health of your arteries is saturated fat. It is found mostly in foods derived from animals – fatty cuts of meat, butter, lard, cheese, full-fat milk and other dairy produce – and is generally solid at room temperature. It is also often present in biscuits, cakes, pastries, pies, burgers, sausages, chips, crisps and many pre-prepared ready meals and deep-fried takeaways.

Most of the 'bad' LDL cholesterol in our bloodstream is made by the liver from saturated fats in our diet. Although people used to worry about eating eggs, because they contain dietary cholesterol, it is our saturated

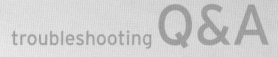

# troubleshooting Q&A

## My doctor says my cholesterol level is too high. Should I use a cholesterol-lowering spread?

It might help, but cholesterol-lowering spreads are not routinely recommended for people who have no other signs of cardiovascular disease. Many spreads, yoghurt-type drinks and soft cheeses contain added plant chemicals called sterols and stanols, the plant equivalents of cholesterol in humans. They reduce the uptake of cholesterol from the intestines, and this has been shown to reduce levels of total and 'bad' LDL cholesterol. However, although foods containing these plant chemicals may help to lower your cholesterol, it is still not clear whether they can reduce your risk of developing cardiovascular disease.

fat intake, not how much cholesterol we eat, that is mainly responsible for high blood cholesterol levels. On average, about 40 per cent of the energy we get from fats comes from saturated fats – and that is much too high.

## BEWARE TRANS FATS

Trans fatty acids, or trans fats, are synthetic ingredients found in many margarines, spreads and products such as cakes, pastries, biscuits, sweets and pre-prepared meals. In recent times, consumption of trans fats has been linked with the increased prevalence of heart attacks and stroke. One Dutch study suggested that cutting out trans fats altogether from our food supply would reduce deaths from heart disease by 20 per cent. In the UK that would mean 12,000 fewer premature deaths every year.

Trans fats are chemical by-products of an industrial process called hydrogenation. While experimenting with hydrogen molecules, chemists discovered that they could turn liquid vegetable oil into a solid at room temperature. It seemed a golden opportunity. Why not use this process to produce cheap and readily available alternatives to products known to be high in unhealthy saturated fats, such as butter and lard? We know now that, far from being a healthier option, these artificially hardened fats behave in the body just like – or possibly worse than – saturated fats.

As evidence against trans fats grows, many UK manufacturers have removed them from their products. Others voluntarily label foods such as margarines and spreads with their trans fat content, though it is not yet compulsory to do so. When buying packaged food, look for the words 'hydrogenated' or 'partially hydrogenated' fats on the list of ingredients (these must be declared). If you find them, do your arteries a favour and put the product back on the shelf.

# choose unsaturated

There is every reason to switch to unsaturated fats if you care about the health of your cardiovascular system. The two types, monounsaturated and polyunsaturated, are found mainly in plants and fish – think olives, olive oil, nuts, avocados and salmon. Olive oil and rapeseed oil are especially rich in monounsaturates, and sunflower oil and corn oil are packed with polyunsaturates, including omega-6 fats (though you should avoid consuming too many of these – see page 105).

Many studies have shown that monounsaturated fats in particular can boost the health of your heart. For example, researchers at the University of Pennsylvania found that a diet high in 'monos' was twice as effective as a typical low-fat diet at reducing the risk for cardiovascular disease.

That is good news for food lovers. Try cutting down on butter (full of saturated fat) and replace it with olive oil drizzled on to crusty bread, or toss a crisp green salad in olive oil mixed with balsamic vinegar (made from health-giving grapes).

# time for an oil change?

**O**ils with the most monounsaturated fat and the least saturated fat should be your first choice. The chart shows the proportions of different types of fat in oils commonly used for cooking.

TYPE OF OIL

SATURATED FAT ▮ MONOUNSATURATED FAT ▮ POLYUNSATURATED FAT ▮

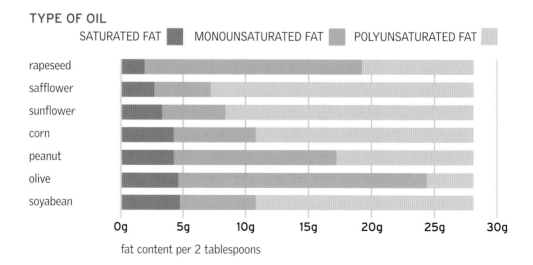

fat content per 2 tablespoons

Omega-3s found in oily fish such as kippers help to prevent blood platelets from clumping together and causing heart-stopping blood clots.

# and omega-3s

The other form of 'good' fats that help to maintain a healthy cardiovascular system are omega-3 fatty acids, also known as essential fatty acids or EFAs; although they are essential for many body functions, we can't make them in our bodies, so we must take them in as food.

Omega-3s are found in oily fish, such as salmon, fresh tuna, sardines, kippers, trout, mackerel, pilchards, herring and swordfish. They are also present in nuts, leafy green vegetables and a few vegetable oils such as rapeseed or flaxseed.

Studies indicate that omega-3s help to prevent blood platelets from clumping together and causing heart-stopping blood clots. In the same way they lower the risk of strokes caused by clots. They reduce inflammation, high blood pressure and triglyceride levels (see page 101). And there are signs that a diet rich in fish oils blocks the build-up of LDL cholesterol in the aorta, the main artery leaving the heart.

## OMEGA-3 vs OMEGA-6

Omega-6 fats, found mostly in processed vegetable oils, are polyunsaturated but should be consumed in limited quantities. It has been demonstrated that very high levels of omega-6 fats in the body can offset the beneficial effects of omega-3s on the cardiovascular system.

The ideal ratio of omega-3s to omega-6 fats is reckoned to be 1:1. But the modern diet tends to include a far higher proportion of omega-6 fats than used to be the case since they are present in popular cooking oils, such as sunflower, safflower and corn oils, as well as in other processed foods. These days, the typical ratio may be 1:12 or even higher. This imbalance is thought to play a role in the development of inflammation, which encourages the formation of plaque in the arteries, one of the characteristics of cardiovascular disease.

# eat to beat ...

Your food choices really can help you to live longer. In one study of nearly 4,000 older people, eating oily fish at least once a week was linked with a 44 per cent lower risk of dying from a heart attack. Other research shows that omega-3s offer increased protection against a second heart attack.

In one Spanish study, 40 men on a cardiac rehabilitation programme were split into two groups. One consumed a dairy product, supplemented with omega-3s and vitamins A and D; the other consumed milk with just vitamins A and D added. Both groups also underwent a programme of supervised exercise. Over the following year, blood homocysteine, a marker of cardiovascular risk, decreased in both groups, but the omega-3 group also had reductions in other cardiovascular disease markers and levels of blood cholesterol.

## FEAST ON FISH

Eating just two servings of oily fish a week can reduce your risk of heart disease by a third or more. And because of the significant benefits of omega-3s, people who have had a heart attack are recommended to increase their intake to two to four portions weekly. (But it is advisable to eat no more than one portion a week of swordfish, shark or marlin as they can contain high levels of mercury; pregnant women or those trying to conceive should avoid them altogether.) To get the maximum benefit from omega-3s, poach, steam, bake or grill your oily fish, rather than frying it.

# good fats in fish

Oily fish are better sources of omega-3 fatty acids than white fish. Here are some popular types of fish rated according to their quality as a source of omega-3s.

| GREAT SOURCES | MODERATE SOURCES | POOR SOURCES |
| --- | --- | --- |
| mackerel | bass | cod |
| pilchards | halibut | flounder |
| salmon (canned and fresh) | smoked salmon | haddock |
| sardines | sea bass | snapper |
| sturgeon | | sole |
| trout | | tuna (canned) |
| tuna (fresh) | | |

If you don't like eating fish, consider taking 1g of fish oil supplement daily. In one four-and-a-half-year study of over 18,000 people in Japan, adding fish oil to cholesterol-lowering statin drug therapy after a heart attack reduced the risk of further major coronary events by around 20 per cent.

# secret ingredients

Certain important nutrients such as folate and isoflavones have a significant role to play in preventing strokes and heart attacks.

## FOLATE

A high level of the protein homocysteine in the blood has been linked with increased rates of cardiovascular disease. For the body to metabolise homocysteine, it needs to take in folate, a B vitamin present in raw fruit and vegetables. Homocysteine and folate levels tend to move in opposite directions. The level of homocysteine increases in people with high blood pressure and is lowered in response to a good dietary intake of folate and other vitamins.

**KEY SOURCES:** Peas, broccoli, Brussels sprouts, asparagus, chickpeas, brown rice, oranges and bananas.

The level of homocysteine increases in people with high blood pressure and is lowered in response to a good dietary intake of folate.

## ISOFLAVONES

A group of plant chemicals called phytoestrogens mimic some of the effects in the body of the female hormone oestrogen – the hormone that, up until the menopause, underlies a woman's protection against heart disease. Chief among these phytoestrogens are isoflavones, found particularly in soya and chickpeas.

Dietary isoflavones have been shown to reduce inflammation and to stop damaging cells being drawn into arterial plaque. People who include plenty of soya in their diet have lower blood pressure and lower cholesterol levels than those who don't; they are also less likely to become obese, and seem to have more protection against heart attacks and strokes. Isoflavones may help someone avoid a second stroke.

Continued on p110 ▶

# Mediterranean magic

For many hundreds of years, the people of southern Europe have enjoyed a colourful and delicious diet that has now been shown to provide some protection against heart disease, diabetes and stroke.

## FRESH LOCAL CUISINE

The so-called Mediterranean diet – steeped in the culinary traditions of the region, especially southern Italy and Greece – is one of the healthiest diets in the world. As well as being rich in locally grown foods such as olives, olive oil, fresh fruit and vegetables, whole grains and beans, it gives more prominence to freshly caught fish than to red meat.

Even though people in the southern Mediterranean consume relatively high levels of fat, they have far lower rates of cardiovascular disease than in Britain or the USA. The type of fats widely eaten in the region actively protect against heart disease by lowering cholesterol, blood pressure and blood sugar. In Britain, by comparison, we tend to favour polyunsaturated cooking oils such as sunflower oil, which contains omega-6 rather than omega-3 fats (see page 105) and foods heavy in saturated fat.

## SECRET weapon

### NUTS

If you eat just a small handful of (unsalted) nuts every day for a year – in combination with a Mediterranean diet rich in fruit, vegetables and fish – you are far less likely to die of heart disease or diabetes than people who rarely eat nuts.

Nuts, especially walnuts and pecans, are packed with beneficial omega-3 fatty acids. Walnuts are also rich in vitamin $B_6$, which helps to control homocysteine, and they provide the amino acid arginine, which stimulates production of nitric oxide, a molecule that relaxes constricted blood vessels. Some research indicates that eating a handful of walnuts four or five times a week can lower your risk of heart attack by up to 40 per cent. Nuts can help to control blood sugar, too. Hazelnuts and cashews contain copper, a nutrient vital for people with diabetes. Harvard scientists found that women who regularly eat a few nuts – any nuts – several times a week are less likely to develop Type 2 diabetes than those who don't.

## THE POWER OF 5 A DAY

A key element of the Mediterranean diet is an abundance of fresh fruit and vegetables which does wonders for cardiovascular health, as research shows. In one study, scientists at the universities of Cambridge and East Anglia measured the vitamin C intake of more than 20,000 men and women, then followed their progress. Nine years later the people who were consuming higher levels of vitamin C had a 42 per cent lower risk of having a stroke. In another study, American researchers followed the health of 832 men over a period of 20 years. After analysing the data and adjusting for age, they found that, on average, each additional three servings of fruit and vegetables a man ate a day lowered his risk of a stroke by more than a fifth. Fruit and vegetables contain a number of

# menu magic

**P**ick a dish, almost any dish, and add a few nuts to it – for taste and added nutrients. Here are a few simple ideas for incorporating nuts into everyday meals.

- Stir chopped walnuts or pecans into rice dishes.
- Add pistachios to chicken salad.
- Sprinkle your favourite chopped nuts and some dried cranberries on green salads.
- Mix pine nuts or chopped walnuts into pasta dishes along with olive oil, basil and some chopped sun-dried tomatoes.
- Create your own snack mixture with dried fruit, high-fibre cereal and some of your favourite nuts.

vitamins and minerals, such as beta carotene, vitamin C and vitamin E, known as antioxidants, which protect the body's cells from harmful free radicals. Fruit and vegetables also add soluble and insoluble fibre to our diet, helping to lower blood cholesterol. That is one reason why medical experts recommend that everyone should eat at least five portions a day – a total of at least 400g. And the more the better. A 2006 analysis of several different studies found that eating more than five servings a day lowered the risk of stroke by 26 per cent.

Oranges are rich in vitamin C – an antioxidant which helps to protect against cardiovascular disease.

## WHAT IS A PORTION?

A portion of fruit is any medium-sized piece of fresh fruit, such as an orange, a banana or an apple; a medium-sized serving of salad or vegetables; or 6 tablespoons (about 140g/5oz) of stewed or canned fruit. A small glass (100ml) of fruit juice also counts but provides much less useful fibre. If you make just one change to your diet after reading this step, let it be to include fruit and vegetables in every meal you eat. We are lucky to have such a wide variety to choose from – a distinct benefit of the global market that makes so many countries' produce available to us all year round.

## THE GOOD LIFE

A further element of the Mediterranean lifestyle is a love of good, red wine, savoured over a leisurely home-prepared family meal that can last for a couple of hours. See page 111 to learn how red wine can help to protect you against cardiovascular disease.

Researchers from the University of Hong Kong studied 102 patients with well-established cardiovascular disease who had experienced a stroke caused by a blood clot in the previous six months. Half the patients received a daily supplement of 80mg of isoflavones and the other half were given a placebo. After 12 weeks, there had been a significant improvement in arterial widening among those patients taking isoflavones. The fact that the patients in this trial had relatively advanced cardiovascular disease and had already sustained either a first or second stroke makes the results even more impressive. The greatest benefit was seen among those with the most severe disability. Further research is planned, but the results suggest that eating more isoflavone-rich foods could help to reduce cardiovascular risk in stroke patients – even at a late stage.

**KEY SOURCES:** Soya, chickpeas, beans, peanuts and green tea.

## POLYPHENOLS

Many fruits and vegetables contain antioxidants – chemicals that reduce the level of free radicals in the blood. Free radicals are unstable molecules which, if left to accumulate, cause cell damage. A key group of antioxidants are known as polyphenols, or flavonoids. They reduce inflammation and blood clots, improve the health of arterial linings, and lessen other cardiovascular risk factors. In one study of 805 older men, those who consumed the most polyphenols had a 68 per cent lower risk of developing cardiovascular disease than those consuming the least.

**KEY SOURCES:** Berries, apples, beans, peas, cherries, pomegranates, grapes, broccoli, cabbage, onion, sweet potatoes, celery, red wine, green tea, olive oil and chocolate.

# calling chocoholics

Chocolate-lovers will be delighted to hear that dark chocolate provides protection against heart attacks and strokes. Thanks to its high content of polyphenols and other antioxidants, dark chocolate reduces inflammation, lowers blood pressure, reduces 'bad' LDL cholesterol, boosts 'good' HDL cholesterol and protects the health of your arteries. It also contains

**ERRATUM**

**Page 123 - Reductil**

**✱ Another drug, Reductil (sibutramine)
works by altering chemical signals to the
brain, making you feel full more quickly
than usual, and therefore more easily
satisfied by a smaller meal...**

On January 22, 2010 (after *Conquering
Heart Attack & Stroke* was printed), the
European Medicines Agency (EMA) banned
Reductil. From a study of 9,800 patients, it
concluded that the drug raised the risk of a
heart attack or stroke, and that the risk
outweighed Reductil's benefits. The ruling
was endorsed by the UK's Medicines and
Healthcare products Regulatory Agency
(MHRA). Current users were advised to
consult their GP about alternative treatments.

# power foods for healthy arteries

**W**hile eating more fruit and vegetables should be high on your list of priorities for boosting the health of your heart and arteries, there are other elements of diet that can offer significant protection against cardiovascular disease:

● **Red wine** – A polyphenol called resveratrol is thought to be the main ingredient in red wine responsible for its well-documented effect in protecting against heart attacks. Researchers from Queen Mary College, University of London have found that other heart-protecting chemicals called procyanidins are especially high in red wines from Sardinia and south-west France.

● **Garlic** – A review of ten studies looking at the effects of garlic on blood pressure showed that, among patients with high blood pressure, garlic supplements produced an average reduction of 16.3 mmHg in systolic and 9.3 mmHg in diastolic blood pressure, compared with patients taking placebo tablets; however, neither had any effect in patients with normal blood pressure.

● **Grapeseed extract** – According to a study involving 24 patients with metabolic syndrome, taking grapeseed extract can lower blood pressure by an average of 12 mmHg systolic and 9 mmHg diastolic after just one month. Participants taking the extract also had reduced LDL cholesterol levels.

Both green and black tea have been shown to
offer protection against cardiovascular disease.

● **Tea** – Both green and black tea have been shown to offer some protection against cardiovascular disease. In one study of 1,900 people admitted to hospital after a heart attack, moderate and heavy tea drinkers had a 31 and 39 per cent reduction in the risk of a further event compared with those who hardly drank any tea. However, you may need to take your tea black – according to a study published in the *European Heart Journal*, the protective effects of tea are negated if you add milk.

● **Broccoli** – A diet rich in brassica vegetables such as broccoli is known to reduce the risk of heart attacks and strokes. Now scientists from the University of Warwick have shown that a key broccoli nutrient called sulphoraphane can reverse the damage to coronary arteries caused by high blood sugar levels in people with diabetes.

● **Cocoa** – Dutch research reveals that cocoa can lower blood pressure and reduce deaths from cardiovascular disease.

● **Persimmon** – Also called Sharon fruit, persimmons look a little like orange tomatoes. According to research in Israel, they contain a magic cocktail of atherosclerosis-busting chemicals including minerals, antioxidants and trace elements, as well as high levels of dietary fibre – in fact, the researchers recommend a persimmon a day instead of an apple a day to keep the doctor at bay. There is also evidence from animal research that persimmons improve the metabolism of fats. But, if you have had ulcer surgery, avoid the fruit, especially unpeeled. Very rarely they can cause intestinal blockages in people with insufficient stomach acid to digest them properly.

PERSONAL
REPORT

Dean Tarleton

# A new attitude to food

When Dean Tarleton suffered a haemorrhagic stroke in March 2007, it left his left arm and leg partially paralysed. That he had also lost his sense of taste might have seemed a minor problem - except that Dean, then aged 43, was a chef, running a restaurant at the busy hotel he then owned in Southport.

Dean's stroke happened in the early hours as he lay in bed. He remembers trying to get up and just falling to the floor. 'It felt as though my arm was made of foam,' he says. 'My speech had gone and I was gibbering like an idiot.' His wife, Vivienne, immediately called an ambulance.

Within 30 minutes Dean was treated in a hospital stroke unit. He regained his speech but the weakness down his left side meant he could no longer cook; instead he supervised the menus.

'Then, after six months, my taste came back,' he recalls. 'It was wonderful. I really appreciated the flavours.'

'Then, after six months, my taste came back,' he recalls. 'It was wonderful. I really appreciated the flavours.'

By then, his approach to food had changed - and not just his own food, but his customers', too. High-cholesterol dishes such as creamy peppercorn steaks, deep-fried chicken kievs and goujons of plaice came off the menu, to be replaced with dishes such as grilled fish and steamed vegetables, mostly sourced locally so they were at their peak of freshness. 'Southport shrimps became very popular,' he says.

Dean has gained personally, too, from adopting a healthier diet, losing 4½ stone (28.6kg) reducing his cholesterol from 8 to 3mmol/L and lowering his blood pressure as well.

'I've really embraced the flavours of good food, and realised the benefits of losing weight.' He advises moderation and is keen to spread the healthy-eating message.

'So many things implode in your life after a stroke. Like losing the ability to drive, or small irritations like being unable to reach the end of your trouser belt when it's behind your back.' But one good thing has come out of it: 'It has really helped me to rediscover the excitement of food.'

chemicals that prompt the release of endorphins, the body's pain-relieving and pleasure-promoting hormones. As you will find out in Step 9, a sense of wellbeing is vitally important to keeping your cardiovascular system in top condition.

In one major review of 139 studies conducted over nearly 40 years, researchers concluded that chocolate consumption could lower the risk of cardiovascular death by around 19 per cent. That's the good news. The bad news, for some, is that all you need to eat to improve your health is 6.7g per day. That's equivalent to one small square two or three times a week – the heart benefits tend to disappear with consumption of larger amounts. A little dark chocolate may even help to curb our appetite for unhealthier foods, according to research at the University of Copenhagen, which reveals that dark chocolate is more filling than milk chocolate and reduces cravings for salty, fatty or sugary items.

### SECRETweapon

### CHICKEN SOUP

Researchers in Japan have shown that chicken legs and chicken breast contain chemicals that act like blood-pressure-lowering drugs called ACE inhibitors. Early tests were on animals but in February 2009, they published the first human study – on 15 patients with slightly raised blood pressure, who took a small daily dose of chicken soup ingredients over four weeks. Their systolic blood pressure (the top figure in a blood pressure reading) dropped by an average 11.8mmHg.

## Eating chocolate could lower the risk of death from cardiovascular disease by around 19 per cent.

The key to eating chocolate is to know when to stop and when not to indulge. If you are a chocoholic – and a craving for chocolate is the most common of all food cravings in both men and women – try taking a brisk 15 minute walk. Researchers at the University of Exeter found that a walk allayed cravings in chocoholics, even in tempting situations.

# drink to your health

It is now broadly accepted that regular, moderate alcohol consumption, especially wine-drinking, is not only enjoyable but can also reduce your risk of coronary artery disease. According to researchers at the Joseph Fourier University of Grenoble in France, wine also lowers the risk of a second or further heart attack. When the team studied 353 men who had

Indulge in a glass of red wine if you wish and
savour a little dark chocolate in the knowledge that
it is doing you good. Your weight should stay stable.

recently suffered a heart attack, they found that drinking two or more glasses of wine regularly halved their risk of a second attack, compared with men who did not drink.

The benefits of red wine, in particular, are so impressive that a UK hospital in Swindon offers two glasses a day to selected heart patients. The key ingredient seems to be a powerful antioxidant called resveratrol, derived especially from grapes grown on Pinot Noir vines in wet and humid regions. If you don't drink, resveratrol can also be found in weaker amounts in grape juice, and in peanuts. Scientists at the Pavese Pharma Biochemical Institute in Italy are trying to capture its benefits in a pill.

## THE ADVANTAGES OF MODERATION

In the course of a major health study, researchers from University College London made some interesting findings about alcohol consumption. They recorded the average weekly alcohol intake of 9,655 civil servants, then logged what happened to them over the following 17 years.

The study concluded that among the group classified at the outset as exhibiting 'unhealthy behaviours' – those who smoked, took little or no exercise, or had poor dietary habits – moderate drinking was associated with a significant reduction in both fatal and non-fatal heart attacks, compared with abstinence or heavy drinking. In this research, there was no additional benefit derived from alcohol among those categorised initially as exhibiting 'healthy behaviours' – who took 3 hours or more of exercise per week, ate fruit or vegetables daily and didn't smoke.

# healthy weight healthy heart

In terms of cardiovascular health, the messages are clear. Eat as much natural food – vegetables, fruits and whole grains – as possible; enjoy oily fish such as salmon; and choose olive or rapeseed oil whenever you can. Indulge in a glass of red wine if you wish and savour a little dark chocolate in the knowledge that it is doing you good. Your weight should stay stable. But read on if you are already carrying a little more weight than is healthy. The same dietary principles apply, but Step 6 explains how you can reduce your calorie intake and shed the excess pounds.

# the polymeal

The idea of a polypill that could cure all ills – or, at least, reduce the risk of cardiovascular disease in the majority of the population – was described in Step 1 (see page 34). Well, instead of popping a pill, how about indulging in a delicious meal? That's the proposal made by a team of researchers from the Netherlands, Belgium and Australia. Writing in the *British Medical Journal*, they suggest that their 'polymeal' is a more natural, safer and probably tastier alternative to the polypill, and that it could reduce the incidence of cardiovascular disease by as much as 76 per cent.

The scientists took published scientific papers to assess the cardiovascular protective effects of various food ingredients and came up with an 'evidence-based recipe', employing the most efficacious ingredients. Then, using data from major studies of heart disease, they worked out a model of the potential benefits of the polymeal in men and women over the age of 50.

The meal was based on seven food ingredients or categories for which scientific evidence showed specific individual effects (not as part of a diet) in either reducing the incidence of heart attacks and strokes or in reducing cardiovascular risk factors. These were: wine, fish, dark chocolate, fruit, vegetables, garlic and almonds. Here are the specific calculated effects of each of these ingredients:

- 150ml wine daily – reduces cardiovascular disease by 32 per cent (though it is advisable to have at least one alcohol-free day a week).
- 114g fish four times a week – reduces cardiovascular disease by 14 per cent.
- 100g dark chocolate daily – reduces systolic blood pressure by 5.1mmHg and diastolic blood pressure by 1.8mmHg, equivalent to reducing heart attacks and strokes by 21 per cent (although a little as 6.7g a day is effective, which is worth bearing in mind if you don't want to put on extra weight).
- 400g fruit and vegetables daily – gives the same effect as 100g dark chocolate.
- 600 to 900mg of dried garlic powder a day, equivalent to 1.8 to 2.7g of fresh garlic – reduces total cholesterol by an amount equivalent to a 25 per cent reduction in heart attacks and strokes.
- 68g almonds daily – reduces total cholesterol by half the amount seen with garlic, equivalent to a reduction in cardiovascular disease of 12.5 per cent.

A diet that combined all these ingredients would give a 76 per cent reduction in the risk of cardiovascular events in later life, the team calculated. For men, sticking to the polymeal principles after the age of 50 could increase total life expectancy by 6.6 years and yield an extra nine years free of cardiovascular disease. For women, it could add 8.1 years free of cardiovascular disease and 4.8 years to their total lifespan.

Eating garlic can help to lower cholesterol.

# self-defence plan

LOSING EVEN A FEW EXTRA POUNDS CAN MAKE AN ENORMOUS DIFFERENCE TO YOUR HEALTH AND WELLBEING. YOU'LL NOT ONLY LOOK YOUNGER, YOU'LL FEEL RE-ENERGISED — AND YOU'LL HAVE THE WONDERFUL SATISFACTION OF KNOWING THAT YOUR WILLPOWER HAS PROBABLY ADDED YEARS TO YOUR LIFE.

# Reach your
# target weight

**D**o you think you might be carrying too much weight? You're not alone. More than half of us are overweight, according to official figures, and one in four people is obese. The reasons for this modern Western affliction are simple: we tend to eat too much of the wrong types of food and many of us have inactive lifestyles – which means that we are consuming far more calories than our bodies need.

## SMART FOOD CHOICES

Step 6 explains how to counter the imbalance between calorie intake and energy expended, and how to compensate for the sedentary working life that is now all too common. As already indicated, the types of food that you consume have a huge effect on your weight and the health of your arteries. Simply by making healthier food choices you will be able to lower your cholesterol and blood pressure and reduce your risk of heart attack and stroke, as well as that of diabetes, osteoarthritis, liver disease and several forms of cancer. You'll learn, too, why carrying too much fat is more dangerous in certain areas of your body than in others – and when you should worry about the possible health effects.

## SECRET OF SUCCESS

Losing weight doesn't have to be a form of punishment. There is no need to spend your days counting carbohydrates, fat grams and calories.

**MYTHS X**

### I WOULD KNOW IF I NEEDED TO LOSE WEIGHT

**T**his is not necessarily the case. More than a quarter of individuals who would be classed by doctors as overweight or obese don't realise that they have a weight problem, according to research carried out by University College London. Another British survey of 4,000 men and women found that more than half were overweight or obese. As many as 87 per cent of obese people and 32 per cent of those who were overweight failed to recognise how heavy they were. Many believed they were a normal weight.

By applying the lessons you learned in Step 5 – which foods to eat more of and which to cut back on – you'll make the changes that will ensure you are still trim and healthy ten years from now.

# recognise your risk
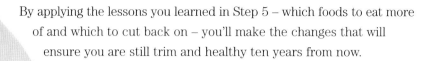

You may already be aware that you are carrying too much weight. If this is the case, it is helpful to know just how heavy you are, so that you can follow your progress as you begin to lose weight. The most reliable indicator of how much body fat you have is the body mass index, or BMI. As explained in Step 3 (see page 66), you can calculate your BMI by working out the square of your height in metres and dividing it by your weight in kilograms. Look at the information below to find out which weight band you fall into. If you are classed as overweight, it means that you weigh more than the ideal for your sex, height and build; broadly, men who are 20 per cent or more over their ideal weight, and women who are 25 per cent or more over theirs, are obese.

## WHAT THE RESULTS MEAN

● A BMI between 18.5 and 24.9 is healthy. For example, the maximum healthy weight of someone who is 5ft 7in (1.7m) tall – male or female would be around 11st (70kg).

● If your BMI is between 25 and 29.9, you are officially overweight – you weigh more than you should do based on your age, sex and height. You are more likely to have high blood pressure and are at moderate risk of cardiovascular disease.

● If your BMI is over 30, you are clinically obese and storing far too much fat. You have a high risk of coronary artery disease, high blood pressure, diabetes, heart attacks and strokes.

● A BMI of 40 or more is classed as very or 'morbidly' obese, signalling a very high risk of cardiovascular disease and other complications.

If you are overweight or obese according to the height–weight chart, with a BMI of 25 or more, a waist measurement of more than 80cm (32in) if you're female or 94cm (37in) if you're male, or a waist to hip ratio above 0.80 (women) or 0.90 (men), you will experience clear health benefits by losing weight. If you are on the obese side of overweight, it is worth talking to your GP to see if you can get help to do this (see page 122).

## Both my parents had a struggle with obesity. What's the best way for me to avoid getting fat?

People with an obese parent are more likely to be obese themselves. Scientists don't know how much of this is due to genetic inheritance and how much to learning bad eating habits as a child. They do know that we can inherit a tendency to overeat, possibly caused by faulty appetite-control mechanisms that affect the signals by which our brain detects when we are full. It is not inevitable that people with this tendency will become obese, though they may struggle more than most to control their weight. It is important to be vigilant about diet – about what, and how much you eat – and to build exercise into your daily routine to help to burn off any extra calories.

## FIND YOUR MOTIVATION

There are no quick fixes to achieving long-term weight loss. In order to succeed you must really want to change your eating habits and believe that change is worth the effort. Think about your reasons for wanting to lose weight. You are far more likely to reach your goal if you are pursuing it for your own satisfaction (rather than to appeal to your partner or to impress your boss or to stop your neighbour thinking you're fat).

Try to find some inner motivation – such as being able to climb a flight of stairs without panting. Visualise yourself at your ideal weight, feeling attractive, in favourite clothes you haven't been able to wear for a few years – and having the energy and confidence to go swimming with your children. You know what's important to you.

## inside information
# is obesity caused by a virus?

**C**ould there be a virus that causes obesity? The idea may seem far-fetched, but a nutritional biochemist at Wayne State University in the USA thinks he has identified just such an organism. In laboratory tests, human adenovirus, or AD-36, which is responsible for some cases of respiratory infection, has been shown to cause dramatic weight gain in animals. In an analysis of 1,000 people, another biochemist, Nikhil Dhurandhar, found that those with AD-36 antibodies – a sign that they have been infected with the virus – are significantly more likely to be overweight.

How could a virus make you fat? When fat cells are exposed to AD-36, they begin to multiply, Dhurandahr found. 'I'm not saying all obesity is caused by a virus,' he says. 'Genes, metabolism, habits, all play a role. But at least one other possibility appears to be infection.' Scientists are now suggesting that 'infectobesity' is worth further investigation.

# living life to the full

For many of us, the most powerful motivation for losing weight is the prospect of feeling fit again, and of being able to live a fuller life. In fact, a landmark study by Oxford University clearly indicates that if you lose weight you will live longer. The scientists analysed BMI data relating to a million people worldwide, who were then followed for up to 20 years. The results show that, if you have a BMI of 30 to 35, which is now common, you shorten your life by three years; while the seriously obese, with a BMI of 40 to 50, will die ten years earlier than they should. 'If you are becoming overweight or obese, avoiding further weight gain could well add years to your life,' says the Oxford epidemiologist Dr Gary Whitlock.

## TARGET ABDOMINAL FAT

Abdominal fat is especially dangerous because it releases 'messenger substances' that promote the development of chronic diseases. It is also linked with metabolic syndrome (see page 30) and the inflammation that provokes the formation of plaque in arteries. Abdominal fat puts you at risk of heart disease, diabetes, high blood pressure and some cancers – even if your overall weight is normal. In a ten-year study involving some 350,000 people, scientists from Imperial College London and the German Institute of Human Nutrition found that a waist measurement of over 100cm (39in) in women or 120cm (47in) in men more than doubled the risk of premature death, compared to people with a healthy waist size. Other research has found that men and women with high waist:hip ratios are almost twice as likely to have calcium deposits inside their coronary arteries – one of the early signs of atherosclerosis.

## inside information
# the hunger 'switch'

Scientists at the Lawson Health Research Institute in Ontario, Canada, have found that abdominal fat releases a hormone called neuropeptide Y, or NPY, that makes more fat cells. High levels of the same hormone in the brain are known to produce constant feelings of hunger and to stimulate appetite. If NPY is transported in the blood (and the next phase of research will establish this one way or the other), it may be possible to develop a simple blood test to detect increased levels of NPY in people at risk, and to develop a treatment to 'turn off' the hormone.

# foods that fight
## 'middle-age spread'

**A**bdominal fat is notoriously difficult to get rid of, but here are four foods to include in your healthy diet that will help you to achieve a flatter stomach.

● **Olive oil** Foods that are rich in monounsaturated fat, such as olive oil, contain anti-inflammatory phytochemicals that can help to curb the build-up of abdominal fat. In a 2004 study, 180 people with metabolic syndrome were divided into two groups – with 90 following a Mediterranean diet, rich in olive oil, whole grains, fruits, vegetables and nuts, and 90 following a relatively high carbohydrate, low-fat diet. Two years later, more than half the dieters in the first group no longer had metabolic syndrome – they had lost weight and had healthier cholesterol levels. Inflammation in their arteries dropped dramatically, and tests indicated that the lining of their blood vessels was much healthier too. They also showed less evidence of insulin resistance, which increases the risk for Type 2 diabetes and heart disease. In the control group, who didn't follow the diet, 78 of 90 participants still had metabolic syndrome.

> Green tea stimulates fat-burning in the body and abdominal fat in particular.

● **Nuts** Eating a small handful of nuts every day could help to reverse metabolic syndrome. That's the implication of a Spanish study in which participants who ate a Mediterranean diet along with extra nuts for a year reduced their abdominal fat, blood pressure and cholesterol levels. Nuts contain anti-inflammatory substances such as fibre and antioxidants such as vitamin E. **A note of caution.** Adding nuts, which are high in calories, to a diet already packed with too many calories and junk food could lead to weight gain.

● **Soya protein** In one small study, women who drank a soya-based drink daily gained less abdominal weight than those who drank a milkshake. The researchers speculate that it is the isoflavones in soya that protect against laying down fat in this area. Try edamame, fresh green soya beans, available shelled or in the pod, soya nuts, tofu, miso soup and soya milk.

● **Green tea** In one study, volunteers were given a daily drink of green tea, which contains catechins, an antioxidant. (The daily dose was 625mg; an average cup of green tea has from 150 to 250mg.) After 12 weeks the group had a significant reduction in abdominal fat and triglycerides. Green tea may also increase the body's sensitivity to insulin, lowering the risk of diabetes.

If you've tried to lose weight but just can't make any progress, then talk to your GP.

# How your doctor can help

**I**f the brutal truth is that the enemy has simply gained too much ground, what is to be done? If you've tried to lose weight but just can't make any progress – and, for many people who have high blood pressure, diabetes, metabolic sydrome, angina, or who've had a stroke or heart attack, losing weight is particularly hard – then talk to your GP. He or she will be used to giving advice about this problem, and will probably be delighted that you've decided to tackle it.

Your GP can discuss lifestyle factors with you and help you to set a target weight and a realistic timescale for achieving it. Some surgeries run obesity clinics. Alternatively, your doctor may refer you to a dietitian or nutritionist at the practice or the local hospital who can provide practical dietary advice, or to a weight-loss counselling programme, although these services are not available in all areas.

## PILLS ARE NO PANACEA

If you have a high BMI combined with an existing condition such as high blood pressure, high cholesterol or diabetes, your GP may prescribe medication to aid weight loss. Such drugs are not magic pills, however – nor do they take away the need for dieting and exercise. They are prescribed only to those who have demonstrated that they can lose weight on a calorie-controlled diet.

Xenical (orlistat) works by blocking the absorption of some fats in the intestines, and the makers claim that it can boost weight loss by 50 per cent compared with dieting alone. You need to take care not to eat too much fat while taking Xenical, or you may suffer side-effects such as

## Could my obesity be due to a medical problem?

Medical causes of obesity are fairly uncommon, but if you do have sudden, unexplained weight gain, tell your doctor. It may be due to an underactive thyroid; other symptoms include tiredness, depression, dry skin, constipation, aches and hair loss. If weight gain is accompanied by swollen ankles, it could be a sign of heart failure due to fluid retention. Another disorder characterised by weight gain, which affects one in ten women of childbearing age, is polycystic ovary syndrome. Some medications such as steroids prescribed for other conditions can cause weight gain.

diarrhoea and wind. In 2009, UK pharmacists were given the go-ahead to dispense Xenical without a prescription – but at half the usual dose – to people with a BMI of 28 or more. Another drug, Reductil (sibutramine), works by altering chemical signals to the brain, making you feel full more quickly than usual, and therefore more easily satisfied by a smaller meal.

## THE SURGICAL OPTION

If you are extremely obese, with a BMI of more than 40, and are considered at high risk of complications, your GP can refer you to a specialist to consider whether an operation would help. Surgery aims to reduce hunger or to reduce the amount of food your body can digest, thereby speeding up weight loss.

## GASTRIC BANDING

The most common surgical procedure to treat obesity, called gastric banding, involves placing a band around the upper part of the stomach to restrict the amount you can eat and make you feel full even though you have eaten a relatively small amount. This can be done through keyhole surgery techniques, so scarring is minimal. The band includes a fluid-filled balloon connected to an injection port brought out through the skin. It can therefore be adjusted by injecting or withdrawing fluid to tighten or loosen the band as needed. It can also be removed altogether when required, so the procedure is reversible.

## STOMACH STAPLING

The next most common surgical procedure is gastric bypass, commonly known as 'stomach stapling', which physically restricts the amount you can eat by creating a small pouch stapled off from the main part of the stomach. A section of the small intestine is then bypassed and reconnected to the pouch. As a result all food eaten takes a shorter route through the stomach and less is digested. The procedure may be carried out by keyhole or open surgery and is permanent. The risk of complications is higher than gastric banding and the operation can leave a significant scar. However weight loss is more rapid and more likely to be maintained.

# crash diets don't work

'Some people find it harder than others to lose weight, but in every case it's crucial to avoid fad diets that promise the earth but are impossible to stick to throughout life,' says Lyndel Costain, a leading nutritionist and spokesperson for the British Dietetic Association.

Typically slimmers appear to make good progress in the first few days of a crash diet. They may lose 3 to 5lb (1.4 to 2.3kg) in the first week, but most of this is water, as the body burns up stored sugars that previously soaked up excess water. Then, they reach the 'plateau' phase, after which further weight loss is increasingly difficult, and can become discouraged.

One review of 31 studies shows clearly how often deliberate dieting fails in the long term. While the subjects lost weight in the first six months, within five years, two-thirds put on more weight than they had initially lost; in one study half the dieters were 11lb (5kg) heavier than their initial weight.

The truth is that the human body has evolved to survive periods of reduced food intake by going into 'starvation mode'. This involves adjusting its metabolism – the rate at which it burns calories – to try to conserve energy. So, if you drastically reduce your calorie intake, your body will react by starting to burn fewer calories to keep your body's normal processes functioning. It learns to

Photograph your food ... these snapshots could make you stop and think – before you tuck in.

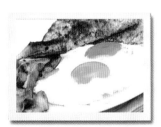

# ten weight-loss winners

The key to successful weight loss involves making small but important changes that you can incorporate easily into your everyday routine – and stick to. After tracking a group of volunteers over eight weeks and monitoring their behaviour relating to food and eating, researchers came up with these ten tips that have proven to be effective:

**1** **Keep to your meal routine** Whether you have two, three, four or five daily meals, try to eat them at roughly the same times each day.

**2** **Reduce fat** Choose reduced-fat versions of foods such as dairy products, spreads and salad dressings where you can. Use sparingly and check the labels carefully; although the fat level has been 'reduced', some may still be relatively high in fat.

**3** **Walk off the weight** Walk 10,000 steps (equivalent to 60–90 minutes of moderate activity) each day. You can use a pedometer to count the steps and spread the exercise through the day.

**4** **Pack a healthy snack** If you like to eat snacks, choose a healthy item such as a piece of fresh fruit or a low-calorie yoghurt, instead of chocolate or crisps.

**5** **Look at the labels** Be careful about food claims. Check the fat and sugar content on food labels when shopping and preparing food.

**6** **Caution with your portions** Don't heap food (except vegetables) on to your plate. Think twice before having second helpings.

**7** **Get up on your feet** Break up the time you spend sitting. Stand up for 10 minutes of every hour.

**8** **Think about your drinks** Choose water or sugar-free squashes. Unsweetened fruit juice is high in natural sugar so limit it to one glass per day (200ml/⅓ pint). Alcohol is high in calories. Try to limit the amount you drink.

**9** **Focus on your food** Slow down. Don't eat while you are walking around or while watching television. Eat at a table if possible.

**10** **Don't forget your five a day** Eat at least five portions of fruit and vegetables a day (400g in total).

Source: Cancer Research UK and Weight Concern

## RELAXATION

Relaxation techniques designed to counteract the effects of stress can also help to reduce unhealthy compulsive eating. One group of women who followed a two-year programme of yoga, meditation and visualisation lost an average of 2.5 kg (5lb 8oz), and kept the weight off, while another comparable group who focused purely on exercise and nutrition did not. The 'relaxed' women were also generally healthier and happier at the end of the research study.

One of the study's co-authors, Dr Caroline Horwath, from the University of Otago in New Zealand, believes that helping women to 'break free from chronic dieting' is the key to better long-term health. 'By learning and practising relaxation techniques as part of a wider lifestyle-change programme, women acquire effective tools to manage stress and emotions without resorting to unhealthy eating.'

expect a lower food intake. As soon as your calorie intake increases, you are even more likely to gain weight until your body adjusts again – and that could take months, during which time you're piling on the pounds.

## FALSE PROMISES

Even worse than one-off crash diets is the phenomenon known as 'yo-yo' dieting, or weight cycling, in which people get trapped in a cycle of weight loss followed by weight gain followed by further dieting to lose weight again. The typical pattern is for someone who is over-zealous about losing weight quickly to pick an extreme diet and – if they can stick to it for a while – to be initially overjoyed at the amount of weight lost in a short time. But diets that deprive you of too much food are impossible to follow for long, and they make you irritable, tired and depressed. They also intensify food cravings and encourage you to eat too much when you stop the diet. As a result you feel a failure, even though it was the fad diet that failed – not you.

## THE BIG DANGER

If you lose weight too quickly through crash dieting alone, the big danger is that you will lose muscle mass as well as body fat, particularly if you are not taking exercise. Since muscle burns far more calories than fat, losing muscle mass is bad news.

When you stop dieting and start to eat more, you will only gain fat unless you are exercising as well. So what crash dieting does is to swap muscle for fat, increasing your fat-to-muscle ratio, as well as slowing your metabolism, and causing weight gain in the long term.

Studies show that crash dieting reduces levels of HDL, the 'good' cholesterol, reduces cardiac blood flow in post-menopausal women, and actually increases your proportion of body fat. You are much more likely to lose weight permanently by making small, sustained changes to your eating habits.

# ways in which the body uses food

**S**cientists believe that arginine, an essential amino acid in our bodies, could be a useful weapon in the battle against obesity. Researchers at A&M University in Texas, USA, fed obese rats either a high or a low-fat diet supplemented with arginine for 12 weeks. They found that, by regulating the quantity of the amino acid given to the rats, they were able to increase muscle mass and significantly reduce body fat in both groups – by 63 and 65 per cent respectively. The scientists say that arginine alters the way the body uses food. They are planning to do follow-up studies in obese adults and children to test the benefits of taking supplements. Arginine-rich foods include watermelon, seafood, nuts, seeds, algae, meat and soya protein.

And to ensure that you achieve steady gradual weight loss, it is best to combine healthier eating with more exercise. Most overweight or obese people should aim to lose between 5 and 10 per cent of their starting weight in the first three months of a weight-loss programme. You should soon notice the positive effect on your health, particularly if you are already suffering from high blood pressure, diabetes or arthritis.

Diets that deprive you of too much food are impossible to follow for long and make you irritable, tired and depressed.

# your healthy eating plan

The key to successful weight loss is to eat healthy foods in moderation. So, when you're thinking about adopting a new eating plan, start by taking a long hard look at your current diet. Review the results of the questionnaires in Step 3, then apply the lessons you learned about 'good foods' in Step 5.

Your target is to eat more natural, unprocessed foods and to cut down on takeaways, ready meals and fried foods that are high in saturated fat, sugar and salt. Choose more fruit, vegetables, fish, lean protein and unsaturated fats. And don't forget whole grains such as

## Breakfast reduces cravings for high-fat or sugary snacks later in the day, and increases people's fruit and vegetable intake.

wholemeal bread, brown rice and cereals that still have the nutritious grain and fibre-rich outer layer. The benefit of whole grains lies in the fact that they take a long time for your body to break down; they satisfy your hunger but don't pile on the calories. Try to have three servings every day. These are nutrient-dense rather than calorie-dense foods that provide substantial amounts of vitamins and minerals and fewer empty calories.

### NICE AND SIMPLE

The beauty of the healthy eating plan outlined above is its simplicity. There is no need to spend hours counting carbohydrates, fat grams or calories. You simply learn which foods to add more of to your diet and which foods to cut back on. Even the small changes in calorie intake that this will generate will make a difference and – provided that you continue to take in fewer calories than your current level, and that you burn off more energy than you take in as food – you will soon start to shed unwanted pounds.

## SUSTAINING WEIGHT LOSS

'Once you have made a decision to manage your weight, it is something you need to continue to do for the rest of your life,' says Dr Ian Campbell, the chairman of the National Obesity Forum. The plan described in these pages adds up to a life-long strategy, not a short-term (and potentially dangerous) fix. The encouraging news is that these minor adjustments can contribute to significant weight loss over time. Depending on the quality of your diet at the moment, you may find that just following the good-diet guidelines in Step 5 will help you to take off the pounds gained over years of less healthy eating.

## A NOTE ABOUT CALORIES

When referring to energy intake and expenditure, we usually talk about 'calories', but when you study a food label, you'll notice that the energy content of food is listed kilocalories or kcal. This may seem confusing but it's because a calorie, in strict scientific terms, is a tiny unit of heat energy, so it's easier to measure in thousands of calories – kilocalories.

## inside information
# men may be able to 'switch off'

**M**en may find it easier than women to avoid tempting food when they are on a diet and could also find it easier to lose weight. In a brain-scan study, researchers flashed tempting foods in front of men and women who hadn't eaten for a day, then told them to fight their hunger. The men's brains showed far less activity in areas of emotional regulation, memory and motivation than the women's – as if men were more easily able to 'switch off' their cravings for favourite foods, which included fried chicken, lasagne, ice cream and pizza.

Whether you are male or female, however, your willpower can be undermined by stress and anxiety. So, if you are trying to lose weight and you have just had a difficult day at the office, don't walk home past a bakery.

# golden rules

During the first weeks of adjusting to a healthy eating plan, your willpower will probably be sorely taxed. Described below are some golden rules to help you to keep on track. One very useful tactic is to keep a food diary.

For the first week, make a record of every item of food and drink that you consume, at what time and how you feel (or take pictures, see page 124). The diary will enable you to review your food choices and to take stock of what prompts you to eat. You need to learn how to distinguish between true biological hunger, the sign of a healthy appetite, and false alarms, when you feel the urge to eat because you are bored or stressed.

## PORTION PROPORTIONS

We have become so used to seeing (and eating) big portion sizes that many of us don't recognise what a moderate-sized serving actually looks like.

Here are some examples of moderate servings with illustrative comparisons:

- 85g of meat **the size of a pack of cards**
- 1 baked potato **a clenched fist**
- 45g porridge oats (uncooked) **⅓ mug**
- 25g cheese **four stacked playing dice**
- Butter or margarine on bread/toast **a 5p coin**
- Nuts or dried fruit **a golf ball**
- Pasta, rice, mashed potato **a computer mouse**
- 180ml juice **a small yoghurt container**
- Potato crisps **a cupped handful**
- 1 small bun **half of your fist**

(Generally, there is no need to limit portion sizes of fruit and vegetables.)

## SCHEDULE SMALLER MEALS

Scheduling breakfast, lunch, dinner and snacks in the same way that you schedule other daily appointments can help to prevent overeating, so take your meals at regular, set times. Eating little and often improves appetite control, reduces hunger and avoids the blood-sugar swings that can induce you to eat more. In one study, men who increased their frequency of eating consumed up to 27 per cent fewer calories. So, instead of three large meals, try to build five or six small portions of healthy foods into your daily routine.

## CHOOSE HEALTHY SNACKS

Whenever you reach for a snack, think about why you are doing it. Because the food's there and other people are tucking in? Because you feel upset or tired? Eating can be an emotional reaction, and once you understand why you crave a sugary doughnut or biscuit, you may find it easier to resist.

It's also worth keeping healthy snacks to hand so you can satisfy momentary hunger without upsetting your general diet. Choose snacks that add nutrients and keep you feeling full, such as fruit or cut-up vegetables – keep a stock of chopped carrots and broccoli in the fridge.

# sensible **snacking**

**M**ost of us love to nibble. In fact, we eat an average of three snacks a day. While there is nothing wrong with snacking in itself, all too often we fill ourselves up on high-calorie, high-fat snack foods, then either skimp on meals that contain important nutrients or eat normal-sized meals and consume too many calories in total.

There is a way to snack sensibly, however: Choose nutritious snacks and think of them as part of your daily food intake rather than as 'extras'. This will satisfy your cravings and also help you to meet your nutritional needs. Instead of potato crisps, try a piece of fruit or a pot of low-fat yoghurt.

| SNACK | KCAL |
|---|---|
| 250ml (9fl oz) tomato juice | 35 |
| 25g (1oz) ready-to-eat dried apricots | 40 |
| 1 medium apple | 47 |
| 100g (4oz) grapes | 60 |
| 1 slice malt loaf | 86 |
| 1 medium banana | 95 |
| 1 low-fat cereal bar | 95 |
| 1 crumpet with 2 teaspoons reduced-sugar jam | 100 |
| 1 oatcake with cottage cheese | 100 |
| 200g pot low-fat yoghurt | 125 |
| 150g pot low-fat rice pudding | 150 |

**AVOID THESE TREATS** – they may seem light, but they pack a high-calorie punch:

| | |
|---|---|
| 1 small croissant | 230 |
| 2 chocolate digestive biscuits | 168 |
| 1 small packet potato crisps | 150 |
| 1 small packet cheese puffs | 155 |

## EAT SMALLER PORTIONS

Many of us have got used to eating far more than we need. One reason is that average portion sizes of ready meals, takeaway foods, pastries and puddings have increased dramatically over the last two decades, says the Food Standards Agency. Some have nearly doubled in size, and the same is true of restaurant meals. We tend to serve more at home too – portions are now up to eight times as large as those recommended.

Try serving food on smaller plates – this can cut the amount of food eaten by as much as 25 per cent, according to psychologists at Cornell University in New York State. Other studies reveal that people consume 34 per cent fewer liquid calories when they drink out of tall, skinny glasses instead of short, stubby ones.

## EASY EATING ADJUSTMENTS

- Cut your portion sizes by around 10 per cent; when you have got used to the smaller size, reduce portions by another 10 per cent.
- Use slightly less butter and slightly less cooking oil; consider switching to a low-fat margarine.
- If you tend to splurge on snack foods such as biscuits, buy individually wrapped items. Having to open each packet in turn will discourage you from over-indulging.
- Bake, steam or grill food instead of frying it.
- Have one meal each day that excludes starchy carbohydrates (no rice, potatoes, pasta or bread). Try a lean chicken breast with salad, or two portions of different vegetables, for example.
- Trim all visible fat from meat and remove the skin from poultry.
- Replace sugary breakfast cereal with a slice of wholegrain toast and a piece of fruit.
- When eating out in restaurants, choose tomato-based sauces rather than creamy ones.

# make every meal a pleasure

As described in Step 5, people who live in the Mediterranean countries of southern Europe eat a very different diet from most people in the UK. They eat more healthily and are less likely to gain weight as they get older – two factors that are thought to explain at least some of the variations across Europe in the risk of heart disease and stroke. But is the content of their diets all that's involved?

Southern Europeans generally take more time over their meals, and tend to ensure that they eat in pleasant surroundings, at an attractively laid table free of clutter; TV dinners are not part of the agenda. They savour their food, lingering, chatting, making meals into social occasions. This style of dining is beneficial to health in all kinds of ways – being sociable is good for your heart, as indicated in Step 9, and it may also hold a clue to losing weight.

Habitually hurrying your meals doubles your risk of being overweight, according to one study of 3,000 people. Why? Eating fast could mean that there's not enough time for your stomach to send 'I'm full' signals to your brain to tell you to stop eating before you consume too much. And the simple act of chewing may send other signals that cause your brain to feel satisfied and to release appetite-suppressing hormones – but only

# A good night's sleep can help you to resist food cravings.

20 minutes or more after you start to eat. Those in the study who both ate fast and continued eating until they felt full were three times as likely to be overweight as those who did neither of these things. So if you wolf down too much too quickly, your body's natural feedback mechanisms are unable to keep up. It appears that some 'fast food' may be dangerous because of the speed at which it's generally eaten as well as on account of its contents.

## SLOW DOWN

Deliberately trying to savour your food could have other benefits. Several studies suggest that obese people actually derive less pleasure from food than people of normal weight – and that they eat more in an attempt to increase their sense of satisfaction. In reinforcement of this theory, researchers have now shown that some people have a particular genetic make-up that adversely affects the quantity of gratification-promoting chemicals in their brain.

So eat slowly, take time to relish your food, put your knife and fork down at intervals. Never eat lunch at your desk, while talking on the telephone or answering emails. If you do, you are more likely to overeat.

# a winning combination

Reducing the amount you eat or taking more exercise will help you to lose weight, but for maximum effect you need to do both – and this approach is also the best way to protect your cardiovascular system.

## ENERGY STORAGE

One reason why many of us put on weight in middle-age is because we are less physically active as we get older. That tendency is made worse by the fact that we don't have to expend as much energy as we used to simply to survive. Nor, in the days of central heating, do we need fat layers to keep us warm. We have cars and buses and trains to save us from travelling under our own steam, and a vast range of machines and gadgets to save us from effort in everyday life. But humans have evolved to store body fat as a reserve for times of famine. And some people will do this more efficiently than others. An obese person can store up to a year's worth of energy as fat. The problem is that, when food is in plentiful supply, that is just too much to get used up during ordinary living.

## A TWO-PRONGED ATTACK

In one study of obese, inactive men and women with poor glucose tolerance (suggesting a high risk of diabetes), a 12-week programme of aerobic exercise reduced body fat without affecting lean muscle mass, and improved both fitness and blood sugar levels – but greater improvements were seen among those who also followed a reduced-calorie diet. In another study, reported in the *International Journal of Obesity*, researchers proved that exercise is vital to reducing the size of abdominal fat cells – calorie restriction alone just didn't work. That's important, because fat-cell size has been shown to predict the risk of diabetes, whether or not someone is actually obese.

**REDalert !**

### COUCH POTATOES

The more time you spend watching television, the more likely you are to become obese and to develop diabetes. That's the conclusion of a six-year study involving 50,000 women. Researchers found that an additional 2 hours' television time was associated with a 25 per cent greater risk of obesity and a 14 per cent increased risk of diabetes. What's more, the dangers persisted even when the statistics were adjusted to take account of other factors such as diet and smoking. So it's not just increased snacking while you're watching that's responsible; nor is it simply sitting – the perils of which are discussed in the next chapter. The researchers discovered that risks were also increased when office workers sat for similar periods, but not by nearly as much as television-watching. They recommend limiting the time you spend watching television to no more than 10 hours per week; people in the UK currently watch, on average, 26 hours of television a week.

## A PLAN FOR ALL AGES

You're never too old to benefit from a health programme. Researchers in Taiwan identified 52 younger and 50 older people, all of whom were obese and had diabetes, and put them on a one-year programme that combined a calorie-reducing diet and a moderate aerobic-exercise regime. At the end of the year, improvements in BMI, total cholesterol and triglycerides were the same in both age groups, while improvements in body-fat levels, waist circumference and various metabolic markers were actually better among the older participants.

## DEFENCEtactics

### A MIX OF EXERCISE IS BEST

For the most effective weight loss, make sure that you do both aerobic exercise and strength training. Aerobic exercise – the type that makes you breathe faster and stimulates blood circulation – is ideal for the health of your cardiovascular system. It also speeds up metabolism (the rate at which you burn calories), but only for a short time. Strength training – which builds up muscle mass – helps to boost your metabolism overall, because the muscle mass that you are gaining burns up more calories than the fat that you are shedding. And it's beneficial to incorporate some stretching exercises too, to enhance flexibility and to help keep you mobile. See Step 7 for more details.

## SET REALISTIC TARGETS

Avoid setting over-ambitious targets. The key to success in any weight-loss regime is to make changes that you can easily incorporate into your everyday life. As an example, if you can burn just an extra 58kcal each day – from 10 minutes' dancing, for example – while keeping the same food intake, you will lose half a pound a month. Take in 58kcal less food each day – the equivalent of one biscuit – as well, and you'll double this. That could add up to 12lb (5.5kg) in a year, with scarcely any extra effort. Obviously, with a little bit more exertion and a little bit less food, you'll lose even more. Sticking to one element of a plan – whether it's to take more exercise or to cut down on junk food – boosts your willpower and self-control, making you more likely to succeed in other areas.

A two-pronged attack – tackling both diet and exercise – is vital if you're serious about losing weight.

Jackie Herbert

# Weight-loss triumph

When Jackie Herbert was diagnosed with diabetes five years ago, at the age of 52, her weight was 16st (102kg). She'd mentioned to her GP that she had to get up frequently at night to pass urine and was also very thirsty. 'He tested my blood sugar and told me I had diabetes. Then he said I needed to lose weight.'

Jackie managed to lose more than 2st (13kg) in eight months. 'I simply stopped buying fatty foods such as sausage rolls and cake, and I used only small amounts of oil in cooking,' she says. Before eating anything she'd ask herself, 'Should I eat this? Is it fattening?' Slowly the weight began to drop off - and she helped her husband, Eddie, to lose 2st (13kg) too. 'It was easier with Eddie's support, but I would have lost weight on my own because I knew this time I had to do something.'

Jackie had gained weight after the menopause, and thinks her diet was largely to blame. Now she eats more fresh food, and moderation is her motto. 'Life is for living. I'm not going to give up everything. If I want some chocolate, I have some, but a small amount - and I make sure it's good quality.'

## Before eating anything, Jackie would ask herself, 'Should I eat this? Is it fattening?'

She also keeps active, looking after her four-year-old grandson four days a week, plus her own cleaning, cooking, washing, ironing and household chores for her daughter when required. It all helps to keep the weight off, she says.

'I've lost another 7lb (3kg) in the last eight weeks,' Jackie adds, and thinks this may also be due to a newly acquired taste for Japanese food. 'I've been making lots of sushi, which is small in terms of quantity but filling. I also make bread - pounding the dough is quite good exercise.'

Her new lifestyle is paying dividends. While Jackie still needs medication for diabetes and cholesterol-lowering drugs, her cholesterol levels are normal and her blood sugar is down.

'Diabetes is in my life, but I don't let it rule me. It only becomes an issue if you ignore the rules. I take my tablets, watch what I eat and keep my blood sugar under control. But I live life to the full, just as before. I won't let it change me.'

## BUILD UP YOUR ACTIVITY LEVEL

Small daily additions to your activity level can often make more difference than an all-out crash exercise programme that you probably won't be able to sustain (and which may be harmful if you do).

It takes 3,500kcal to make 1lb (0.5kg) of fat, and you need to burn this amount to lose it. Half an hour's brisk walk will burn up about 150kcal; if you do that five days a week, you'll burn enough calories to lose 11lb (5kg) in the course of a year, as long as you don't increase your food intake.

# the neat solution

All of us use up energy each day simply to stay alive and keep our bodies in working order. This is known as 'basal metabolism'. It takes on average, about 1,300kcal for women and 1,600kcal for men – that's what we would use up if we did nothing but lie down or sleep all day. For those people who have a fairly inactive lifestyle, basal metabolism may account for as much as 60 per cent of their total energy expenditure.

In addition to this, of course, we use up energy – burn calories – in the course of physical exertion. According to Dr James Levine of the Mayo Clinic in the USA, we do this in one of two ways: 'One is to go to the gym and the other is through all the activities of daily living called NEAT – Non-Exercise Activity Thermogenesis (thermogenesis means heat generation, a product of the breakdown of food to create energy). NEAT is the energy used up in routine daily activities, when we're doing more than just lying down, but not actually 'exercising' – washing up the dishes or taking out the rubbish, rather than jogging or playing football.

For most people in Western societies, NEAT is by far the most significant form of energy expenditure, says Dr Levine. 'In people who have sedentary lifestyles, NEAT is responsible for less than 15 per cent of total energy expenditure, whereas it may account for more than 50 per cent in highly active people. It appears that NEAT is far more important for calorie-burning than exercise in

---

**MYTHS** X

### SWEAT MORE, SLIM MORE

The common belief that the more profusely you sweat during exercise the more calories you burn – and, consequently, the more fat you lose – has no basis in fact. It is true that strenuous exercise burns up more calories than gentle exercise, but sweating is not a reliable indicator of strenuous exercise. What's more, sweating simply sheds water – so any weight lost directly as a result of sweating will be put straight back on when you have a drink afterwards.

nearly everyone.' A study of 20 volunteers at the Mayo Clinic proves his
point. The results demonstrated that 'It's metabolically more effective to
put more NEAT into your life to achieve a healthy body weight than to
seek organised exercise.' Even minor changes in physical activity
throughout the day can increase daily energy expenditure by 20 per
cent, it seems.

## ON THE GO

So how do you get more NEAT into your life? The answer
is through just about anything involving movement
that's not strictly 'exercise'. Examples include certain
aspects of your work, your housework and leisure
activities – even fidgeting counts. According to
researchers in the USA and Germany, some people
have a 'fidget' gene – and inveterate fidgets are less
likely to be overweight than others. If you are one of

## You're on the way to taking control of your weight – rather than letting it control you.

those who shuffle and shift in your seat, fiddle with pencils or
tap your feet (and the tendency runs in families), you're getting
valuable daily exercise without even knowing it, they say. In
a study at the Mayo Clinic, Dr Levine fed 16 people an extra
1,000kcal a day. After two months the natural fidgeters in the
group weighed the same; those who barely moved had gained 12lb
(5.5kg). Fidgeting can burn up to 350kcal a day. Over the course
of a year, that's equivalent to up to 40lb (18kg) of fat worked off.

## in the driving seat

Step 6 has explained why the best way to keep your weight down is to
make small changes to your eating patterns and daily activity levels. You
don't need to embark on a crash diet or join a gym, but you do need to be
patient. Most people who weigh more than is healthy have put on weight
gradually over months or years, and it may take some time to lose it. Don't
weigh yourself more than once every week or, preferably, every two weeks.

There are two reasons for following this advice. First, you may be fooled by an initial improvement that is in fact mostly water loss, then get downhearted when it's not sustained. Second, you may see no change at all, or even – if you have started exercising when you've previously been sedentary – an early increase because muscle weighs more than fat. Again, this can be disheartening. Keep a note of your waist measurement as well as your weight; waist measurement is actually more important – but again, don't measure too often.

And remember that you're most likely to succeed if you adopt realistic goals. The key is small, steady changes of around 1lb (0.5kg) a week, so there's no point weighing yourself more often. Many people find interim goals help their progress – aim to lose 4½lb (2kg) by Easter, trim an inch in time for your summer holiday, or drop a clothes size in three months.

## KEEP IT UP

If you have begun to adopt more careful eating habits, you're already on the way to controlling your weight, rather than letting it control you. Now you have to plan how to keep the weight off in the long term. Many people need as much support to maintain their reduced weight as they did to lose it in the first place. Your chances of success will be boosted, and you'll be far more likely to carry on with your healthy diet, if everyone in the family adopts similar habits (which will improve their health as well) than if you have to shop for and cook separate meals for yourself.

Support can come from many sources, not just from your family but also from friends, your GP, a weight-loss support group, or an exercise class including other people who have the same aim as you.

## TIME TO GET MOVING

You know the dangers of being overweight. You have assessed your own risk and can apply what you have learned about different types of food that can help you to fulfil your weight-loss programme.

Of course, no plan for losing weight and protecting your heart and arteries is complete without regular exercise. In Step 7 you will discover how to get started on an exercise regime. You will learn some do's (exercise should be enjoyable and fun) and don'ts (if you push yourself too hard and too fast, you are much more likely to give up). And as you put into practice a strategy for incorporating more physical activity into your life – to help both to shed the pounds and to keep them off – you may find it's easier than you think.

# self-defence plan
## STEP
# 7

YOU KNOW THAT EXERCISE IS GOOD FOR YOUR HEALTH, BUT THE HARDEST PART IS GETTING STARTED. OR IS IT? AS YOU'LL DISCOVER, YOU DON'T HAVE TO JOIN A GYM OR RUN MILES TO GIVE YOUR ARTERIES A WORKOUT. ALL IT TAKES IS A CONSCIOUS DECISION TO GET UP AND GET MOVING IN EVERYDAY LIFE.

# Get in
# shape

The word 'exercise' with its overtones of an energetic gym workout or a 5 mile run discourages many people. But you don't have to be a dedicated athlete to maintain the healthiness of your heart and arteries. What counts is keeping as active as you can in your daily life and squeezing a bit more physical activity into everything you do. If you adopt this holistic approach, you will be able to watch your energy levels rise as your weight falls.

## BREAKING BAD HABITS

As far as our bodies are concerned, 21st-century life can be surprisingly static, and it takes a determined effort to change habits that have become deeply ingrained. In our technologically advanced, automated world, more and more of us spend our days doing sedentary office jobs. In addition, thanks to 'labour-saving' devices, work at home is much less arduous than it used to be. So the seemingly frantic pace of our lives does not often involve physical challenges. To get things done quickly, we rely on cars to take us everywhere. After a stressful, mentally tiring day, we frequently relax in front of the television.

Only one in five adults in Britain follows the official advice to take moderately intensive exercise for a minimum of 30 minutes a day – the level required to protect the cardiovascular system. And, as we get older, we exercise less. According to a survey by Sport England, while one in three 16 to 24-year-olds is physically active, this falls to one quarter of 35 to 44-year-olds, one in six 55 to 64-year-olds, and just one in 17 of those aged 75 to 84. It is hard to break free from a vicious cycle: you put on weight as you get older, you take less exercise, you put on more weight, and so on. This pattern of behaviour is clearly damaging. According to the Department of Health, as many as one in five deaths of people aged over 35 can be partly attributed to a lack of exercise.

## EXERCISE IS FUN

The key to change in your own life is to opt for activities you want to do – go dancing, enrol in a yoga class, kick a football with your children, take the stairs instead of the lift, or just walk in the countryside on a glorious summer's evening. It is up to you to choose which physical activities you incorporate into your daily routine – and every little counts.

Kick a football with your children.

# powerful **health** benefits

The benefits of exercise are so stunning that if they could be packaged as a pill it would be regarded as a miracle cure. Regular, moderate exercise halves your risk of heart disease and stroke over the long term and makes you five times less likely to die from cardiovascular disease than someone whose daily routine involves no physical exertion. One study estimates that reducing levels of inactivity by just 1 per cent a year for five years would, in Scotland alone, prevent 2,162 deaths from heart disease and 128 from stroke.

Exercise can even bring benefits to people who already have heart disease. A Norwegian study that was conducted over a period of 18 years clearly indicated that both women and men with coronary heart disease who exercised for just half an hour a week were likely to live longer than those who took no exercise. The more exercise they took, the greater their longevity.

## troubleshooting Q&A

### I'm 68. I used to be pretty active but I've got out of the habit. What sort of exercise would be best for me?

The best activities for someone in your situation include brisk walking, Pilates and isometric exercises (see pages 160–61), which will all help to prevent the muscle loss that tends to occur with age. Since muscle naturally burns more calories than other tissue, you will also store less fat.

It is never too late to build up your muscle strength. In one study of volunteers in their nineties who followed an eight-week strength-training programme, some increased their strength threefold. As you get more active, you will also build up your aerobic capacity (how well your heart and lungs cope with exercise). Just remember to take it in slow, steady stages if you've been inactive for a while.

Exercise that strengthens muscles also aids in the prevention of height loss as well as preserving strength, flexibility and stamina, helping you to maintain your balance and coordination, protecting your bones and even safeguarding your mental agility. So you have much to gain.

## A WELL-OILED MACHINE

As you exert yourself during exercise, your heart pumps blood through your body more efficiently, flushing out the arteries, and protecting them from plaque build-up. Exercise strengthens your heart, reducing your resting pulse rate (your regular heart rate without physical exertion). A well-trained athlete has a resting heart rate as low as 40 beats a minute, but if you take no exercise, your heart has to work harder – at as many as 100 beats a minute in the really unfit – to pump the same amount of blood.

## SELF-PROTECTION

Research indicates that adopting a relatively active lifestyle, including exercise such as a 30 minute brisk walk every day, could prevent nearly a third of new cases of obesity and more than 40 per cent of new cases of diabetes (a condition strongly linked to heart disease and stroke, see page 30). Giving your muscles a workout makes it easier for your body to process energy in the form of blood sugar, or glucose. Researchers from Glasgow University underlined this when they found that insulin resistance in women at high risk of diabetes dropped by 22 per cent after seven weeks on an exercise programme that involved running, cycling, using a rowing machine and aerobics.

## THE SECRET OF YOUTH

It is no myth that exercise helps to keep you young. Studies have shown that women who stay physically active after the age of 50 are as fit as, or even fitter than, women 20 years younger who take no exercise. And a long-term American study found that men who get fit in middle age reduce their risk of dying over the following 20 years by almost a quarter.

Giving your muscles a workout makes it easier for your body to process energy in the form of blood sugar, or glucose.

# regular exercise
# can change your life

If you exercise regularly, you will experience a large number of benefits to your health. All the following advantages associated with exercise are also linked with reducing the risk of heart attacks and strokes.

- Regular exercise lowers total cholesterol levels and levels of 'bad' LDL cholesterol, while boosting levels of 'good' HDL cholesterol, reducing plaque build-up in your arteries.
- It controls weight and reduces body fat.
- It lowers blood pressure.
- It boosts your heart rate while you are in the process of exercising – providing a cardiovascular workout – but lowers it in the long term, meaning that your cardiac capacity and fitness improve.
- It improves circulation and breathing, so your heart and lungs work more efficiently and you get more oxygen to vital organs and tissues.
- It stabilises blood sugar and improves glucose metabolism, thereby lowering the risk of diabetes.
- It relieves stress and anxiety (which, as you will read in Step 9, is important in lowering the risk of heart disease).
- It lifts mood and reduces depression by releasing endorphins, the body's natural 'feel-good' chemicals. And it may also improve any decline in mental alertness associated with depression.
- It helps you to sleep better.

Keeping physically active offers these additional benefits:

- It halves the risk of hip fracture among people over 45 and combats the crippling bone disease osteoporosis, reducing your chance of disability and dependence in old age.
- It reduces the risk of breast, bowel and lung cancer.
- It boosts general fitness, muscular strength and endurance.
- It enhances flexibility and balance.
- It tones your body, so that you look better.
- It reduces the risk of erectile dysfunction in men.
- It lowers your risk of respiratory disease.

And, above all, it may prolong your life – so there would seem to be no argument against the advice that we should all take regular exercise.

# stand up
## and stay healthy

Sitting for long periods – as many of us with sedentary jobs or an inactive lifestyle tend to do – may be a health hazard, disrupting the way our bodies should function, recent scientific studies suggest. In the UK, we spend an average 36 years of adult life sitting compared to just over a year (387 days) taking exercise.

## SITTING SYNDROME

Many of us have desk-bound jobs. And we also tend to sit down while relaxing – whether we're watching television or DVDs, playing computer games, or chatting to friends on social-networking websites.

What makes sitting for long periods so hazardous, say researchers, is that, while sitting, we don't make even the normal brief but frequent muscular contractions that occur when standing or walking; these small, intermittent movements may be necessary to keep our bodies in good working order.

For instance, when we are sedentary for too long, certain chemicals in the body that play a part in burning fat stop functioning. An enzyme called lipase which, when we are engaged in some activity, helps muscles to take up fats circulating in the bloodstream, virtually shuts down when we sit down. With nowhere else to go, blood fats either stick in artery linings, causing the build-up of plaque, or are stored as body fat. And sitting for long periods reduces levels

**Action station** Dr James Levine of America's Mayo Clinic has developed a desk that can be used without sitting down. It is built on the principle of a treadmill, to which, if you prefer, you can add an exercise ball to sit on while you work. He claims that, compared with sitting in a chair, people burn an extra 100kcal an hour walking while they work – equivalent to a weight loss of 4st (25.5kg) a year if they use the desk for 8 hours daily. The adjustable model (left) is a version from TrekDesk, which fits onto an existing treadmill.

of 'good' HDL cholesterol by almost one quarter, increasing the risk of heart problems and metabolic diseases, such as diabetes. This may explain why light activity has been shown to reduce levels of blood sugar.

## ON YOUR FEET

By contrast, every 2 hours we spend standing or walking around at home reduces our risk of obesity by 9 per cent and diabetes by 12 per cent, according to the results of a study by Dr Frank Hu, an expert in nutrition at Harvard School of Public Health. Standing burns an extra 60kcal an hour compared with sitting. That may not seem much, but over an 8 hour working day that's 480kcal – or roughly 2st 5lb (15kg) in a 46 week working year. So, if you habitually sit instead of stand, you need either to take an equivalent amount less as food, or burn off this many calories more through activity. Dr Hu's prescription for a healthy lifestyle is to take at least half an hour's brisk walk every day and to limit the time you spend watching television to 10 hours a week. It is as important to decrease sedentary behaviour, especially watching television, as it is to take more physical activity, he says. To deal with the challenge, Dr Hu's personal solution is to have a treadmill in front of the television, so that he can exercise while watching the news.

## MOVE YOUR MUSCLES

If you are obliged to sit for prolonged periods, try to change position regularly. You could also exercise your legs under the desk, stretch your neck, shoulders and arms, wriggle in your chair, clench your buttocks and abdominal muscles – anything that gets parts of your body moving that would otherwise be still. Most importantly, you should get up and move around at regular intervals. Take a short break every hour, if you can, and do something active, even if it's simply walking to the photocopier or doing sit-ups or star-jumps while the adverts are showing on television.

# defeat desk-bound disease

**W**hether you work from home or in an office, you can fight off the afflictions that come from sitting at a desk for hours at a time. Try the routines described below. You will find that they relieve tension and stress, and ease headaches and tiredness.

- **Neck tilt** Keeping your shoulders loose and your face turned forwards, lean your head towards your shoulder on one side then the other. Bend your head forwards to touch your chin to your chest, then gently lean it back as far as you can go in comfort. Repeat sequence twice.
- **Shoulder roll** Raise your shoulders as high as they will go and roll them forwards and backwards until you feel the tension release.
- **Chest expansion** Clasp your hands behind your head and pull your elbows backwards, moving your shoulder blades together. Repeat three times.
- **Arm stretch** Push your arms out straight to the sides, palms up, as far as they will go, then bend your arm and touch your shoulder tips with your fingers. Release.
- **Arm strengthening** For this, you need a chair with firm armrests. Sit normally with your feet on the floor and place your palms on the armrests, pushing yourself up with your hands as if getting up from the chair. Hold when your legs are almost straight, then slowly lower yourself. Repeat twice on the first day, four times on the second, etc., aiming for ten repetitions in total.
- **Wrist pull** Keeping your shoulders relaxed, make a fist with one hand and flex it inwards as far as you can towards your forearm. Press your fist gently with the other hand and hold for three seconds. End by circling your wrist and clenched fist inwards and outwards three times. Relax and do the same on the other side, then repeat the whole sequence.
- **Back stretch** Fold your arms across your chest until your hands are as far around to your back on the opposite side as possible, as if trying to hug yourself. Hold for 10 seconds, then repeat with the opposite arm on top. Next, place your palms in the small of your back, elbows out, and arch your back forwards, pulling your shoulder blades inwards. Hold for three seconds and relax.
- **Thigh stretch** Place one foot on top of the opposite knee, then bend forwards to touch your forehead on your knee. Repeat on the other side.
- **Leg lift** Sitting with your feet away from your desk, stretch your legs out as far as you can and raise each one in turn until it lifts your thigh away from your chair. Repeat ten times on each side.

# the key to **motivation**

Since everyday life in the early 21st century is relatively sedentary, most of us who want to improve our fitness have to make conscious decisions to be more physically active. The strength of our motivation will make a huge difference to our prospects of success.

In general, formulating positive reasons for taking exercise is far more effective than dwelling on negative ones, according to psychologists. So, if you are thinking about taking up regular exercise because someone close to you has had a heart attack, try to re-frame this as a positive wish to stay healthy and have lots of energy. People who are strongly motivated tend to exercise more and to persist for longer than those who are not – and they are more likely to enjoy exercising. You may feel that you are more tired and stressed than you used to be, you have aches and pains that you didn't used to have, or you simply don't feel as well as you once did. The trick is to harness these complaints into positive long-term incentives for exercising – such as wanting to feel fit, to sleep better or to maintain your muscle strength and stay independent as you get older.

And remember that the longer you can keep going with your exercise programme, the more likely it is that health-giving exercise will become a permanent part of your life.

> **SECRET**weapon
>
> ### EXERCISE BUDDY
>
> You can increase your chance of sticking to an exercise programme by arranging with a friend to go for a walk together every week at a set time, or by joining a walking group. Studies show that people who undertake activities with a spouse, partner, friend or in a class are more motivated. If you make a firm commitment, you are much less likely to change your mind because it's raining or because you just feel too tired.

## EXERCISE THAT FITS INTO YOUR LIFESTYLE

Some people believe that only intense or structured exercise such as aerobics counts as a cardiovascular workout, but it is the total amount of activity in your daily life that matters most. As the World Health Organisation points out, there are four major 'domains' to most people's day: work, travel, home and leisure – and there are opportunities for physical activity during all of them. Exercise that fits into your lifestyle can be more effective than structured exercise. So perhaps the key is to abolish the 'E' word altogether, and just think about how, when and where in the course of your everyday life you can add to your physical activities. Try to find opportunities for activity throughout the day, every day.

Richard Winterflood

# The runner

Richard Winterflood took up running when he went to university as a mature student. 'Hours of studying texts, alone, in a smallish room, left me with an overpowering desire to get out into the open air. I'd been a keen sportsman when I was younger and my body seemed to need it,' he says.

'The exercise itself is a source of great pleasure - the enhanced feeling of wellbeing, a greater alertness of mind, the awareness that you can undertake all sorts of physical activity, or respond to physical challenges,'says Richard. 'But also, as I run throughout the year, it is the increased awareness of nature - the cycle of birth, growth, fruition and death witnessed in the gardens, hedgerows, allotments that I pass.'

'The exercise itself is a source of great pleasure,' says Richard, 'the enhanced feeling of wellbeing, a greater alertness of mind ...'

Now retired and living in north London, Richard runs every day early in the morning on Hampstead Heath or in Highgate Wood. 'As I've grown fitter and leaner, I run with greater ease. Increasingly, as my body takes over the basic rhythm of the running, my mind is left free to scan the path ahead, the choice of paths between the trees, the speed with which I feel I want to run, the kind of step I want to use. The rhythmic variation links with my mood and what I'm thinking and feeling.'

What also delights him is that his enthusiasm appears to be infectious. 'Some months ago a wiry middle-aged man exercising on a set of parallel bars in the wood called out and told me that he'd watched me and was now following my exercise example - albeit in his own way.'

More recently, during his daily runs he noticed that an older denim-clad man whom he'd seen for years regularly walking his dog was suddenly absent. Where was he, Richard wondered?

'Six months earlier, he had told me that his dog was getting too old to give him any real exercise,' says Richard. 'Recently, I've glimpsed him twice: the first time walking - without his dog. Then a few days later, I saw him again - running and still in his habitual denim. I couldn't help smiling as I watched him disappear through the trees.'

## MAKE IT EASY

Here are a few simple psychological incentives to increase your motivation and help you to stay on track:

- **Change your mindset** Don't think I should/must/ought to exercise. Think 'a quick stroll now would clear my head' or 'a swim in the morning would give me more energy for the day'.
- **Do something you enjoy** Some people love going to the gym; others feel intimidated by all the equipment. Some feel motivated if they take classes with other people; others prefer a solitary jog. Some people are most energetic first thing in the morning; others are better in the afternoon. Make your chosen activity fit your personality and lifestyle.
- **Start small** If you find exercise hard, aim to do just 10 minutes on three days a week to start with … then 15 minutes … then four times a week and so on. Take at least one day off from your routine each week.
- **Make exercise fit into your routine** If you have to travel a long way to reach your place of exercise, and go there at a time of day that makes it hard to fit around other commitments, you'll probably give up in a week. Schedule activity at a convenient place and time.
- **Get the right clothing** Choose loose, comfortable clothes for exercising. If you decide to go running, get proper footwear; nothing undermines exercise plans faster than pain or injury. If it boosts your confidence, buy some attractive running gear or a new swimsuit.

# before you start running

Jogging is a very effective way to achieve cardiovascular fitness and burn calories, but you must start cautiously, particularly if you haven't done any running before. Make sure that you follow these guidelines:

- Buy a comfortable pair of good running shoes that cushion and support your feet. You should buy a new pair every six months if you run regularly.
- Always warm up and stretch thoroughly before you start (see page 155).
- Take things slowly to begin with – for instance, start by walking much of the way and gradually include periods of jogging. As you become fitter, you can gradually increase the time you run.
- You should need to breathe a little harder (to get more oxygen into your body) but you should still be able to chat while you jog – a sign you are not overdoing it. If you get uncomfortably out of breath, slow down or walk until you have recovered.

Bear in mind that, although jogging is less stressful than sprinting, it is still a relatively high-impact activity and not always suitable for people with knee or ankle problems.

- **Stick to the schedule** If you can't face a 30 minute workout, don't just sink into the nearest armchair – go for a walk instead. But keep to your routine. If it starts to rain just at the time when you had planned to have a cycle ride through the park, vacuum the living room or clean the windows instead (yes, housework does count, see page 166).
- **Be honest** Don't fall back on the excuse that you are 'too busy' to take exercise. Think about how much time you spend sitting during the day (on average, we each spend more than 3½ hours daily just watching television). And if you're truly pushed for time, spread activity into shorter bursts throughout the day.

## BEFORE YOU START

Although in general most of us need to take more exercise, people who have been inactive for a while may have health concerns about embarking on an exercise programme. If any of the following applies to you, you must talk to your doctor before starting any programme:

- You have had a heart attack or stroke.
- You have heart disease or diabetes, or are seriously overweight.
- You have asthma or lung, liver or kidney disease.
- You have osteoporosis or arthritis, or have had joint surgery.
- You have had a recent joint, muscle, tendon or ligament injury.
- You have balance problems or dizzy spells.
- You are a man aged over 45 or a woman over 55 with high blood pressure or high cholesterol.

If you haven't exercised for a considerable length of time, it is important to start slowly and to build it up gradually. First, think about adding some walking and gentle stretching exercises to your daily routine, or going swimming with a friend a couple of times a week. If you do join a gym, ask the trainer to help you to plan a programme suited to your own starting fitness level (your resting pulse rate, see page 144, is an indication).

## TALK TO YOUR DOCTOR

Starting an exercise programme can be especially difficult if you have mobility problems. If you have had a stroke or are recovering after a heart attack, discuss your plan with your doctor or rehabilitation specialist. There may be a local scheme already running for people with impaired mobility, or you may benefit from seeing a physiotherapist who can help you to develop an exercise routine to fit your needs.

## I have angina. Will exercise increase my risk of a heart attack?

Yes and no. In people with severe blockages of the arteries supplying the heart muscle, activities such as press-ups or weight-lifting can increase the stress on the heart to the point where it might lead to a heart attack. On the other hand, regular gentle aerobic exercise – such as walking or swimming – should help your angina, making a heart attack less likely in the long term.

## GENTLY ON THE JOINTS

Gentle exercise has been shown to improve symptoms of arthritis. It can reduce joint pain and stiffness, help to build the muscles that support your joints, improve flexibility and increase endurance. Of course, exercise also helps to control your weight, taking the load off your knee joints, and it can reduce the risk of other skeletal problems such as osteoporosis.

Compared to brisk walking, strolling reduces the strain on knee joints by around 25 per cent, helping to burn calories while reducing the risk of injury. In Nordic walking (see page 169), the poles take the load off joints and you burn more calories per mile. Swimming or tai chi are also good options for a safe aerobic workout.

Always begin any exercise routine with warm-up stretching exercises to improve flexibility. If you find even gentle exercises too painful at first, try a water exercise programme (your local pool probably runs one). The buoyancy of the body in water reduces the stress on hips, knees and spine, making movement easier.

## HOW MUCH EXERCISE DO YOU NEED?

To gain cardiovascular benefits, you need to take at least 30 minutes' moderate-intensity exercise five days a week. (Moderate-intensity exercise makes you feel slightly warm and slightly out of breath.) If you find this daunting, then begin with 10 minutes three times a day and gradually build up to an unbroken 30 minutes.

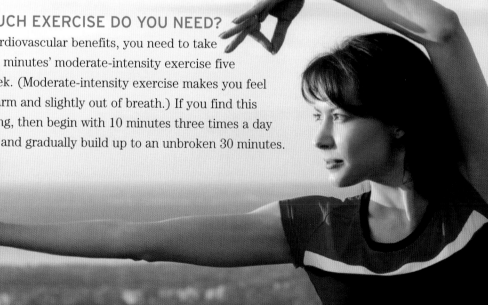

# simple **workout** routines

There are two types of exercise: aerobic and isometric. Aerobic exercise gets your heart beating faster and your lungs working harder. Isometric exercise – also known as resistance training or strength training – builds muscles by making them lift, pull or move something heavy. The classic way to strength-train is with weights in a gym, but you can also do simple exercises using portable dumbbells. An ideal exercise plan incorporating both types of exercise consists of the following components:

- A warm-up at the start of each session to help to loosen your muscles, tendons and ligaments, and to prevent injury.
- Stretching exercises to increase flexibility, improve the range of motion of your joints, enhance posture and boost circulation.
- Aerobic exercise to improve stamina and build cardiovascular strength. Examples include brisk walking, running, swimming, cycling, dancing, and certain household or gardening chores. To be effective, the activity should last for about 20 minutes.
- Strength training through resistance exercises, to maintain and enhance muscle mass and strength, thereby burning calories more efficiently.
- Exercises for core muscles in your lower back, abdomen and pelvis, to enhance balance and stability.

# basic stretching exercises

**S**tretching before exercise helps to prevent injury and keeps you flexible, making it easier to do many physical activities. Here are four simple stretches: calf stretch, hamstring stretch, lower-back stretch and quadriceps stretch.

## CALF STRETCH

Take a step forwards with your right foot. Keeping your left leg straight and both heels on the ground, lean forward. You will feel a stretch in your Achilles tendon, at the back of your foot, and your calf muscles. Repeat with the other leg.

## HAMSTRING STRETCH

Place your left heel on a low stool, step or anything you have to hand, such as an upturned bucket. Put your hands above your hips for support. Bend over very slowly, keeping your back straight and shoulders square until you feel a stretch at the back of your leg. Repeat with the other leg.

## LOWER-BACK STRETCH

Lie on your back with your knees bent. Using both hands, pull your left knee to your chest, pressing your lower back into the floor. You should feel the stretch in your buttocks and lower back. Repeat with the right knee.

## QUADRICEPS STRETCH

Place your right hand on a chair or against a wall for balance. Grasp your left foot with your left hand and pull your foot gently toward your buttocks, keeping your standing leg slightly bent. You should feel a stretch in the muscle at the front of your thigh. Repeat with the right foot.

Aerobic exercise is an excellent way to burn body fat.

## NO PAIN, NO GAIN

It is not true that, to be effective, exercise should hurt. If you are doing enough to benefit your health and burn up calories, you will feel warmer than usual, your breathing will be quicker than normal and your heart rate slightly raised. If you have not generally been very active, your muscles may feel a little sore and stiff the day after exercise, but actual muscle pain during exercise means that you are overdoing it and you need to slow down. So don't 'go for the burn', whatever anyone says. If you develop any of these symptoms during exercise, stop what you are doing and call your doctor straight away:

- Pain in your chest, arms or jaw.
- Shortness of breath that lasts for more than 10 minutes even after you stop exercising.
- Feeling faint or giddy.
- Palpitations.
- Breaking out in a cold sweat.
- Nausea or vomiting.

## AEROBIC EXERCISE

During aerobic exercise, your breathing gets deeper as you take more oxygen into your lungs and your pulse speeds up as your heart pumps blood faster around the body. Your blood vessels dilate to allow more oxygenated blood to your muscles. This is an excellent way to burn fat and lose weight, reducing stress on bones and muscles.

Your heart and the muscles around your lungs respond to aerobic exercise by getting stronger. Your body uses the oxygen it takes in during exercise to convert the energy stored as sugars and fats into usable physical energy. In this way, the more exercise you do, the more fat you burn off.

Any exercise that raises your heart rate will benefit your cardiovascular system and help you to lose weight, so long as it is performed frequently and

# exercise and **heart rate**

**E**ach of us has a maximum heart rate, above which we are over-exerting the heart and putting ourselves at risk. For most people, the maximum heart rate is 220 minus your age. So, if you are 50, your maximum heart rate is 170 beats per minute.

Doctors and fitness experts recommend that, in the course of exercising, people should reach and maintain roughly 60 to 65 per cent of their maximum heart rates – and, to promote good health, this level of exertion should be maintained for at least 30 minutes a day. For a 50 year old, this would be 102 beats per minute. In comparison, the average person has a resting heart rate of about 70 beats per minute.

You can measure your heart rate yourself, either manually or by using a special monitor. If you want to do it manually, start by checking your resting heart rate by counting your pulse for a minute (see page 67). Then do the same again after exercise, to see how close you are to reaching your maximum.

at the correct intensity. Popular activities include running, cycling, rowing, playing football, racquet sports, organised aerobics classes, and gym-based workouts using equipment such as steppers.

If you are devising your own aerobic-exercise programme, structure each session as follows: about 10 minutes warming up, 10 to 20 minutes exercising, and 5 to 10 minutes cooling down. Build up to exercising three to five times a week. (See page 158 for a range of aerobic exercises.)

## ISOMETRIC EXERCISE

Isometric exercise produces muscle tension without moving the joint and increases strength, but does not benefit the cardiovascular system immediately. It is not suitable for some people with heart disease or high blood pressure.

But this form of exercise can prevent the loss of muscle mass that often accompanies ageing and may stop the decline in metabolism that leads to 'middle-age spread' – simply having more muscle on your body means that you burn more calories. In women, it can also increase bone density and help to prevent osteoporosis.

**RED**alert

**WEIGHT LIMITS**

**I**n contrast to aerobics, which exercises your heart and cardiovascular system, isometric exercise, or strength training, is a form of activity designed to exercise your muscles. Using weights sensibly is a good way to maintain and build muscle mass, but it's important not to try to lift weights that are too heavy, since this puts stress on the heart and increases blood pressure. So this is one instance where you can't necessarily incorporate exercise into everyday tasks by, for example, lifting sacks of coal unassisted. People who already have heart disease or high blood pressure should not do heavy isometric exercises.

# an aerobics programme
## ten exercises

**I**f you would like to try an aerobics programme at home, have a go at the exercises described here. You may not be able to do all of them every day – but do them when you can. Some, such as the star jump, are quite demanding, but there are simple bends and strides that you should be able to work into your daily routine.

**1 Spot jog** Lift your knees to waist height as you jog on the spot. Keep your stomach tight and land on your toes. Jog continuously for 30 seconds.

**2 Star thrust** Squat on your toes with your hands on the floor just over shoulder-width apart. Keep your stomach tight and your back straight. Jump your feet back so that your legs are extended behind you in a push-up position. Jump your feet forward into the squat position again and move back up into standing position. Repeat continuously for 30 seconds.

**3 Bridge** Lie on your back with your legs bent and your feet flat on the floor. Place your hands flat on the ground beside your body. Exhale as you use your abdominal muscles to push your buttocks up away from the mat, straightening your body. Inhale as you come back onto the floor. Repeat continuously for 30 seconds.

**4 Speedball** Bend your arms to 90 degrees and hold them in front of you at chest level. Circle your arms around each other continuously for 15 seconds. Change direction and circle them for another 15 seconds.

**5** **Star jump** As you jump up in the air, open your legs wide and move your arms up and out, so that your body forms a star shape. Move down into a squat position as you land, ready to jump again. Repeat continuously for 30 seconds.

**6** **Side stride** Stand with your feet together, your hands on your hips and your back straight. Step sideways with your right foot, then follow with your left foot so that your feet are together. Step back to the side with your left foot and follow with your right foot. Repeat continuously for 30 seconds.

**7** **Lunge** Stand with your feet together. Inhale and take a large step forward. As your foot touches the floor, bend your knee and lower your body until your leg is at a 90-degree angle. Exhale and push yourself back up to standing. Alternate legs continuously for 30 seconds.

**8** **Side jump** Stand with your feet together. Imagine a straight line on the ground heading away from you. With your feet together and your knees slightly bent, jump from one side of the line to the other. Repeat continuously for 30 seconds.

**9** **Wall press-up** Stand facing a wall, about an arm's length away from it. Place your palms flat on the wall at shoulder height and slightly wider than shoulder-width apart. Inhale as you bend your arms, leaning your body in towards the wall. Keep your stomach tight and your back straight. Exhale as you push yourself back up to the starting position. Repeat continuously for 30 seconds.

**10** **Cross jump** Stand with your feet together. Imagine that you are standing at the centre of a cross with one line extending in front and behind you and the other out to your sides. With your feet together and knees slightly bent, jump forward along the imaginary line then back to the centre point. Jump backwards along the line and then return to the centre. Jump out to the right and return and out to the left and return. Repeat continuously for 30 seconds.

# strength training

**B**y building muscle mass, strength training is the best long-term strategy for burning more calories and reducing body fat. The isometric exercises below require a few inexpensive items – dumbbells, a stability ball and an exercise mat (see 'Exercise aids', page 154).

## BACK AND BICEPS

**1 Back fly** Sit on the edge of a stability ball or a chair with your feet flat on the floor. Hold a dumbbell in each hand. Keeping your back flat, bend forwards at the waist and lower your chest to about 7–10cm (3–4in) above your knees, letting your arms hang down on either side of your legs with your hands by your feet. Squeeze your shoulder blades and raise the weights out to the side until your arms are outstretched parallel with the floor. Pause, then slowly return to the starting position.

**2 Bent-over row** Stand with your feet shoulder-width apart, your back straight and your knees slightly bent for support. Hold a dumbbell in each hand. Keeping your back straight, bend 90 degrees from the waist and let your arms hang towards the floor, palms facing your legs. Squeeze your shoulder blades together and bend your elbows, raising the dumbbells on either side of your body, as if rowing. Pause, then slowly return to the starting position.

## CHEST AND TRICEPS

**1 Stability-ball push-up** Place a stability ball against a wall, then kneel in front of it so that it is between you and the wall. Place your hands on the ball so they are directly below your shoulders. Walk back on your knees until your body forms a straight line from your head to your knees. You should be leaning forwards into the ball. Keeping your torso straight and your abdominal muscles contracted (concentrate on pulling your belly button to your spine), bend your elbows and lower your chest towards the ball. Stop when your elbows are in line with your shoulders. Pause, then return to the starting position.

**2 Triceps pressback** Sit on a stability ball with your knees bent and your feet flat on the floor. Hold the dumbbells in front of you with your arms bent at a 90-degree angle and your elbows at your sides. Keeping your back straight, bend slightly from the hips. Straighten your arms and extend the weights behind your back, turning your palms towards the ceiling once your arms are fully extended. Pause, then return to the starting position.

## LEGS AND CORE

**1 Side plank** Lie on your left side with your knees bent. Bend your left arm so your forearm is extended in front of you perpendicular to your body, then lift your torso off the floor. Your upper body should form a straight line from your hips to your shoulders. Place your right hand on your hip and hold for 5 to 15 seconds. Return to the starting position, then repeat on other side. Work up to holding on each side for 30 to 60 seconds.

**2 Hover** Lie facing down on the floor with your upper body propped on your forearms. Your elbows should be directly beneath your shoulders and your palms flat on the floor. Raise your body so that your torso, hips and legs are off the floor and your body is in a straight line, supported on your forearms and toes. Don't let your back arch or droop, and hold for 10 to 20 seconds.

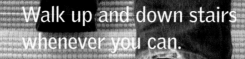

Walk up and down stairs
whenever you can.

# find time for fitness

It is often difficult to find time to fit exercise into a busy schedule. There is a tendency to think that, if you can't do the recommended daily minimum of 30 minutes, there is no point in doing any exercise at all. In many surveys, lack of time is the main excuse people give for not being more active. But bear in mind that you don't have to do it all at once. You can achieve your daily quota by breaking it up into three shorter bursts of exercise lasting 10 minutes each. The trick is to build activity into your everyday life.

## BOOSTING DAILY ACTIVITY

Here are some ways in which you can boost your daily activity when you just don't have time for a traditional exercise regime:

- Get up half an hour earlier once a week. Use the extra time to do some floor exercises (getting an exercise DVD can help), or go for a walk or a swim. Once you're happy with that, do it twice a week.
- Walk up and down stairs whenever you can. If you use a lift at work, get out two floors below your usual level. Walking up just two flights of stairs a day can add up to 6lb (2.5kg) weight loss over a year.
- During the lunch break at work, instead of eating at your desk or sitting in the staff restaurant, have a quick snack and go for a walk outside.
- Get off the bus one stop earlier than usual and walk the rest of the way.
- Park a little further away than you really need to each time you arrive at the office or the shops, and walk the rest of the way. From time to time, increase the distance and try to walk a little faster.
- Think about how to incorporate activity into your regular routine. Could you cycle to the shops, for example, or swap your regular cinema trip with a friend for a bowling or ice-skating session?
- Treat waiting times as opportunities for action. Don't simply stare at your computer screen while waiting for a page to load; do a quick arm stretch

or three. Waiting for the kettle to boil? Try a few squats, holding the edge of the worktop or the back of a kitchen chair, if necessary.

● While watching television, make sure you spend at least 10 minutes in each hour doing something else as well – sit-ups, leg lifts, stretching exercises. Getting up during the adverts to load the dishwasher and tidy the kitchen can add up to 15 minutes' activity an hour.

● Do the ironing while watching a film, or set up an exercise bike or treadmill in front of the television. In 10 minutes you'll burn 62kcal ironing or 97kcal on the bike or treadmill.

# take the high-intensity route

Busy workers with little time for exercise may be heartened by a recent small study at Heriot-Watt University in Edinburgh which concluded that short bursts of intense exercise every few days could dramatically reduce the risk of certain diseases.

'Many people feel they simply don't have the time to follow current guidelines on exercise,' says James Timmons, Heriot-Watt's Professor of Exercise Biology. These guidelines recommend that we perform moderate to vigorous aerobic and resistance (isometric) exercise for several hours a week. 'The risk of cardiovascular disease or Type 2 diabetes is greatly reduced by regular physical activity,' says Timmons, 'but we also found that short bursts of exercise can be highly beneficial.'

The team at Heriot-Watt studied 25 inactive men, each of whom did four to six 30 second sessions, as fast as they were able, on an exercise bike, taking 4 minutes' rest between each sprint. They did this three times a week for two weeks. The result – based on a total of just 15 minutes of intensive exercise over the course of a fortnight – was a 23 per cent improvement in insulin sensitivity, demonstrated by the speed at which the subjects' bodies removed glucose from the bloodstream after exercise.

The explanation for this is that intense muscle contraction is the only way to remove glycogen – the body's stored form of glucose – from muscles.

'Think about diabetes as being glucose circulating in the blood rather than stored in the muscles where it should be,' says Professor Timmons. 'If we take out the glycogen from the muscles through exercise, then the muscles draw in that excess glucose from the blood.' He recommends four all-out 30 second sprints on an exercise bike three times a week. You could gain similar benefits, he says, by running up and down four flights of stairs three times twice a week. The exercise routine, known as 'high-intensity interval training', or HIT, can work for men and women of all ages.

# exercise to suit yourself

The favourite way for most people to get exercise is through brisk walking. In a recent survey of popular physical activities by Sport England, walking came top, followed by swimming, going to the gym, cycling and football. Jogging came just above golf, while aerobics was low on the list.

Walking for half an hour just three times a week is one of the best forms of exercise, offering significant benefits to cardiovascular health. A team from Queen's University in Belfast studied 106 adults aged 40 to 61 who were healthy but inactive. Two groups were asked to do 30 minutes of brisk walking on either three or five days per week, while a third group did not change their activity level.

After 12 weeks, the walkers in both active groups recorded significant falls in their blood pressure and in waist and hip circumference, as well as improvements in their overall level of fitness. There were no changes among the control group.

## WALK TALL

If you are not used to doing much walking, start slowly and gradually pick up your pace after the first minute or two. Keep your shoulders back and relaxed and your abdomen tucked in to protect your lower back. The best rhythm and stride are the ones that feel most comfortable. If you want to increase your pace, take short quick strides – your feet will more easily get into a rhythm and you will move at a faster speed.

## HOW MANY STEPS DO YOU TAKE?

A pedometer is a cheap step-counting device that is very useful if you are trying to increase your overall level of daily activity. Just strap one on to your waistband and go about your life. This is a simple and clever way of measuring just how active you are. You won't be able to resist having a look at your step count and, with luck, making the effort to increase it.

If you are fairly inactive, you probably take around 3,000 steps a day; an average daily level is 7,000 steps for men and 5,000 steps for women. In trials, people wearing pedometers take an average of 2,491 more steps a day than people not wearing them (2,000 steps is about a mile, so that represents nearly 9 miles a week). Wearing a pedometer will increase your level of physical activity, and users also experience significant reductions in blood pressure and BMI (see page 66). Having a target number of steps to aim for has been proven to increase step counts more effectively than aiming for a 30 minute brisk walk daily. Experts recommend aiming for at

## The ideal is to complete at least 10,000 steps a day.

least 10,000 steps a day, which will burn around 500kcal, or 3,500kcal in the course of a week. As long as you don't increase your calorie consumption, you will be a pound lighter in weight for the price of a little extra footwork. If your starting level is a lot lower than the average, simply set interim goals – 5,000 steps a day, then 6,000, and so on.

The more you can do the better. A 2008 study involving 14 researchers from around the world showed that, for effective weight control, women under 40 and men under 50 should aim for as many as 12,000 steps a day.

### WANT TO JOIN A GYM?

If you would like to become a member of a gym or fitness centre, but feel too embarrassed to make the initial approach, take a friend with you. Most gyms will be only too happy to give you a personal tour and, once you've

Building up your muscle power could increase your life span.

# be strong, live long

**B**uilding up muscle power can increase a man's life span. That's the conclusion of a study in Sweden in which researchers tested the strength and fitness levels of 8,762 men aged between 20 and 80 and followed them for almost 20 years. They found that men with greater muscular strength at the outset had lower rates of death from all causes, including cancer. The strongest group of men were 23 per cent less likely to have died at the end of the follow-up period than the weakest group – and they had 29 per cent fewer deaths from cardiovascular disease.

seen the equipment and met the staff, it will seem less intimidating. It may well be a good plan to go in January, when many fitness centres offer special reduced rates to mark the start of a new year.

Avoid fitness centres with gleaming wall-to-wall mirrors. According to researchers at McMaster University in Toronto, Canada, exercising in front of a mirror makes women feel less energised, relaxed and upbeat than exercising without a mirror. Even women who feel good about their bodies experience negative feelings after working out in front of their reflections.

# home is where the heart gets healthy

Performing household chores, window-cleaning, gardening and DIY are among the ideal ways to increase your heart rate. They all involve NEAT, Non-Exercise Activity Thermogenesis (the heat or energy we use up in routine daily activities) – see pages 137–38. Dr James Levine of the Mayo Clinic, whose team led the reseach into NEAT, estimates that the many labour-saving machines associated with our homes – everything from cars

## Put on some lively, invigorating music.

and lifts to dishwashers and television remote controls – deprive us of 100 to 200kcal per day of NEAT that we could be expending, and this, according to Dr Levine, may be the cause of 'the entire obesity epidemic'.

When you are next doing housework, try the routine described below. It is guaranteed to get you moving up a gear.

- Put on some lively, invigorating music to keep the pace going, and sing along with it so that you exercise your lungs and chest muscles.
- Start with a light chore, such as dusting, as a warm-up.
- Make a conscious effort to contract abdominal and thigh muscles when you bend and stretch (such as when making beds), holding for 10 seconds each time.
- Run up and down the stairs as often as you can. This is a wonderful aerobic workout, especially if you are carrying a heavy load.
- When you are cleaning windows or polishing, deliberately trace wide energetic loops to help to tone and strengthen arm muscles.
- Push the vacuum cleaner as far forwards as you can on each sweep.
- When you are picking things up to tidy a room or to fill a laundry basket, do a separate squat for each item, bending from the knees and keeping your back straight.
- Use a low stool to do step-up exercises when cleaning windows or dusting shelves and picture frames.

## HOUSEHOLD MUSCLE

Did you know that climbing a flight of stairs in a typical house burns 2kcal in under 15 seconds? Have a look at the table overleaf. As you can see, there are plenty of ways in which you can use a little muscle and get fit – and at the same time save the money you would otherwise have spent on getting someone else to do the tasks for you. The figures represent extra calories burned, over and above what you expend by simply existing. They are averages. The heavier you are, the more calories you burn.

Energetic gardening – one of the ways to add activity to your life

# household muscle

| activity | kcal/hour | kcal/10 minutes |
|---|---|---|
| decorating/DIY | 383 | 63.8 |
| energetic gardening | 340 | 56.7 |
| mowing the lawn | 333 | 55.5 |
| mopping the floor | 268 | 44.7 |
| washing the car | 250 | 41.7 |
| weeding | 248 | 41.3 |
| window-cleaning | 180 | 30 |
| dusting | 174 | 29 |
| washing up | 171 | 28.5 |
| ironing | 142 | 23.7 |
| standing | 91 | 15.2 |

## ENJOY YOURSELF

The key to staying active is doing things that are fun. Exercise doesn't have to be confined to working out in a gym or pounding pavements, and there is a huge variety of ways to add activity to your life without regarding it as a penalty. Are there any activities that you've always wanted to do but never got round to trying, such as playing golf, scuba diving, or climbing a wall with ropes (something the whole family can do at a local sports centre or climbing centre)? Here are some more ideas to inspire you:

● **Join a walking club** Walking with others is an excellent way to get fit. Being part of a club means that there are other people to socialise with and to motivate you, and that you are regularly required to be present at a specific time and place. Before joining a club, find out how far the members generally walk and whether it is suitable for your current fitness level. You don't want to find yourself on a 20 mile (32km) hike when you'd been anticipating a half-hour stroll in the park.

- **Nordic walking** Try this Scandinavian form of walking that's catching on in Britain. It uses special poles to help to propel you forwards, taking some of the weight off your knees and providing a great cardiovascular workout. A bit like cross-country skiing, pole walking exercises both upper and lower body at once. It uses more muscles and burns more calories than ordinary walking, while seeming to require a lot less effort, and it aids flexibility and helps people with balance problems.
- **Be a child again** Children are the world's best exercise aid. They won't stay indoors because it's raining, sit down because they feel like a nap, or get distracted because they're worried about a deadline. And children need exercise too – as a diversion from watching television and playing computer games. They make activity fun and they spread their infectious enthusiasm for life. So go bike riding with your children, play football in the park, kick leaves and splash in puddles, throw a Frisbee, fly a kite, skip, play hide-and-seek, take them to the beach … the possibilities are endless.

## If there's no child in the house, how about getting a dog?

- **Get a dog** If there are no children in your home, have you thought about getting a dog? Dogs won't put up with excuses when you don't feel like taking them for a walk, and they offer companionship and a chance to meet other dog-owners. Studies show that dog-owners are less stressed, get more exercise and have lower blood pressure and lower cholesterol levels than the general population. What's more, they tend to be healthier overall, having fewer minor health niggles and other medical complaints.
- **Skip yourself fit** Skipping is good for the heart, bones, flexibility and coordination. Ten minutes' skipping will burn between 70kcal and 110kcal.
- **Get in the swim** If the thought of swimming lengths without a break keeps you away from the pool, try alternating length-swimming with a few water exercises.

- **Yoga** You're aware of it, but have you tried it? Yoga can boost cardiovascular fitness, lung capacity, muscular strength and flexibility, as well as being a very effective stress-reliever. One review of 70 studies worldwide showed that doing yoga regularly can reduce numerous risk factors associated with cardiovascular disease.
- **Sing your heart out** Singing exercises your heart and lungs, boosts your circulation, improves cardiovascular efficiency, increases oxygen uptake, enhances alertness and is a great workout for upper body muscles – as well as making you feel energised and more positive about yourself. Singing can also reduce pain and help people to recover from strokes and heart attacks. Even if you do it only once a month, singing can make an extraordinary difference.
- **Tai chi** This ancient Chinese technique has been described as an art form as well as a type of exercise. It involves a series of flowing, coordinated body movements sometimes known as 'moving meditation', and aims to harmonise mind and body while developing flexibility, strength, balance, posture and calm. Since the movements are so gentle, tai chi is suitable for almost anyone, even people recovering from injuries or frail older people. It has been shown to be as effective as an aerobic workout in lowering blood pressure.

Singing exercises your heart and lungs, boosts your circulation and improves cardiovascular efficiency.

### FIND OUT HOW FIT YOU ARE – THEN AIM TO GET FITTER
Whatever your current state of fitness, and however you decide to exercise, it is good to have a goal and a way to measure your success. So, before you start, do a few checks and note down the results. Check again every six weeks, and watch as your fitness level climbs. Make your goals realistic – and be sure to reward yourself when you hit your target.

- Find out your fitness level by establishing your resting pulse rate (see page 67). Generally, the lower the rate, the fitter you are – in well-trained athletes, heart rate may drop as low as 40 to 60 beats per minute. A high resting heart rate is a predictor of heart attacks and coronary deaths in both men and women. Aim to bring yours down.

- Take what you would regard as a reasonable walk at a reasonably brisk pace. Record your pulse rate immediately afterwards and 2 minutes later; note how far you walked and how long it took you. Your aim is to walk further and faster each week and to see your pulse return to its resting level more quickly.

- Next, look back at the various measurements you have taken earlier – BMI, waist and hip circumference, waist-to-hip ratio (see pages 66-67). If you are overweight, you should aim to reduce all these figures.

- If you have a pedometer, record how many steps you take during an average day of the week and a typical day at the weekend. Try to increase this number – the more steps the better. Settle on a realistic short-term target at the start, depending on your initial step count, and aim for at least 10,000 as your final goal.

- Improve your 'recovery rate'. Your resting pulse rate gives you some measure of your fitness level, but for an accurate assessment you need to know how quickly your heart rate returns to normal after exercise. If you have been unable to take strenuous exercise, or if you are not very fit and you are just beginning to be physically active, use the measurements you took from the self-paced walking test described above. Otherwise, do some form of short-burst exercise that noticeably increases your pulse rate, such as press-ups, skipping or star jumps for as long as you can manage between 2 and 5 minutes (but stop if you develop any pain or discomfort). Take your pulse immediately after stopping the exercise, and again 2 minutes later.

# feel good

If you manage to make physical activity part of your routine, the idea of '30 minutes a day' will no longer seem daunting. You'll start to notice an improvement in your health. You will look better, feel more alert, and your energy levels will soar. You'll sleep better, too, and cope better with stress. It feels good to be active, independent and healthy. Start gently, build up gradually, and do it regularly – and you will reap the rewards of exercise.

# self-defence plan

## STEP 8

EATING WELL AND STAYING FIT ARE EXCELLENT WAYS TO PROTECT AGAINST THE WEIGHT GAIN AND INACTIVITY THAT CAN RESULT IN HEART ATTACK AND STROKE. BUT YOU SHOULD ALSO BE AWARE OF OTHER EVERYDAY ENEMIES THAT CAN CAUSE CARDIOVASCULAR PROBLEMS. THIS STEP DEALS WITH TEN COMMON HAZARDS AND HOW TO COMBAT THEM.

# Safeguard
## your body

**W**e all know how good it feels to be out in the countryside, away from noise and traffic, breathing clean, fresh air. For air polluted by vehicles, smoke and fumes is not only unpleasant; research suggests it also threatens cardiovascular health. Similarly, the constant rumble of heavy traffic on major roads and other loud noises can pose a threat to your heart, as can cold weather and even lack of sunshine.

Every day our bodies are exposed to a variety of toxins in the environment, some of which are easier to escape from than others. You undoubtedly know about a few of the culprits already – smoking, for example, which is especially damaging to the heart and arteries, and shortens lives. Most people are rather less aware of other potentially dangerous toxins, such as chemicals in the plastic packaging widely used for food and drinks.

Various types of infection can also put your arteries at risk, contributing to the body-wide inflammation that underlies the development of arterial plaque (see page 18). Colds and flu can have more serious consequences than simply keeping you in bed feeling miserable for a few days. And, while moderate consumption of alcohol, especially red wine, seems to protect against the development of cardiovascular disease, heavy drinking – especially binge drinking – can greatly increase your risk.

### POISON PURGE

Step 8 explains how we can protect our arteries from ten noxious enemies that potentially threaten all of us in our daily lives, and gives an abundance of helpful advice on how to combat their harmful effects. You may not be able to change, for example, the weather, the air that you breathe when you step outside, or the level of traffic noise – but there are many things you can do to limit your exposure to them.

# alcohol units

**T**he UK government's recommended safe drinking limit is 2 to 3 units a day for a woman and 3 to 4 units for a man. Use the table to work out your own consumption. (One unit in a drink is equivalent to 10ml of pure alcohol.)

1 pint of strong lager = 3 units
1 pint of ordinary lager, bitter or cider = 2 units
175ml (large glass) wine (11 to 12 per cent alcohol) = 2 units
125ml (small glass) wine (11 to 12 per cent alcohol) = 1.5 units
1 alcopop = 1.5 units
1 measure of spirits (25ml) = 1 unit

# no.1 excess alcohol

Drinking a glass or two of red wine every few days can provide you with some protection against cardiovascular disease – but it is important not to overdo it, since drinking too much will increase your risk of having a heart attack or a stroke.

Many people in the UK are habitually drinking much more than they used to. Consumption of wine grew by 180 per cent in the 20 years to 2005 and is still climbing. It is easy to underestimate your intake since bars and restaurants regularly offer 175ml or even supersized 250ml measures of wine (equivalent to a third of a bottle), and the alcohol content of many beers and lagers is far higher than it used to be. Many premises have also increased spirit measures from 25ml to 35ml, and offer doubles (50ml) as standard. The information in the panel above will help you to calculate how much alcohol there is in a variety of popular drinks.

## BEWARE OF BINGE DRINKING

Consuming little or no alcohol during the week does *not* mean you can 'save up' your units for a Friday night or a weekend party. Binge drinking – irregular bouts of heavy consumption – is especially dangerous for your heart and increases your risk of a stroke. Each episode causes a surge in blood pressure and, if it's a regular pattern, you may develop high blood pressure, which is especially likely to promote atherosclerosis, doubling your risk of a heart attack. If you regularly consume 6 or more units at a single sitting (that is, within a 6 hour period, according to the Stroke Association), you are twice as likely to have a stroke as a non-drinker.

The amount you need to qualify as a binge drinker is 8 or more units a day for a man, 6 or more units for a woman. According to UK government figures, 40 per cent of men and 33 per cent of women drink at least double the advised maximum on their heaviest drinking day in the week. If you regularly drink enough to be intoxicated, you increase your risk of dangerously abnormal heart rhythms, heart failure, stroke and sudden death – even if you have no pre-existing heart disease.

## TIPS FOR STAYING SOBER

Here are some tips for having a good night out while staying fairly sober. First, have something to eat before you go out; food slows down the process of alcohol entering the bloodstream. Pace yourself: drink slowly and alternate alcoholic drinks with soft drinks. You could also order a glass of water as well, and take regular sips of that. Order light or low-alcohol beers, avoiding strong continental brands. Drink single shots with plenty of mixer. If you need an excuse for not drinking, say that you are driving or taking medication.

**RED**alert **!**

### ALCOHOL AND YOU

If you think you may be drinking too much, have a look at the statements below and see how many apply to you.

- You often have six or more units at one time.
- You have a bit of a reputation as a drinker.
- You drink to escape from your problems or worries.
- You avoid social occasions where you won't be able to drink.
- Friends or relatives express concern about the amount you drink.
- You are late for work, or have missed work, because of a hangover.
- You drink – or want to – in the morning.
- You sometimes drink on your own.
- You drink because you are shy and need to boost your confidence.
- You hide your drinking, or lie about the amount you drink.
- Drinking has caused problems at work.
- After a night out, you have forgotten what you have done.

If three or more of these statements ring true in your case, your drinking may be getting out of control. The more of them that apply to you, the bigger the problem. It is difficult to change your drinking habits, but skilled and sympathetic support groups can give you the strength you need. See Resources, page 240.

# no.2 gum disease

Gum disease – a chronic inflammation of the gums known medically as periodontal disease – has been shown to have a strong association with atherosclerosis. For example, a study in which samples of dental plaque (the sticky substance that accumulates on teeth) were taken from 659 people with an average age of 69 revealed that those with higher levels of four bacteria known to cause periodontal disease had thicker arterial walls in the carotid arteries supplying the brain. This sign of atherosclerosis is a strong predictor of the risk of strokes and heart attacks.

## DENTAL HYGIENE

Good dental hygiene combined with regular dental check-ups is the key to controlling gum disease, according to Dr Nigel Carter, chief executive of the British Dental Foundation. 'Brush for at least 2 minutes, twice a day, with fluoride toothpaste, flossing daily (alternatively, you can use a small interdental brush), and visit a dentist as often as he or she recommends,' he says. 'And look for an anti-bacterial mouthwash that reduces plaque.' A hygienist can treat more advanced gum problems, removing 'calcified' or hardened plaque round the teeth and below the gums.

If you are not sure whether you are cleaning your teeth effectively, ask your dentist or hygienist to check, or buy some disclosing tablets from the chemist – these leave a temporary stain on any areas of plaque, indicating where you need to clean more thoroughly. The aim is to make sure that dental plaque doesn't build up on your teeth – which also reduces the risk of sclerotic plaque building up in your arteries.

In one study, researchers in Australia and Norway tested the blood of their subjects for blood-clot risk factors and inflammation before and after dental treatment. They noted a marked reduction in risk factors after treatment, which strongly suggests that eliminating advanced gum disease could effectively reduce the risk of heart attack or stroke. People with severe periodontal disease are almost four times as likely to have had a heart attack as those with no evidence of the disease. And recent research indicates that having extensive gum disease doubles the risk of diabetes.

## EARLY WARNINGS

Older people, smokers, people who grind their teeth and those under stress have an increased risk of gum disease. Early treatment can guard against future damage to arteries, so learn to spot the warning signs.

### FLOSSING MADE EASIER

When flossing your teeth, keep to a regular pattern. Start at the top and work from left to right, then move to the bottom. At first it helps to look in the mirror. Here is the British Dental Health Foundation's guide to flossing.

- Break off about 46cm (18in) of floss, and wind most of it around one of your middle fingers. Wind the remaining floss around the same finger of the other hand; as you use the floss, take up the used section with this finger.

- Hold the length of floss tightly between the thumb and forefinger of each hand leaving no slack. Use a gentle 'rocking' motion to guide the floss between your teeth. Don't jerk the floss or snap it into the gums.

- When the floss reaches the gum-line, curve it into a C-shape against one tooth until you feel resistance.

- Hold the floss against the tooth. Gently scrape the side of the tooth, moving the floss away from the gum. Repeat on the other side of the gap, along the side of the next tooth.

- Don't forget the back of your last tooth.

These include:

 Red, swollen or bleeding gums.
- Gums that bleed when you clean your teeth or floss.
- Loose teeth and/or gaps appearing between teeth.
- Gums receding, so teeth look longer.
- Bad breath.
- A metallic taste in your mouth.
- A change in the bite of your teeth or in the fit of partial dentures.

## YOUR DENTIST

It is important to keep appointments for check-ups as often as your dentist recommends, to make sure any subtle changes, such as inflammation of the gums (gingivitis), that can herald periodontal disease are picked up quickly. You should also have regular sessions with a dental hygienist, who will clean areas that it's impossible to reach by brushing and flossing alone.

# no.3 smoking

Quitting is the single most important action you can take to reduce your risk of a heart attack, according to the British Heart Foundation. Research suggests it will also halve your risk of stroke and add years to your life – an extra 14 years, on average, if you are a woman, and an extra 13 years if you are a man. In the UK one in eight deaths from cardiovascular disease is linked to smoking. And research suggests that passive smoking, too, is a risk factor, especially for stroke.

**RED**alert

## POISONED PUFFS

Tobacco plants produce nicotine as a chemical defence against being eaten by insects. In other words, nicotine is a natural insecticide. So, when you smoke, remind yourself that you are taking in a toxin that, drop for drop, is more deadly than strychnine, arsenic and the venom of the diamondback rattlesnake.

Like most people you want to live a long, fulfilling, and active life. So, if you smoke cigarettes, consider for a moment the extensive harm that smoking is doing to your body.

- It damages the lining of your arteries and increases the build-up of sticky plaque which, over time, can clog arteries throughout your body.
- It raises levels of fibrinogen and platelets in the blood, increasing the tendency of the blood to clot.
- It causes nine in ten cases of lung cancer and increases the risk of more than a dozen other cancers, including cancer of the mouth, larynx, oesophagus, liver, pancreas, stomach, kidney, bladder and cervix.
- It raises the risk of dangerous swellings of arteries called aneurysms.
- If you also have diabetes, it heightens an already raised risk of cardiovascular disease.
- It increases the risk of developing diabetic kidney disease or peripheral arterial disease so severe that it requires amputation.

troubleshooting Q&A

## I don't inhale. Am I still a risk?

Unfortunately, not inhaling makes little difference. Nicotine can be absorbed through the membranes that line the mouth as well as those in the lungs.

## Can't I just cut down or switch to a lower-tar brand?

The short answer is no. Any reduction is better than none, but as long as you continue to smoke you remain at risk. Even smoking just one to five cigarettes a day increases your risk of a heart attack by 38 per cent, according to the Interheart Study. Smoke more, and your risk rises in direct proportion to the number of cigarettes you smoke. If you are a two-pack a day smoker, your risk is increased by a staggering 920 per cent.

Low-tar brands contain similar levels of tar and nicotine to normal brands; the main difference between the two types lies in the filter. But research shows that people who smoke low-tar cigarettes smoke harder and more frequently to satisfy their nicotine craving. According to one study, low-tar smokers ended up inhaling about 80 per cent more smoke than those who smoked normal brands and had similar levels of cancer-causing chemicals in their blood.

- It increases levels of total and 'bad' LDL cholesterol, but lowers 'good' HDL cholesterol.
- It promotes an outpouring of the 'fight-or-flight' stress hormone adrenaline, increasing your heart rate and blood pressure, so that your heart has to work much harder.
- It exposes you to a high intake of carbon monoxide, a poisonous gas that reduces the ability of red blood cells to carry oxygen. This makes angina (chest pain on exercise) more likely.
- It changes your shape – smoking alters body fat distribution to a less healthy pattern with more abdominal fat and a higher waist:hip ratio.

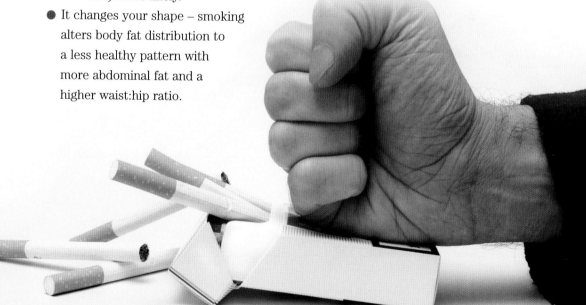

## KNOW YOUR ENEMY

If you want to stop smoking, it helps to understand just how the addictive substance in tobacco – nicotine – maintains its hold. When you inhale from a cigarette, a belt of nicotine enters your brain within 10 seconds. That is faster than the entry of almost any other substance, and helps to give nicotine its powerful grip.

Smoking feels good because nicotine is a stimulant. It can make you feel calmer, more energised and more mentally alert. By prompting release of the body's own feel-good chemicals, called endorphins, it can give you a mood boost and lift depression.

These effects are only temporary, however. To sustain them, you need regular doses of nicotine, and after a while the brain adapts, lowering your natural energy and mood levels. So the consequence is that you need to smoke to feel 'normal' – and, when you try to quit, you are hit hard by nicotine-withdrawal symptoms including anxiety, depression, impaired concentration and tiredness.

## DEVELOP A STRATEGY

That's why it is so crucial to work out in advance a strategy for achieving your aim. Some people manage to quit 'cold turkey' – they just stop smoking and that's it – and this approach can be surprisingly successful, especially if you have the right support.

One helpful tactic is to plan ahead, pick a date on which you will have your last cigarette, and set about dismantling your psychological associations with smoking – to make it easier to deal with when the time comes.

If you decide to choose a stop date in advance, make it a day when you are least likely to be stressed and most able to break familiar habits and routines. Avoid trying to give up at Christmas, during intense work periods, or at times when you are likely to have heavy domestic or family commitments.

Will-power is your main weapon but studies suggest that the more support you have – be it from friends, family or professionals – the more likely you are to succeed. It is a good idea to talk to your GP about the help available on the NHS. He or she will be able to refer you to an NHS

Trying to give up means having to deal with nicotine-withdrawal symptoms, including anxiety, depression and tiredness.

# therapies and medications

Your GP can prescribe nicotine replacement therapy (NRT) in the form of gum, patches, inhalators, lozenges or medications that help to control cravings. These products are also available over the counter at pharmacies. NRT releases nicotine into your bloodstream at much lower doses than in a cigarette, without the tar, carbon monoxide or 4,000 odd poisonous chemicals you get from tobacco smoke. Most people stop using NRT within three months, but heavy smokers may need to use it for longer. And some people find NRT itself hard to quit as it still provides some nicotine.

Zyban (bupropion) and Champix (varenicline) are also available on the NHS to help smokers give up. Zyban is an anti-depressant that affects brain chemicals. It relieves withdrawal symptoms and may double your chances of quitting when used with a motivational programme. Champix, which appears to have a better success rate and fewer side effects, acts specifically on nicotine receptors in the brain, reducing nicotine cravings and lessening the 'kick' of smoking. It, too, is usually taken together with a counselling programme. In one 2008 study, four weeks after starting treatment, 63 per cent of users of Champix were still not smoking, compared with 48 per cent of those on nicotine replacement therapies, and 51 per cent of people who quit 'cold turkey'.

stop-smoking support service, or advise you about one-to-one counselling and stop-smoking groups. Success rates for people who are aiming to quit are substantially improved by programmes that offer support, education, coping skills, counselling and behaviour therapy – virtually anything that means that the smoker is not left to do it alone. Having the support of your family and friends, too, can make all the difference. (See Resources, page 240, for more information.)

## FORWARD PLANNING

Expect the first three days of withdrawal to be the worst, and make plans to ensure that this time is as stress-free but as busy as possible – fill it with activities that you find absorbing and calming. If possible, get out of your usual environment. You could book a three-day activity break over a long weekend, take that long-awaited trip to a health spa, join a gym, or attend a course that precludes smoking during the day.

If you stay at home, plan to do something outside your usual routine that has a clear goal and visibly positive results – decorate or springclean the house, tackle the garden, or do a DIY project. Or simply spend time having long lie-ins, soaking in the bath, reading, listening to music, or however else you like to relax.

## SUPPORT FROM FAMILY AND FRIENDS

Telling your friends, family and colleagues that you plan to stop smoking makes it far more difficult for you to find excuses to put it off and start 'tomorrow' or 'next week'. Ask those around you to give you their support, encouragement and understanding.

## PREPARE YOURSELF

Getting to the bottom of what motivates you to smoke is often important in preparing yourself mentally for giving up. For example, do you use smoking as an excuse for taking a break from work, as an opportunity to sit down and relax for 5 minutes, to combat stress, tension, tiredness or boredom, or as a substitute for a snack? Do you have a cigarette at social events, when you're under pressure at work, or because other people around you are smoking?

Think about what motivators could help you to quit – such as being able to wake up in the morning without coughing, protecting your family from second-hand smoke, avoiding cold winter mornings smoking on the pavement outside work, or the money you'll save. If you've tried to stop before and gone back to the habit, don't regard that as a failure; think of it as a trial run. However long you stopped for on that occasion, it was a success, and now's the time to build on it.

**SECRET**weapon

**BE POSITIVE**

Setting a positive goal is much more likely to succeed than focusing on self-denial. Don't tell yourself 'I want to give up smoking' or 'I mustn't have a cigarette' (which just draws attention to how much you want one). Think 'I want clearer lungs', 'I want to taste my food properly again', or 'I want to stay healthy when I get older'.

Change your routine ... If you are in the habit of having a cigarette with breakfast at home, go to a café instead.

## UNLEARN BAD HABITS

Smoking is not just a physical addiction; it is also a learned behaviour and, to free yourself from it, you need to unlearn the habits associated with it as well as breaking the physical addiction. The more you understand how your habit took hold, the greater your chance of breaking it. If you smoke a packet of cigarettes daily, then in the course of a year you take more than 70,000 puffs, each one giving you a temporary 'high' as the nicotine hits your brain. But your brain links the high not only with nicotine but also with all the associated gestures you make: the way you take the cigarette out of the packet, light it, inhale and hold it; and with all the situations in which you typically smoke: after a meal, with your morning coffee, after sex, on the phone, when you're working, with a drink.

A long time before the date on which you intend to give up, make a mental list of the situations in which you usually smoke, so that during your first three days you can avoid as far as possible your most common cigarette cues. Start to break the habits, preferably by substituting new ones that give you similar relief and are better for your health.

## STOP-SMOKING DAY

When you do stop smoking, take it one day at a time. Simply concentrate on steering well clear of cigarettes for that particular day. Your mind can cope with 'none today', but may go into overdrive with rationalisations for relapsing if you feed it the thought of 'no more ever again'.

## CONQUER CRAVINGS

The average craving lasts just 3 minutes – though it can seem like hours. Here are some tactics that can help to prevent you from caving in:

- **Change your routine** If you usually have a cigarette at the end of a meal, try clearing the plates away immediately you have finished eating, brushing your teeth or putting the kettle on. If you typically smoke while you're on the phone, keep some sugar-free gum or mints next to the handset (or with your mobile) and chew or suck as you chat. If you usually light up with your morning coffee, switch to tea or fruit juice for a while, or go to a café for breakfast rather than having it at home.

- **Make it difficult for yourself** Ideally, there should be no cigarettes in the house at all. If you do have some, keep the cigarette packet on the other side of the room, in a cupboard, or even a locked drawer. Do not carry cigarettes with you when you go out.

- **Relieve work stress** Instead of joining the smoking-break huddle on the pavement outside your office, go for a quick stroll around the block. It will improve your mood and relieve feelings of tension.

- **Distract yourself** Train your brain to unlearn the expectation of an instant nicotine reward. When you think you want a cigarette, persuade yourself to wait 5 minutes … then 10. When you want to give in, find something – anything – to do to take your mind off cigarettes. Have a shower, pull up a few weeds, clean your teeth, take out the rubbish.

**WHAT TO DRINK**

For the first three days after giving up, sip acidic fruit juices such as cranberry, grapefruit or pineapple. They can help to stabilise blood-sugar levels and accelerate elimination of nicotine during the first crucial 72 hours.

Be careful with alcohol, though. Almost half of those who relapse while trying to quit smoking have had a drink first. Alcohol reduces inhibitions and speeds up the metabolism of nicotine, so can exacerbate withdrawal symptoms and make you more likely to give in, especially as people typically smoke when they're drinking. It makes sense to avoid alcohol for 72 hours.

Nicotine doubles the rate at which caffeine is metabolised, so your blood caffeine levels can more than double if you drink the same amount of coffee or tea as you did prior to quitting. As this can increase feelings of anxiety and make giving up all the harder, it is sensible to avoid caffeine or at least cut back on your intake.

# countdown to good health

**S**ome of the health benefits from stopping smoking take place quite quickly. Here is what happens to your body in those first smoke-free days and afterwards. The benefits are similar whether you take the 'cold turkey' approach or use nicotine-replacement products.

| Time since stopping | Health improvement |
| --- | --- |
| 8 hours | The carbon monoxide levels in the blood reduce by half and oxygen levels increase, returning to normal; circulation improves so your hands and feet get warmer. |
| 24 hours | Carbon monoxide is eliminated from the body. |
| 48 hours | Your ability to taste and smell improve. |
| 72 hours | Breathing ability (lung function) is beginning to improve. |
| 14 days | Blood circulation in the gums is virtually back to normal. |
| 1 month | Skin appearance improves. |
| 1 to 3 months | Lung function and breathing improves so walking and all exercise becomes easier. |
| 1 year | The risk of heart attack reduces by up to 50 per cent compared to that of a smoker. |
| 5 years | Your risk of dying prematurely from heart disease or stroke is now almost equal to that of someone who has never smoked. |

- **Don't go without breakfast** When you are a smoker, you can often get away with having no breakfast. When you give up smoking, missing breakfast can make you much more susceptible to a cigarette craving or to snacking on too many of the wrong foods later in the day.

## INSTANT BENEFITS

The great thing about giving up smoking is that, when you do quit, you will gain benefits almost immediately. After just 24 smoke-free hours, the supply of oxygen to your heart muscle begins to improve. After one to three months, you will find that you can exercise more freely.

If you've already had a heart attack, stopping smoking will halve your risk of having another one, and reduce your risk of dying from a further attack by a quarter. Within five years, your risk drops almost to that of a someone who has never smoked, and your added risk of stroke virtually disappears as well, no matter how old you are.

## BODY DETOX

For every 2 hours that you get by without smoking, your body's nicotine reserves reduce by half. That sounds good – but it takes up to 72 hours before your blood, and therefore your brain, is completely free of nicotine. It is at this point, three days after your last puff, that the cravings, tension and anxiety associated with giving up typically reach a peak.

The average smoker experiences six cravings on the third day after giving up. That is just 18 minutes in total on the very worst day. Knowing this can help to put the urge in perspective. If you can persist to the end of three smoke-free days, you have got through the chemical withdrawal symptoms and are well on the way to stopping for good. But remember that a single draw on a cigarette can stimulate up to half of all the brain receptors linked with nicotine addiction. So don't give in to even a single puff!

## AVOID WEIGHT GAIN

Smokers tend to put on a little weight when they give up, perhaps because of a change in metabolism, or perhaps because they are eating more or eating high-fat and sugary foods to compensate for not smoking. The body may be adjusting to what should be its 'normal' weight (smokers tend to weigh less than non-smokers). In addition, recovering smokers are more likely to react to hunger cues by binge eating, because their brains are used to the 'quick fix' of nicotine. Here are some tips on how to avoid weight gain.

- Anticipate hunger – avoid binge eating and carbohydrate cravings by eating frequently and choosing small amounts of healthy foods.
- Plan your meals and don't buy sugary or fatty snacks.
- Don't use sweets as an aid to stopping smoking – if you need something to satisfy oral cravings, try sugar-free gum.
- If you are tempted to satisfy a nicotine craving with a calorie-laden snack, take a couple of deep breaths or sip a glass of cold water instead. Curiously, our brains sometimes confuse hunger and thirst, so we may think we are hungry when, in fact, we need something to drink.
- Step up your activity levels – walk a little bit farther or a little bit faster, or use the stairs instead of the lift.

---

**MYTHS** ✗

### PUTTING ON WEIGHT IS AS BAD FOR YOUR HEALTH AS SMOKING

This is true only if you gain a vast amount of weight. You would need to put on around 5st 5lb (34kg) to expose yourself to the same level of risk as smoking a packet of cigarettes a day – and fewer than 4 per cent of smokers gain more than 1½ stones (9kg). In fact, the average weight gain among people who stop smoking is about 5lb (2.25kg), and about one in five people who stop smoking don't put on weight at all.

Exposure to cold temperatures places a
strain on the heart and cardiovascular system.

# no.4 cold weather

Cold weather is something you cannot escape unless you are fortunate
enough to be able to migrate to a country with a warmer climate. Older
people are particularly vulnerable to cold – partly because they may be
less able to detect a lowering of the temperature, and partly because many
of them cannot afford to heat their homes effectively. Exposure to cold
temperatures puts a strain on the heart and cardiovascular system. In
response, our blood vessels tend to constrict, increasing blood pressure,
as well as making blood more likely to clot. At the same time, the body's
demand for oxygen increases to try to maintain body temperature, so
supplies to vital organs such as the heart may be insufficient.

This helps to explain why there are more deaths from heart disease in
December and January than in June and July. Around 23,000 more people
die in the winter than in the summer, and much of this excess is due to
heart attacks and strokes. Other heart problems, such as heart failure
(where the heart isn't pumping strongly enough) also peak in winter.

Ideally, try to keep your house heated to between 18° and 21°C (64°
and 70°C) in winter. And remember to dress in warm clothes. Keeping
active and eating a healthy diet will also help to protect you.

## AVOID EXTREMES

Avoid sudden changes in temperature. Going from a warm centrally heated
house out into the cold without being properly insulated can be especially
dangerous. So, too, can a sudden increased level of exertion, especially as

people tend to exercise less during the colder months, so their general level of fitness may be reduced. If you really must go outside to clear snow from your drive in the morning – the peak time for heart attacks – do the minimum, take it slowly and make sure you are wearing plenty of layers.

## STOP COMFORT EATING

Another factor in winter-related deaths may be that blood becomes more concentrated in cold weather, so cholesterol levels rise in autumn and winter compared with spring and summer. Avoid eating larger quantities than usual in winter, especially more carbohydrate-rich 'comfort foods'. These dietary changes could contribute to raising cholesterol levels as well as promoting weight gain and metabolic changes. Instead, choose home-made soups, baked apples, clementines and other healthy alternatives.

# no.5 respiratory infections

Each week in winter, about one in five people in the UK is laid low by a cold. While the common cold may not do much harm, a severe infection such as flu, bronchitis or pneumonia more than doubles the risk of a heart attack or stroke, according to an analysis of GP records of more than 2 million patients published in the *European Heart Journal*. Respiratory infections cause a body-wide inflammatory response that affects blood vessels and can precipitate rupture of plaque in artery walls.

For this reason, doctors recommend that people with heart disease have an annual flu vaccination. Even if it doesn't stop you getting the infection, it may make it less severe and reduce complications.

## BACTERIAL CONNECTIONS

Scientists believe that low-grade infection may be implicated not only in atherosclerosis but also in a host of other conditions such as diabetes and even some cancers. The evidence is also growing that infections may be an important trigger of age-related diseases and disorders. One team of Russian doctors has even suggested that infection may be what initiates the very process of ageing. Along with many specific diseases, ageing itself, they say, 'has infectious origins'. This indicates that safeguarding yourself from mild infections such as flu or gum disease may protect you not only against heart attacks, strokes and an early demise but also against many of the other conditions underlying the infirmity and disability that often accompany old age.

## HOW GERMS ARE SPREAD

You may have been brought up with the old saying 'coughs and sneezes spread diseases'. That statement is perfectly true, but what it doesn't tell you is that colds and flu are far more often spread by other means, such as shaking a hand, turning a door handle or picking up a telephone that's been used by someone else.

According to the Common Cold Unit at Cardiff University, it is actually quite difficult to catch a cold. Close-range coughing or sneezing can spread an infection, but the spread is much more likely to occur through contact with contaminated fingers – shaking someone's hand is potentially more risky than kissing them. Recent research has shown that respiratory viruses can lurk on hard surfaces for up to two days. What typically happens is that you shake someone's hand, then rub your nose or your eyes – something that most people do unconsciously all the time. If the person whose hand you shook has a cold, you may well be infected too. Touching your eyes can introduce infection because the tear ducts drain into the back of the nose.

## inside information
# why you need liquids

The inflammation associated with having a cold or flu makes your blood 'thicker' and more prone to clot – and this is made worse if you have a fever, because you then lose fluid from the body too. When you go down with a bug, make sure that you drink plenty to keep yourself well hydrated.

## WASH YOUR HANDS …

The key to protecting yourself is as simple as washing your hands – regularly and thoroughly. So avoid the vigorous handshake whenever you can, and go for the vigorous hand-wash instead. In fact, frequent hand-washing has been shown to reduce the transmission of colds even between different members of the same household.

## … AND SURFACES

Another effective way to ward off colds and flu is regular disinfection of household surfaces – ordinary bleach will do. Door handles, taps and refrigerator doors are particular culprits for transmitting infection, and telephones, computer keyboards, light switches, kitchen surfaces and cleaning cloths may also harbour germs.

For situations where you can't avoid contact with other people's germs, carry a small bottle of alcohol-based sanitising hand gel or spray with you and use it after shaking hands or after touching public surfaces.

## COLD CONTAMINATION

One study assessed how easily cold viruses could be transferred from ordinary surfaces to fingertips. Researchers asked 15 adults with colds caused by rhinoviruses, which cause about half of all colds, to stay overnight in a local hotel, then tested ten hard surfaces in each room. Of the total 150 sites tested, 35 per cent were contaminated with cold viruses. The most contaminated surfaces were door handles, pens, light switches, television remote-controls, taps and telephones.

The researchers then asked five volunteers to touch the light switches, telephone keypads or handsets and tested their fingertips for rhinoviruses. When the tests were made an hour after contamination, the subjects' fingertips had become contaminated 60 per cent of the time. Even 18 hours later, contamination was found in a third of the tests. The researchers conclude that people with colds frequently contaminate surfaces in their environment, and that cold viruses can then be picked up by others during the course of normal daily activities.

The problem with trying to ward off cold viruses is that, when you are out in public, you have no idea which surfaces have been touched before you by someone with a virus. What's worse, most respiratory infections are

# beat off those germs

- **Go Gallic** The evidence for hands as a major route for transmitting infection is so strong that scientists at the London School of Hygiene recommend greeting friends the French way, with a peck on the cheek rather than a handshake. Or improvise, according to the situation. The next time someone approaches you with palm outstretched, try an 'air kiss' or a manly hug instead.

- **Disinfect household surfaces regularly** Door handles, taps, television remote controls and refrigerator doors may all be repositories for germs; other culprits include telephones, computer keyboards, light switches, kitchen surfaces and cleaning cloths.

- **Use your microwave** Keep your kitchen sponge or cloth germ-free by microwaving it on full power for 2 minutes daily. This kills 99 per cent of micro-organisms. **WARNING:** Do this only with a damp sponge or cloth – otherwise it's a fire risk.

- **Take a walk** One study showed that post-menopausal women who took regular, moderate exercise – brisk walking for 45 minutes five times a week – had up to a three-fold reduction in the number of colds they suffered compared with women who didn't exercise.

- **Say cheers** Scientists in Spain have shown that wine, especially red wine, also protects against colds. When they studied 4,000 volunteers for a year, they found that those who drank more than two glasses of red wine daily had 44 per cent fewer colds than non-drinkers.

- **Take garlic** In a study involving 146 volunteers at the Garlic Centre in East Sussex, half were given a garlic supplement daily and the other half a placebo. During 90 days over the winter, those taking garlic had a total of 24 colds, compared with 65 among those on placebo. People taking garlic supplements who did catch a cold also had a shorter duration of symptoms and a lower risk of reinfection.

- **Bolster immunity** A healthy diet – with a generous intake of fruit and vegetables – exercise and 7 hours of sleep daily, can make your body less vulnerable to germs.

caught from close contact with someone in your home, especially a school-age child. Surfaces are readily contaminated too, so when one person – or a visitor – is carrying a virus, everyone in the household is at risk.

## HOW TO AVOID COLDS AND FLU

Research confirms that hand-washing and frequent disinfection of surfaces are the most effective ways to protect yourself against colds and flu.

When researchers ran a campaign promoting hand-washing and giving out hand-sanitiser gel among students in university halls of residence, they found that these students had fewer episodes of colds and flu, and missed fewer classes as a result, compared with students who were not part of the campaign. And, according to a Canadian study, using a disinfectant spray on a surface contaminated by cold viruses reduced the virus counts by more than 99.99 per cent in just a minute.

# no.6 lack of sunshine

Regular exposure to sunlight is essential for good health. Sunlight on skin prompts our bodies to make vitamin D, which may help to protect against heart disease, high blood pressure, strokes and many cancers, as well as warding off disorders such as diabetes and rheumatoid arthritis.

Investigations suggest that Britain's grey skies could be contributing to the high levels of heart attack and stroke by depleting our vitamin D levels. Low levels of the vitamin have been linked with increased rates of cardiovascular disease, more colds and flu, and a variety of other diseases. One ten-year study of 18,000 men aged 40 to 75, who were initially free of cardiovascular disease, indicated that low vitamin D levels more than doubled their risk of heart attack and coronary artery disease.

## NOT GETTING ENOUGH?

Dr Elina Hyppönen, a senior researcher at London's Institute of Child Health, confirms that many Britons simply don't get enough sun. 'About 60 per cent of adults – some 36 million of us – have insufficient levels of vitamin D all year round, and 90 per cent of us aren't getting enough of the vitamin during winter and spring,' she says. On average, obese people and those living in Scotland are twice as likely as slim people living in southern England to have low vitamin D levels.

Low levels of vitamin D could go some way to explaining the higher rates of heart disease in Scotland compared with the rest of the UK – and perhaps even some of the difference between the rates in Britain and southern Europe, which is usually attributed to dietary factors.

> In winter, it's worth trying to increase your intake of foods that contain vitamin D, such as milk.

## VITAMIN D IN FOODS

Most of the vitamin D present in our bodies is made by sunlight, but small amounts can be obtained from foods such as oily fish. So, especially in winter, try to increase your intake of foods that contain vitamin D. As well as oily fish such as salmon, fresh tuna, sardines and herring, good sources of vitamin D include cod liver oil, eggs, dairy produce such as milk and cheese, and fortified foods such as breakfast cereals and margarines.

Just 15 to 20 minutes with your arms, hands and legs exposed will keep your vitamin D at adequate levels.

## THE VALUE OF SUPPLEMENTS

Taking vitamin D supplements can have a beneficial effect on your health. Research studies indicate that supplements reduce levels of inflammation, which is believed to be closely associated with heart disease (see page 22), and that a combination of vitamin D and calcium supplements can lower high blood pressure.

One study in the USA demonstrated that people who took vitamin D supplements had 70 per cent fewer episodes of colds and flu over three years – and, as explained earlier, respiratory infections have also been linked with an increased risk of cardiovascular disease. Other research has indicated a 31 per cent lower death rate from heart disease among women over 65 who took vitamin D supplements, while a European review of 18 studies found that taking supplements for six years reduced the death rate from all causes by 7 per cent.

If you decide to take supplements, the recommended daily amount for adults is 400IU (10mcg), though many experts think the official advice needs updating and recommend that – particularly between October and

March – people should aim to take a daily dose of 1,000IU (25mcg). You mustn't take more than this, however, because very large quantities of vitamin D over long periods can weaken bones.

## GET OUT IN THE SUN

You can't overdose on vitamin D from the sun – and the sun is the best source of the vitamin. More than 90 per cent of the vitamin D in our bodies is made in the skin when it is exposed to the ultraviolet light in the sun's rays. Once the skin has absorbed enough UVB rays to make vitamin D, the conversion process shuts down.

Not much is needed to achieve the desired effect. As little as 15 to 20 minutes daily with your arms, hands and legs exposed will keep your vitamin D at adequate levels. That is why some doctors now recommend spending 15 minutes towards midday outdoors without sunscreen (except on your face) several times a week – unless your skin is very fair and reddens with such brief exposure. If you are Asian or Afro-Caribbean, your darker skin isn't as efficient at absorbing the UVB rays that trigger vitamin D production and may need twice this time.

When the recommended time is up, and if you plan to be out longer, put on plenty of sunscreen to protect yourself against the sun damage that can lead to skin cancers.

By getting enough vitamin D from the sun in the spring, summer and autumn, you may be able to store up a supply to last for the first weeks of winter. From then on, you must rely on diet (and perhaps a daily supplement) until spring – and sunlight – return.

# no.7 extreme heat

Very hot summers have been shown to provoke a small increase in death rates, mainly from cardiovascular and respiratory diseases. While extreme heat is not as dangerous as extreme cold – tens of thousands of mainly older people die from cold-related causes every winter, compared with hundreds of extra deaths even in the worst heat waves – it still makes sense to protect yourself against the risk.

Older people are most vulnerable to heatstroke, but younger people can also succumb. Women are affected more often than men. In one study in London, for every 1°C rise in temperature above 20°C, mortality rates

People in cities are especially at risk of heat-related health problems, since roads and buildings act like storage heaters.

increased by an average of 3 per cent in men and 7 per cent in women aged between 75 and 84. People living in cities are especially at risk of heat-related health problems, since roads and buildings act like storage heaters, creating 'heat islands' with temperatures several degrees above those of surrounding areas.

If your home is in a town or city, it is probably unrealistic to consider moving to the countryside, but – wherever you are – it is advisable to take precautions. Since around a third of the deaths that occur as a result of extreme heat waves are thought to be caused by air pollution (see pages 196–97), it is also worth taking measures to limit your exposure to traffic, and other noxious, fumes.

## WHAT YOU CAN DO

In hot weather, stay indoors during the part of the day when temperatures are highest, and close the curtains on windows that get full sun. When outside, wear a broad-brimmed hat with light-coloured, loose clothing and stay in the shade as much as you can. Make use of electric fans if available. If you are out in extreme heat, try to go to places with air conditioning, even if this involves no more than a stroll around a local shopping centre. Make sure that you drink enough fluid to prevent dehydration. You can tell whether you're drinking enough by the colour of your urine: it should be a pale straw colour at most; if it is any darker, you need to drink more.

# no.8 air pollution

People who live in heavily polluted areas have a higher than average risk of developing cardiovascular disease, and air pollution can worsen symptoms in people with heart and circulatory disease – hospital admissions among patients with heart disease increase during periods of high air pollution.

Pollution raises blood pressure and can trigger heart attacks and strokes, especially in vulnerable people. Exhaust fumes are a major contaminating factor, say epidemiologists; studies suggest they can adversely affect arteries and reduce oxygen supply to the heart.

## WHAT'S IN THE AIR?

It's the minute particles in polluted air, generated by vehicles, factories and electricity generators, which seem to do the damage. These can penetrate deep into the lungs, causing inflammation. A high proportion is retained in the lungs, and a tiny amount gets taken up into the body.

Air pollution causes blood vessels to narrow, even in healthy people, which may explain why high pollution levels increase the rate of heart attacks and other cardiovascular problems in people with cardiovascular disease. Researchers found that after breathing air polluted with fine particles and ozone for just 2 hours, the blood vessels of 25 healthy volunteers narrowed by between 2 and 4 per cent.

Being exposed to diesel exhaust fumes reduces the amount of oxygen that reaches the heart during exercise. When a group of men who had recovered from a heart attack exercised for an hour in a room polluted with low levels of diesel fumes, tests revealed a three-fold leap in the amount of stress on the heart – enough to increase the risk of a heart attack. The concentration of diesel fumes in the room was kept to just 10 per cent of the typical pollution levels in city centres, suggesting that real life exercise in urban environments may be even more hazardous.

People who live in American cities that have implemented cleaner-air policies, it is suggested, add an extra five months to their lifespan, compared with those living in more polluted places. In the UK, despite the implementation of clean-air measures, estimates suggest that pollution can reduce lifespan by an average of eight months.

Doctors frequently recommend that people recovering from a heart attack should not drive in heavy traffic for a few weeks because of the stress that this creates – now there is another reason for everyone to avoid heavy traffic congestion whenever possible.

It's important not to stop exercising, so head for the park.

## CHECK THE FORECAST

It is not always possible to avoid air pollution, but you can take steps to reduce your exposure. You can check your local air-quality-pollution index along with daily weather forecasts. In the car, drive with your windows closed on major roads or in town centres, especially on high-pollution days. If you can, plan a route away from heavily congested areas.

## EXERCISE CAUTION

You are at special risk from the effects of pollution when taking exercise, because you breathe more often and more deeply, inhaling more pollutants and sucking them further down into your lungs. Athletes also tend to breathe through the mouth more than normal, bypassing the effective filters against particles provided by hair and mucus in the nose. So, when possible, try to breathe through your nose.

It is important not to abandon exercise, but try to avoid the rush hour, or exercise in green open spaces away from heavy traffic, especially on days when the pollution index is high. Keep away from roads and, whenever possible, walk, run or cycle in a park or the countryside.

## troubleshooting Q&A

### I live near a mobile-phone mast. Does this increase my risk of having a heart attack?

Probably not. Repeated studies have shown no effect on health of exposure to low-level radio-frequency energies – in terms either of overall wellbeing or of cardiovascular health.

# no.9 noise

There is another reason, apart from pollution, to avoid heavy traffic – the sheer noise may be a danger. Living with chronic noise exposure increases the risk of heart attacks, and the World Health Organisation (WHO) warns that long-term noise exposure above 67 to 70dB (equivalent to traffic noise) can lead to high blood pressure. When researchers assessed people who had been admitted to 32 major hospitals in Berlin following a heart attack they found that environmental noise increased heart attack risk more than three-fold in women, and by 45 per cent in men. Overall, people living in a high traffic area were 46 per cent more at risk than those living in quieter areas.

Theories about why noise can do physical harm include its association with increased stress and irritation, leading to an outpouring of stress hormones and rises in heart rate, blood pressure and blood lipids. People who already have cardiovascular disease may be at special risk, and noise can provoke changes in heart rhythm.

## PROTECT YOUR HEARING

If your work involves loud noise, it is sensible to wear ear plugs or ear defenders at all times as recommended by your employer. Similarly, make sure that you protect your ears if you engage in noisy sports like shooting.

But the harm may start at low levels – and there are countless noisy tasks in daily life that we may do without thinking of the potential damage to our cardiovascular system (or our hearing).

So buy several pairs of good-quality ear plugs with a high noise-reduction rating (NRR) and use them whenever you undertake noisy tasks such as mowing the lawn or using power tools.

Small specialised ear plugs, called flat attenuators or flat response earplugs, are available for use at events such as rock concerts; when using them, you are still able to hear the music clearly, but they protect you from hazardous amplified noise levels.

### REDalert !

### SLEEPING WITH THE ENEMY

If your partner is a snorer, the chances are that you are subjected to noise levels overnight sufficient to disturb your sleep and raise your risk of cardiovascular disease. A loud snorer can emit sounds of up to 95dB – equal to a heavy lorry thundering past at close range. One study from Imperial College London showed increases in blood pressure among people sleeping with snorers. In addition, snorers are themselves at high risk of cardiovascular disease.

The best way to resolve this problem is to persuade your partner to see his or her GP for tests, assessment and treatment. Meanwhile, get yourself some special snore-attenuating ear plugs (see www.britishsnoring.co.uk/ for further help).

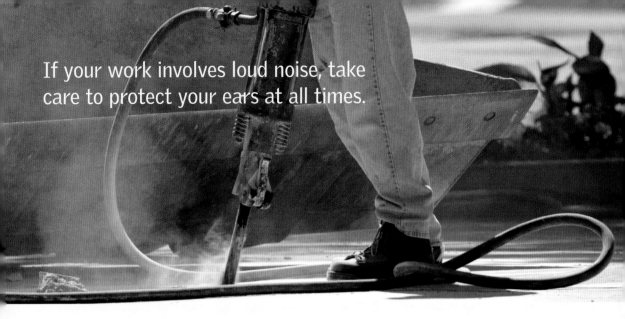

If your work involves loud noise, take care to protect your ears at all times.

# is it **too loud?**

**H**ow can you tell if the sound in your life has the potential to harm your hearing and cardiovascular health? Damage may be occurring if:

- You are exposed to regular heavy-impact noises such as pneumatic drills and hammering.
- You use heavy power tools for more than 30 minutes a day.
- You are exposed to continuous noise during the day – in the workplace, at an airport, on a building site, in a factory that has loud industrial machinery or power tools – or in the evening at a club or disco.
- You experience a ringing in your ears during or after noise exposure.

Hearing impairment can also be caused by prolonged exposure to the noise of a motorcycle engine (90 to 100dB), a loud car stereo (95 to 140dB), or even the interior of a busy pub (90 to 95dB).

## TURN IT DOWN

If you are exposed to loud background noise for long periods, try to reduce the noise level, or minimise your exposure to it, and minimise noise at other times. According to the WHO chronic noise may account for more than 3,000 heart disease deaths annually in the UK.

## NIGHT-TIME NOISE

Chronic night-time noise above 50dB – the level of light traffic – poses a risk to cardiovascular health, says the WHO. Other studies suggest that traffic noise above 30dB may disturb sleep – a hazard in itself. Half of all people in Europe are thought to live in noisy surroundings, and one in three is subjected to night-time noise sufficient to disturb sleep.

If you get traffic noise in your home, hang heavy curtains and consider double-glazing; if it's still noisy at night, lobby your council to install low-noise road surfaces and mend any potholes, which increase traffic noise.

# no.10 toxic chemicals

Chemicals in the environment may be implicated in a variety of medical conditions that have increased in the past hundred years – including cancer, allergies, asthma, skin disease, autoimmune conditions such as rheumatoid arthritis and multiple sclerosis, and cardiovascular disease.

Heavy metals such as lead, mercury and cadmium are known to be linked to the risk of heart disease and strokes – indeed, some experts recommend that anyone who has high blood pressure, heart disease or another vascular disease should be tested for heavy metal toxicity.

- Lead is widespread and long-term low-level exposure has been linked with atherosclerosis, thrombosis (blood clots), high blood pressure and cardiovascular disease. If you live in an old house, make sure that the pipes are not made of lead, which could leach into the water supply. Take care when decorating – old paints often contain lead.
- Mercury increases inflammation, promotes clotting and damages the function of arterial linings. Mercury toxicity is known to cause high blood pressure and cardiovascular disease and to increase the risk of strokes and heart attacks. Pregnant women should avoid eating certain types of fish that may be contaminated with high levels of mercury (see page 106). Taking selenium may help to reduce mercury toxicity.
- Cadmium, used industrially in metal alloys, can cause kidney damage and lead to high blood pressure, blood sugar and body fat imbalances, and zinc deficiency. Eating calcium-rich foods can reduce its toxic effects.
- Iron can promote atherosclerosis, so cutting back on iron-rich foods such as red meat may be protective. In one study of people who had already had a heart attack or stroke, limiting iron intake seemed to reduce the risk of a second attack. But a reasonable intake of iron is required for vital body functions and to prevent anaemia, so talk to your doctor before making any major changes to your diet.

## PLASTIC PACKAGING ALERT

Researchers from the UK's Peninsula Medical School in Exeter have found that people with a high level of the chemical bisphenol A (BPA) in their urine are twice as likely to develop cardiovascular disease and diabetes. Their findings back up similar research elsewhere.

BPA is a phthalate, one of a family of chemical compounds used as plasticisers, mainly to increase the flexibility of PVC and other plastic products. BPA is widely present in hard plastic packaging used for food and drink containers, including water bottles and plastic (polycarbonate) babies' bottles and the lining of food cans – but it is not clear how readily it may leach from packaging and containers into food.

Following a similar ban in Canada, a handful of American companies have banned the use of BPA in babies' bottles. The UK's Food Standards Agency says that BPA levels in plastic products are 'well below the levels considered harmful' but advises that plastic food and drink containers, including babies' bottles, should not be filled with or washed in boiling water or used in microwave ovens, or used when scratched or worn. Glass, or phthalate-free bottles are probably safer for babies.

## PHTHALATES ARE EVERYWHERE

It is almost impossible to avoid some exposure to phthalates. For example, many foods are sold in plastic packaging (it may be wise to remove it soon after purchase). Phthalates may be present in cosmetics, shampoos, adhesives, detergents and paints. As the kind of paint used on the outside of ships usually includes phthalates, the chemicals are increasingly present in fish. BPA is also found in drinking water and on skin – and consequently in household dust (largely derived from shed skin cells). US research has found that more than 90 per cent of people have detectable levels of BPA.

## CARDIOVASCULAR LINK

The evidence linking phthalates and other so-called 'endocrine-disrupting' chemicals with obesity has been growing – so much so that many of these substances are now dubbed 'obesogens', or obesity-promoting chemicals.

Clearly, their association with obesity is one mechanism by which chemicals such as BPA could influence the development of cardiovascular disease, and some studies have demonstrated links between phthalate breakdown products in urine and BMI, waist circumference (a measure of abdominal obesity) and insulin resistance.

# ten times safer

Sensible caution and finding ways to break the grip of any potentially harmful addiction are the best responses to the physical hazards outlined here, and the strategies suggested will help you to combat them effectively.

Your self-defence plan is almost complete. But, as you'll discover, after physical hazards, there are mental games to play. Step 9 outlines the psychological factors which also influence your cardiovascular health.

# self-defence plan

## STEP

# 9

CONTENTMENT, SENSE OF HUMOUR, HAPPY RELATIONSHIPS AND STIMULATING INTERESTS WILL ALL HELP TO PROTECT YOU AGAINST CARDIOVASCULAR PROBLEMS. STRESS, ANGER AND DEPRESSION, BY CONTRAST, CAN RAISE BLOOD PRESSURE AND ACCELERATE THE PROGRESSION OF ATHEROSCLEROSIS. BUT THERE ARE TACTICS YOU CAN ADOPT TO COUNTER THE NEGATIVE ELEMENTS OF LIFE AND PUT YOU BACK IN CONTROL.

# Relax and enjoy life

**N**othing can have a greater impact on your wellbeing than the way you look after yourself – and one of the best ways to maintain both physical and mental health is to act and think positively. Calm resistance to the adverse influences of stress, hostility and hopelessness can work wonders in the fight against heart attacks and strokes. And, as you will see, friendship, laughter and an outgoing, optimistic attitude are golden tickets to a longer life.

## taking stress seriously

Stress is one of the most significant indirect causes of illness in the modern world and plays a key part in triggering cardiovascular emergencies. It is one of the nine factors that, according to the Interheart study (see page 17), underlies 90 per cent of all first heart attacks. Recent research has revealed that, if you are permanently stressed at work or at home, you double your risk of a heart attack. Factors carrying the highest risk include a major conflict between family members and intense financial pressures such as a business failure. Stress is also a significant risk factor for stroke.

### THE EFFECTS OF STRESS

When we experience an event or situation as stressful, our body's learned defence mechanism against danger – the 'fight or flight' response – kicks in. This leads to an increased release of adrenaline and other stress hormones, causing the heart to beat stronger and faster, raising our blood pressure and breathing rate, promoting sweating (in anticipation of intense activity, as sweat helps to regulate body temperature), and shutting down digestion and other non-essential functions. This response would have been helpful in the Stone Age when confronted by a wild animal; it is much less so in the

face of irritating, automated telephone-answering systems and traffic jams. Persistent stress can lead to high blood pressure and a raised clotting tendency – a risk factor for both heart attack and stroke. Stress also prompts the body to release a hormone called cortisol, long-term exposure to which has been linked with abdominal obesity, high blood pressure and Type 2 diabetes.

A sudden rise in blood pressure, stimulated by acute stress, can also cause haemorrhagic stroke (bleeding in the brain). Stress increases your risk of stroke by as much as 40 per cent.

People under stress are more likely to smoke, drink, eat unhealthily, take less exercise and find it hard to sleep.

### OFFICE OFFENSIVE

British people work some of the longest hours in Europe, and more than half of us admit that work stress spills over into our private lives, making us grumpy at home. Medical research links stress at work to an increased cardiovascular risk. In 2008, when scientists at University College London (UCL) analysed data from a 12-year study of 10,000 civil servants they found that men and women under 50 who reported long-term work stress had a 68 per cent increased risk of coronary artery disease. Among those of retirement age the risk was lower. Those reporting the highest levels of work stress had high morning levels of the stress hormone cortisol and a consistently raised heart rate – evidence of increased cardiac instability.

Dealing with an unfair boss can send your blood pressure soaring. In one study, researchers measured the blood pressure of female healthcare assistants over three working days. When some of the women worked under a supervisor they perceived as unfair, they showed average increases in systolic blood pressure (the top reading) of 15mmHg, and in diastolic pressure (the bottom reading) of 7mmHg – more than enough to produce a significant increase in the risk of both heart attack and stroke. Having a boss you rate as incompetent raises your risk, too.

## I'm under a great deal of pressure right now. Am I at risk of having a heart attack or a stroke?

Pressure or stress can have a detrimental effect on your health, but it is all a question of how you handle it. You may not be able to avoid pressure, but you can learn ways to cope with it – and some people positively thrive under pressure. If your stress is making you tense or miserable, or interfering with your sleep, or if you react by smoking, eating high-fat sugary foods or drinking more alcohol, then your unhealthy habits are putting you at increased risk of a heart attack or a stroke. Changing your lifestyle can help you to feel fitter and better able to cope with demands, and there are plenty of things you can do to help you relax and manage stress.

## EASING THE TENSION

If your manager's behaviour makes your blood boil, it is important to learn ways of handling your frustration (see page 210). Try not to tense up in a difficult situation. Standing straight, with a relaxed posture, will give you more confidence and control. If you do have a confrontation, get away from the scene of conflict as soon as you can. Even if it's just for 5 minutes, go out for a walk and give yourself a chance to breathe, loosen up and clear your mind.

While you may not be able to affect your levels of cortisol in the mornings, you can make a substantial difference to other lifestyle factors that increase your risk. The UCL researchers also found that people under stress smoked more, ate fewer fruit and vegetables, took less exercise, and were more likely to have features of metabolic syndrome – factors that explain the increase in cardiovascular risk of almost a third caused by stress at work. So if your work is piling on the pressure, don't pile on the pounds, or engage in other unhealthy coping strategies. Take extra care with your diet and keep active. And remember that exercise will help to relieve stress and anxiety.

### REDalert

### DEADLINE DANGER

Meeting a demanding work deadline can make some people more susceptible to heart attack over the following 24 hours. Swedish researchers assessed 1,381 men and women who had survived a heart attack and asked them about their work in the previous year.

It turned out that 8 per cent of the group – almost one in ten – had faced a high-pressure deadline at work in the 24 hours before their attack, and that such pressure was linked to a staggering six-fold increase in heart-attack risk over the following day. This short-term pressure was far more dangerous than an accumulation of less stressful events over the previous year.

Try to manage tight deadlines by planning ahead. If your workload is unmanageable, talk to your line manager or your human resources team – that's what they're there for.

## WEEKDAY BLUES

Stress levels are at their highest on Monday mornings – also the peak time for strokes, heart attacks and heart-rhythm problems. Heart attacks are around 20 per cent more common on Mondays than on other days, among retired people as well as those employed. Just getting ready for work on Monday can cause some people's blood pressure to rise. The prospect of the week ahead is not the only cause. For some, it's the after-effects of a weekend of heavy drinking, which can cause dangerously abnormal heart rhythms and raise blood pressure (see page 175). For others, it's the pressure of the daily commute. Commuters' heart rate and blood pressure rise so much as they struggle to and from work on public transport that their stress levels are higher than those of fighter pilots going into combat or police officers facing a rioting mob, according to neuropsychologist and author Dr David Lewis, the founder of the research consultancy MindLab International.

To improve your commute, travel later or earlier one morning a week if you can to avoid queues and congestion on your way to the office. You'll probably get a seat – and if you go early, you'll arrive in time to sip a cup of coffee as you quietly plan your day.

## COPING STRATEGIES

Here are some simple but well-tried techniques to help you to stay on top of your workload:

- Ask to work flexi-time so you can travel outside peak hours. (As long as you get the work done, most employers are sympathetic.)
- Cycle or walk part of the way to work. You'll burn up stress hormones and get some exercise.
- Make a task list for the day.
- Set realistic goals. Make them clear and achievable.

### EMAIL MANIA

Many people underestimate the extent to which the advent of email has ratcheted up our levels of stress. The average manager spends 4 hours every day dealing with the onslaught of electronic correspondence. One in three of us admits to feeling stressed by the sheer number of emails we receive, according to a study at the universities of Glasgow and the West of Scotland (formerly Paisley), and some of us check our inboxes up to 40 times an hour. Each message requires you to make multiple small judgments that tax your neural networks. And stopping what you're doing to check the contents of a new email is distracting, so you lose your train of thought, your productivity plummets, and you get tired. One study showed that workers distracted by emails had a 10-point fall in tested IQ – double the reported drop from smoking cannabis.

There are ways to deal with email excess – but you have to stick to them. First, turn off the alert that tells you a message has arrived. Check your emails only at set intervals, and don't interrupt another task to reply unless it's truly urgent.

- Manage your time. Don't try to cram too much into your schedule, and avoid taking on anything else until you've completed the task in hand.
- Break big tasks into small steps.
- Settle for less than perfect. Work at 90 per cent of your capacity rather than 110 per cent – and delegate.
- Regulate the time you spend dealing with emails. Your could set up an automatic email response that reads 'I answer emails at 10am, 1pm and 4pm. If you need a quick reply, please phone.'
- Let your phone switch over to voicemail while you're finishing a task.
- If you spend most of your time sitting at work, do some exercises at your desk (see page 148) to relieve the strain.
- Always stop work during your lunch hour and, preferably, have a change of scenery. Try not to discuss work during the break.
- Learn some rapid stress-relief techniques to use at times of tension (see page 213). Simply closing your eyes for a few moments and clearing your mind can re-energise you during a frenetic day.
- Leave work on time.
- Don't take work home.
- Don't check your work email out of hours or while you're on holiday.

## PERSONAL PROBLEMS

Stressful relationships at home can increase your risk of having a heart attack or a stroke by more than a third. Relationships are an important barometer of your happiness. If you can't resolve sensitive family issues, consult a counsellor (see Resources, page 240).

Catastrophic events such as a death in the family or serious illness can cause a surge in stress hormones that temporarily 'stun' the heart. Some people develop symptoms such as chest pain and breathlessness that mimic those of a heart attack – and, in some cases, heart failure may occur after a severe emotional trauma. Fortunately, however, any damage to heart muscle is usually reversible.

## HOLIDAY ATTACK

Stress is also partly responsible for the rise in heart attacks and strokes in the festive season. There are two noticeable peaks – at Christmas and on New Year's Day. It's not just over-indulgence in fatty foods and alcohol that's to blame. Research indicates that the cause is the emotional stress of the Christmas holidays – dealing with relatives, too much travelling, not enough sleep, the expense, and even cooking Christmas dinner.

Continued on p212 >

# know yourself:
# your reaction to stress

**S**ome stress is necessary in our lives; it keeps us motivated and enthusiastic. For example, being under pressure to complete a piece of work on time can boost creativity. But it's important to get the balance right.

Everyone reacts differently to stress. Some people take it in their stride; others become tense, angry, irritable or tearful; and some lose concentration or reach for 'comfort foods', drink or cigarettes. None of these responses is good for you.

When scientists from University College London studied 34 men who had recovered from heart attacks or acute chest pain, they found that 14 had experienced emotional stress, such as an argument with a neighbour or sadness about a sick or deceased relative, less than 2 hours before their heart attack. The remaining 20 men reported no stress before their heart attacks. All the men were given a series of mentally challenging tests, such as making a speech, to raise stress levels, and they all showed short-term increases in blood pressure and heart rate. But the blood pressure levels of the 14 men who had reported stress, anger or depression just before their heart attack took longer to return to normal. They also had higher levels of platelets in their blood, which increases the chances of dangerous blood clots forming; in the other men, the levels were unchanged.

## ARE YOU SUFFERING FROM STRESS? FIND OUT HOW MANY OF THE FOLLOWING SIGNS AND SYMPTOMS APPLY TO YOU:

- ☐ Feeling sweaty or shivery
- ☐ Pounding heart or palpitations
- ☐ Needing to go to the toilet more often than usual
- ☐ Feeling sick in the stomach (having 'butterflies')
- ☐ Dry mouth
- ☐ Feeling tired, having no energy
- ☐ Odd aches and pains
- ☐ Smoking more than you used to
- ☐ Drinking more (needing a drink to relax)
- ☐ Working to exhaustion
- ☐ Headaches

- ☐ Disturbed sleep, waking unusually early
- ☐ Being easily irritated
- ☐ Thinking 'I can't cope with this'
- ☐ Loss of appetite for food, fun or sex
- ☐ Eating too much or too little
- ☐ Loss of sense of humour
- ☐ Little interest in personal appearance
- ☐ Loss of interest in other people
- ☐ Feeling everything is pointless
- ☐ Tearfulness
- ☐ Forgetfulness

If you ticked more than five boxes, you may already be suffering from stress. On pages 210–211 you will find expert advice on how to control stress now and in the future.

## ELIMINATING STRESS

The findings of the Interheart study (see page 17) highlight how important it is to eliminate stress from your life. The study showed that psychological influences, including stress, account for almost a third of heart attacks, almost as high a proportion as smoking. But it also identified one positive psychological factor in the battle against stress and cardiovascular disease. People with a high 'locus of control'– those who feel themselves in charge of their own destiny – have a 25 per cent lower risk of heart attack than those who feel buffeted by random forces beyond their control. They are generally happier and less likely to become depressed. And if you adapt well to stress, you are 25 per cent less likely to suffer a stroke. The good thing is that you can apply these findings to your own work or home life straightaway. For example:

- Recognise that in most situations you do have a choice, if only about how to react, and it is your own choices that largely determine what happens to you. So, at times of uncertainty, repeat to yourself: 'I have a choice.'
- Counteract negative thinking. If you find yourself thinking 'There's nothing I can do about this,' remember that there is usually some aspect of your situation that you can influence.
- Work at becoming more decisive and developing your problem-solving abilities.

Everyone reacts differently to stress. Some people take it in their stride; others become tense, angry, irritable or tearful.

REDalert

### PANIC ATTACK

Acute feelings of panic can occur at any time, usually for no clear reason. And they put you at an increased risk of heart disease, according to researchers at University College London, who found that people under 50 diagnosed with panic attacks or panic disorder were 38 per cent more likely to have a heart attack and 44 per cent more likely to develop heart disease than others. Risks were raised to a lesser extent in people over 50. Possible reasons include the effect of intense nervous activity on the heart and blood vessels.

In one GP survey, 8.6 per cent of patients said that they had panic attacks, and at least one in ten of us experiences them occasionally – twice as many women as men. Symptoms include faintness, breathlessness, rapid heartbeat, pains in the chest, nausea, trembling and dizziness, accompanied by a feeling of deep anxiety or dread.

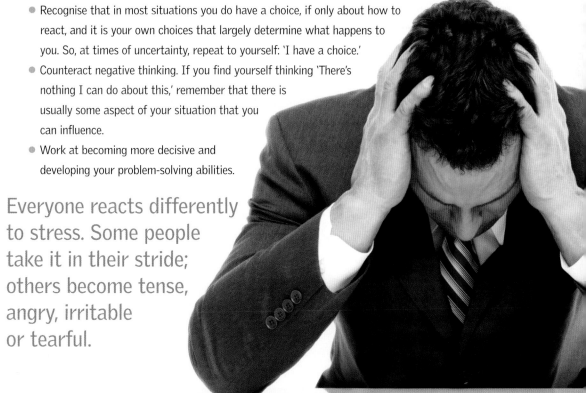

Eat healthily, sleep soundly and
develop your sense of humour.

# banishing stress
# in the long term

**A**s well as knowing how to react well to situations that
provoke sudden feelings of stress, you can devise a
more long-term strategy for a stress-free existence.

- **Learn to relax** If you feel constantly under pressure, it is vital to carve out some
time that is just for you, even if it is only half an hour a week. Progressive muscular
relaxation can really help to alleviate the effects of stress on your body. It doesn't
take long and it is really simple to do. Start by tensing the muscles in your feet, then
relax. Then work your way up your body doing the same thing in sequence from your
feet to your head. Sometimes it's only by experiencing muscle tension like this and
letting it go that we become aware of just how much tension our bodies are retaining.

- **Let it out** If stress accumulates to such a degree that you feel like crying, take heart. Emotional tears are quite different from the sort you produce when you're in pain or peeling an onion. Scientists think that a good cry actually clears out stress-related chemicals produced when we're under pressure. Some doctors speculate that this is why men, who cry less often, are more at risk of stress-related diseases than women.

- **Get high on exercise** Physical activity is one of the best stress-busters and, as explained in Step 7, one of the best exercise aids is easy to use and almost universally available – a staircase. When daily life starts getting on top of you, run up and down stairs a couple of times or, if you can spare 10 minutes, go for a brisk walk around the block in the fresh air.

- **Eat healthily** A healthy diet helps to keep your immune system and metabolism functioning efficiently and protects you from the effects of stress.

- **Talk about it** Cultivate a support network. You might find it hard, but start sharing your feelings on a regular basis with at least one family member or trusted friend.

- **Control your use of imagery** Avoid using dramatic or overblown descriptions of problems in thoughts or speech, such as: 'This job will be the death of me.' We all do it, but exaggerating everyday difficulties increases their emotional intensity. If you say something of this nature inadvertently, counteract it with a strong dose of reality: 'I'm still alive ... so that's obviously nonsense.'

- **Sleep soundly** Not only can stress interfere with your sleep, but also not getting enough sleep can add to your stress levels. See pages 224-27 for advice on how to make sure that you have a good sleep every night.

- **Create a sanctuary** Try to designate one place in your home that's truly 'yours', where you can retreat when you need to get away from it all. Keep it free of clutter and make it as calming and restful as possible – with, for example, a favourite chair and a few objects you find visually pleasing.

- **Meditate or do yoga** When scientists measured the amount of atherosclerosis in arteries of volunteers with high blood pressure, they found a significant reduction after nine months among those who'd learned to meditate (see page 213). And studies show that heart rates drop dramatically during a yoga class.

- **Take a view** Nature is a great stress-reliever. Studies have shown that patients experience less pain after surgery if they have a view of trees rather than a brick wall. And tests on students given a stressful task showed that their heart rates returned to normal faster when they gazed at a real fountain rather than at a digitally created image. Even photographs of restful scenes can help, so, if the view from your window isn't great, try hanging a wonderful scenic photograph on the wall or putting a plant or a small vase of flowers in the place where you spend most time.

- **Develop your sense of humour** Laughter is a brilliant way to release tension from your body and help you to feel relaxed (see page 214).

# dealing with anger

Anger can be a normal, healthy emotion that helps us to respond to a threatening situation. But it can also get out of control, and uncontrolled anger – sudden, intense fury – can actually provoke a heart attack or stroke. In fact, the risk of having a heart attack increases between nine and 14 times in the 2 hours after an angry episode.

The effect of anger was apparent in research involving more than a thousand people with implanted defibrillators – devices that automatically deliver a shock to the heart to control sudden dangerous disturbances to heart rhythm. The researchers discovered that shocks were often needed following episodes of anger. An episode of moderate anger increased the risk of heart-rhythm abnormalities four-fold in the subsequent 30 minutes. Two hours later, people who got very angry had a risk ten times higher than that of people who remained calm.

## LET IT OUT OR HOLD IT IN?

However you deal with it, intense anger is detrimental to health. Letting it out and holding it in can both do harm to your cardiovascular system.

A study that tracked 1,055 medical students for 36 years found that, by the age of 55, the men who showed the most anger were six times more likely to have had a heart attack and three times more likely to have developed any form of cardiovascular disease such as a stroke.

In another study, involving 200 women, those who regularly displayed hostile attitudes, held in their anger and were more negative and self-conscious had a significantly higher risk of atherosclerosis in the carotid arteries supplying the brain ten years later.

## STOP YOUR ANGER IN ITS TRACKS

First, note your flash points. What is it that really drives you wild? Think in advance about how you might react differently next time. Recognise the warning signs of anger – rising irritation, a faster pulse or breathing rate, for example – and react to them by taking a break while you get things in perspective. Take deep breaths and give yourself a vital few seconds to release tension and head off an impending explosion.

Regular exercise and relaxation will make you less prone to angry outbursts and more able to brush aside the little things that used to bother you. If you have a serious problem with anger, think about doing an anger-management course – it could improve your life as well as save it.

# stay cool, stay calm

**R**elaxation techniques such as meditation are effective antidotes to stress, anger and unhappiness. There is no need to take a whole hour out of your day for a relaxation regime – a mere 15 minutes' quiet time will help you to unwind.

## AN OASIS OF CALM

The notion of meditating may strike you as a bit New-Ageish – a fringe activity for hippie types. In fact, it's something much more practical – in just 10 or 15 minutes you can escape from the thoughts churning through your mind. Meditation and related activities, such as visualisation, can be highly beneficial for people who feel anxious, hostile or angry. And the added beauty of these techniques is that you can practise them safely and easily at home or, perhaps, even in a quiet room in your workplace. Just follow these simple steps:

- **Comfort** Wear loose-fitting clothes and pick a quiet corner of your home (or an empty room at work) where you can relax – in an easy chair, perhaps, but don't slump in it as a straight posture helps breathing and keeps you mentally alert; some people prefer to sit on the floor. Look at your watch or a clock and decide to distract yourself for 10 or 15 minutes. Then choose a word or sound like 'om' on which you can focus while you meditate.
- **Focus on breathing** You can close your eyes or keep them open, whichever feels most comfortable and helps you best to concentrate. Breathe deeply and repeat your chosen word or sound in your head every time you exhale, making sure you consciously direct your mind away from other thoughts and back to the sound. Keep everything else outside this little bubble of peace that encloses you. Focus only on the sound and on your rhythmic breathing; this will boost the oxygen supply to your body, reduce your heart rate and help you to relax. Your goal is to be awake and alert but not at all tense.

## ESCAPE IN YOUR MIND

Or try visualisation – which requires only your imagination. You simply sit, close your eyes and, using all your senses, you conjure up a favourite scene – a beach perhaps, where you can feel the sun on your face, see the seagulls swooping, taste a salty tang. Just be there ... until you unwind.

Escape in your mind ... conjure up a favourite scene.

# have a good laugh

Laughter is a marvellous way to relax and release tension, which would suggest that a lively sense of humour can boost your cardiovascular health. To test this hypothesis and to investigate how laughter might protect arterial linings from the damaging effects of stress, cardiologist Dr Michael Miller and his team at the University of Maryland School of Medicine in the USA, asked healthy volunteers to watch comedy films and studied the effects. They found that laughter relaxed their subjects' blood vessels and boosted blood flow by almost 25 per cent – equivalent to the increases seen with light exercise or cholesterol-lowering drugs. Conversely, when the volunteers watched a tense dramatic film, their blood flow was reduced by more than a third – an effect similar to that caused by dwelling on bad memories or doing stressful mental arithmetic.

Intriguingly, laughter is also catching; the saying 'laugh and the world laughs with you' has an element of literal truth. When researchers scanned volunteers' brains while playing tapes of sounds that ranged from people laughing and whooping with triumph to screaming and retching, the positive sounds created much stronger responses. And the area of the brain that 'lit up' in response to triumphant sounds or laughter was the same as that involved in smiling, which suggests that the brain actually primes us to respond to other people's smiles by smiling back. This is also, of course, why producers of certain television programmes or comedy shows build in canned laughter at the end of gags – they hope it will prompt a studio audience, listeners or viewers to laugh along too.

## LAUGHTER YOGA

For those who want to combine getting fit with having fun, there is an international laughter movement that runs 'laughter yoga' classes. This gives you a chance to get together with other people and simply laugh. It's an excellent aerobic workout, combining the physiological benefits of laughter with yogic breathing, which brings more oxygen to the body and brain. Laughter produces endorphins, making you feel good, reducing tension and relaxing your body. (See Resources, page 240, for advice on finding a class near you.)

## PERSONAL REPORT

Janine Capstack

# 'I'm a survivor'

In 2002, Janine Capstack experienced a day she will never forget. Janine, who lives in Plymouth, was just 37 and recently divorced. She worked full-time as a personal assistant to a company finance director while looking after her two small boys. 'I'd just returned home after a trip to Scotland,' she says. 'I did some washing, made the children's tea and started to mow the lawn. Halfway through, I got a sudden sharp headache. I told the children to ring my Mum, went inside and collapsed on the bed.'

Her mother telephoned the doctor, who suggested she take two paracetamol. When pressed, he made a home visit, and after one look at Janine, phoned an ambulance, which took her to hospital. Doctors diagnosed a subarachnoid haemorrhage - bleeding inside the brain. Janine was paralysed down her right side.

## 'I'm a believer in accepting what's happened and making the best of it. I'm a survivor.'

'For what seemed like ages, my life was in ruins,' she says. 'I had to learn to walk and talk again.' She was in rehabilitation for six months and still has some weakness on her right side.

Janine believes that her stroke was caused by the stress of her divorce and looking after the children on her own while working full-time. 'I'd had high blood pressure since my younger son was two, but I never dreamed I was at risk of a stroke. I thought I was too young.' As she recovered, Janine gave up smoking and made sure that the pace of her life slowed down. She now reads much more and takes naps in the afternoons. 'Just half an hour, then I feel fine again. But I've got to sleep.'

She also works only one day a week, as a shop assistant, and could drive, but prefers not to: 'I walk everywhere. And when I want to let off steam, I really stride out.' Her diet is healthier, she has cut out salt and eats plenty of vegetables, but says that chocolate is still a weakness.

Janine admits that it has been a tough time but her advice to anyone in the same situation is to think positively. 'I'm a believer in accepting what's happened and making the best of it. I'm a survivor.'

## THE BEST MEDICINE

When you're laughing, just as when you exercise, your blood pressure and heart rate rise slightly, but in the long term regular laughter reduces blood pressure and boosts your immune system. And remarkable research from the University of Tsukuba in Japan has shown that laughter may even help to control blood-sugar levels in people with diabetes. Volunteers' blood-sugar levels were significantly lower after watching a comedy film than after a dry lecture.

Simply thinking about humour has been shown to have positive health benefits. The anticipation of watching a favourite comedy programme reduces levels of stress hormones such as cortisol and increases levels of stress-relieving endorphins, the 'feel-good' and pain-relieving hormones produced naturally by the body.

In fact, laughter gives your body something of a cardiovascular workout. When you laugh, your breathing rate rises, helping to transfer oxygen around the body – and around 400 different muscles are activated in the process, including abdominal and internal muscles that aren't involved in most exercise routines.

The positive effects of laughter were demonstrated in a small study of people on a cardiac rehabilitation programme after a heart attack. A group of 24 patients watched a 30 minute comedy video each day for a year, and a similar group of 24 didn't. Only two of those who watched the video had a further heart attack, compared with 10 of the 24 people who didn't.

It seems that all human beings are born to find life fun, but that this capacity diminishes as we get older. On average, children laugh between 100 and 400 times daily, but once the stresses of adult life take hold, the frequency drops to between five and 15 times a day.

# the power of happiness

Feelings of happiness, just like laughing or smiling, counteract the effects of stress. When scientists tested men and women taking part in a major study of heart disease risk, levels of cortisol were almost a third lower among people reporting their most happy moments during the day.

Regardless of your age, you can start feeling happier straightaway by making an effort to be more extrovert and energetic in your activities. According to psychologists, almost any active behaviour – singing, dancing to music you hear on the radio – has a positive effect on your mood. And, like laughter, happiness is contagious. According to data gleaned from the massive Framingham Heart Study in the USA, which spanned three decades, happiness spreads from person to person. Analysis of the social networks of the inhabitants of one American town revealed that the happiness of a friend living within a mile of you increases the likelihood of your own happiness by 25 per cent.

## SHARED PLEASURE

The effects of happiness are stronger between friends of the same sex and can be seen at three degrees of separation – your friend's friend's friend's happiness affects your own. And again, say researchers, 'clusters of happiness result from the spread of happiness and not just a tendency for people to associate with similar individuals'. Curiously, in this study, the influence of friends seems significantly greater than that of spouses or siblings. Having a happier partner increased subjects' happiness by only 8 per cent, and a happier sibling by 14 per cent – but a next-door neighbour who became happier boosted a person's chance of happiness by 34 per cent.

What seems clear is that, in general, a key determinant of human happiness is the happiness of those around you. This accords with other research showing how emotions can be contagious, both in the short-term – 'service with a smile' really does make customers more cheerful (and more inclined to give a large tip) – and over longer periods. Similarly, students sharing with a mildly depressed roommate are more likely to become depressed themselves. 'People's happiness depends on the happiness of others with whom they are connected,'

## A FURRY FRIEND

The companionship of a pet may benefit your health in important ways by reducing stress levels. Studies have shown that pet-owners have better than average survival rates following a heart attack, and a lower risk of succumbing to cardiovascular disease in the first place. And older people who own pets are generally healthier and happier than those who don't. According to researchers at Queen's University, Belfast, having a dog does more for your heart than having a cat – dog-owners in the study had lower than average blood-cholesterol and blood-pressure readings, possibly because of the extra exercise they get while taking their pets for walks.

the Framingham team concluded. Detailed analysis of the statistics from the happiness study demonstrates that each happy person you know increases the likelihood of your own happiness by 9 per cent.

## FIND A FRIEND ...

Perhaps not surprisingly, other research indicates that the more friends people have, the more likely they are to be happy. When Britain's National Lottery organisation commissioned a study to investigate happiness among lottery winners and others, it turned out that people who described themselves as 'extremely satisfied' with life had twice as many friends as those who were 'extremely dissatisfied'. The optimum number of friends for happiness seems to be ten.

## ... AND LIVE LONGER

The number of friends you have may even affect how long you live. In one Australian study, conducted over ten years, people over 70 who had a strong network of friends lived longer than those with weaker social links. Other studies show that people with more friends are more likely to survive a heart attack, less likely to have a stroke, and also do better after discharge from hospital. Men who are less sociable have a greater cardiovascular risk, and score higher in blood tests for inflammation (see page 22).

## MARRIED OR SINGLE?

While deaths from heart attacks and strokes are higher in unmarried than married men, having a close group of friends can protect you if you're single. As explained above, friends can have a powerful influence on your happiness – and your health. In a study at the University of Warwick, the health risks to men of living alone were worse than those of people who smoked, while being married reduced mortality in men by 9 per cent over a seven-year follow-up period – greater than the effect of not smoking. However, for married women, the risk of dying within seven years was reduced by only 2.9 per cent compared with single women. Being divorced actually seems to protect women – but not men – against heart disease.

### SECRET weapon

**A HOT DRINK**

If you are trying to make new friends, asking people round for coffee could have surprisingly successful results. If you want someone to warm to you, give him or her a hot drink, say scientists. In one study, volunteers who had just held a cup of hot coffee rated characters in a story as 11 per cent 'warmer' (more generous and caring) than they had just after holding a cup of iced coffee. Holding something warm also makes people feel warmer and more generous themselves since physical warmth promotes trust between people.

## GENDER GAP

The fact that men are generally more reticent than women appears to increase their risk of cardiovascular problems. But what accounts for this phenomenon? One theory is that women are more likely to have close friends in whom they can confide, and therefore benefit more than men from external social support – so being married makes relatively little difference to their risk of heart disease or to their mortality rates. By contrast, men are much more likely to confide primarily in their wives or partners than in friends, so being single puts them more at risk.

Another explanation for the gender gap is that, when it comes to health, being married affects men's behaviour more than women's. Single men – whether divorced, separated or never married – are much more likely to eat pre-prepared meals than married men, are less likely to take up health screening, and have a higher mortality from cardiovascular disease and other causes, whereas such differences are either not seen or appear to a lesser extent between single and married women.

## HUG YOUR WAY TO HAPPINESS

A hug is good for your emotional health and four of them a day is also one of the ingredients of a happy marriage, according to a survey of 4,000 couples by the market research company Onepoll.

Couples who described themselves as happy or very happy were also likely to share at least two dinner dates and one breakfast in bed every month, as well as taking romantic walks and making romantic gestures. Other research has shown that hugs and physical displays of affection such as stroking or holding hands can reduce high blood pressure, speed up recovery from a heart attack, lower levels of the stress hormone cortisol, and reduce the strain on the cardiovascular system caused by stress and anger.

Four hugs a day is one of the ingredients of a happy marriage.

# mind over matter

The healthier you believe yourself to be, the less likely you are to die prematurely – irrespective of how healthy you actually are. One of the earliest studies to highlight this phenomenon used data from a survey of 7,000 older people in California in 1965 and compared their own reports on their health with mortality levels over the next nine years.

Men who initially reported their health as 'poor' were more than twice as likely to have died as those who said their health was 'excellent', even after the data had been adjusted to take account of age, physical health status, health practices, health relative to people of the same age, income, level of education, social and psychological factors. The outcome for women was even more startling. Women who saw themselves as being in poor health were more than five times as likely to die as those who thought themselves to be healthy, irrespective of their actual health status.

Other research has demonstrated that men who believe themselves to be at lower-than-average risk of cardiovascular disease actually had a three-fold lower risk of death from heart attacks and strokes over the following 15 years, even though almost half of them would have been classified medically as at high or very high risk.

Are you an optimist? If so, you are lucky. Optimists have a powerfully beneficial effect upon their own health.

## POSITIVE THINKING

If you are an optimistic person, you are lucky. Optimists have a powerfully beneficial effect upon their own health – and are much less likely than pessimists to die of cardiovascular disease, according to a study of older people in the Netherlands. Over a nine year follow-up period, those who reported high levels of optimism were 23 per cent less likely to die of heart disease or stroke, and 55 per cent less likely to die at all, than those with lower levels. By contrast, people who displayed a sense of hopelessness had a higher incidence of cardiovascular disease.

## THE KEY TO SURVIVAL

A study that followed the fortunes of 96 men who had had a first heart attack revealed that having an optimistic outlook also reduces the chance of a further attack. The researchers kept a close eye on their subjects'

## PERSONAL REPORT

Joanna Cruddas

# Finding a haven

In a corner of south-west London, Joanna Cruddas has found a haven from inner-city pressures. Two years ago she acquired an allotment in Fulham Palace Meadows, close to the Thames, where she spends several hours a week. Gardening is in Joanna's blood. Her aunt was a professional gardener and her parents were keen amateurs. 'I remember, as a child in the West Country, the immense satisfaction of weeding a flower bed, then watching the plants flourish, of sweeping leaves in the autumn and sitting in the first warmth of spring sun surrounded by daffodils.'

Now in her fifties, she still experiences that contentment and finds gardening an antidote to hectic modern life. 'Shutting the gate of the allotment is shutting the gate on the outside world,' she says. 'Once I start to dig or plant, it becomes a totally absorbing relationship between me, the earth and the plants, and I lose all track of time.'

Focusing on a simple task - what you have to cut back or tidy next - allows you to forget about your problems. Gardening is an excellent form of exercise, too. Weeding, digging and

'Once I start to dig, it becomes a totally absorbing relationship between me, the earth and the plants.'

mowing all count as moderate physical activity. Energetic gardening for 10 minutes can burn 55 to 60kcal. Weeding or pruning burns 300kcal an hour, and digging 400kcal. 'There is nothing like sweeping leaves to get the heartbeat going,' says Joanna. 'For me the best benefit has been in building upper-body strength. In this age of labour-saving devices, it's easy for muscles to weaken. Pumping water manually, carrying watering cans, lifting and spreading compost - they've all made a huge difference to the strength of my spine and shoulders.'

At the end of an afternoon's physical work, relaxing with a cup of tea and being able to see the results of your exertion is wonderfully fulfilling, she says. 'That's when I sit on my bench and plan what I'll do in the future, while enjoying the companionship and banter of neighbouring plotholders.'

moods and reactions to events. Over the following eight years, 15 of the 16 most pessimistic men had died of another heart attack – whereas among the most optimistic group 11 of 16 had survived.

## THINK YOURSELF HEALTHY

Several scientific studies have demonstrated that it is perfectly possible to think yourself fit and healthy. Psychologists who observed 84 female hotel workers found that, although the women were clearly getting plenty of exercise, each cleaning 15 rooms per day on average, most didn't count their work as exercise – two-thirds claimed not to exercise regularly, and more than a third insisted that they got no exercise at all. The most amazing finding was that the workers' cardiovascular health, as measured by blood pressure, weight, body fat, BMI and waist-to-hip ratio, was related to how much exercise they *thought* they were getting – not how much they actually got.

The psychologists then went a stage further. They took aside half of the hotel workers and spent an hour explaining to them how the amount of exercise they took in their jobs more than met the requirements of a healthy and active lifestyle. They also gave out fact sheets showing how many calories are burned by various cleaning activities. The other group of workers were given no such information.

Four weeks later, both groups were reassessed. Activity levels had not changed in either group, but those given information about the health benefits of their work now perceived themselves as doing more exercise. And they had become healthier as well. They had lost weight, removed inches from their waist measurements, reduced their body fat, BMI and waist-to-hip ratios, and improved their blood pressure – simply as a result of being given the information and believing that they had a healthier lifestyle than they had formerly thought. The study is an especially compelling example of the power of positive thought.

# never stop learning

You may be aware that by continuing to be mentally active you can help to stave off the decline in cognitive function that often accompanies the onset of late middle age and reduce your risk of dementia – in fact, mental exercise, just like physical exercise, seems to be protective. But did you know that exercising your mental muscle may also help to stave off cardiovascular disease?

## USE IT OR LOSE IT

Scientists know that people whose mental function declines as they get older have a higher risk of coronary artery disease. But until recently it was not clear whether the same mechanism – atherosclerosis – underlies both heart attack risk and reduction in cognitive ability. Now researchers from the University of Bristol have a possible answer.

They studied data from more than 11,000 people born in Aberdeen in the early 1950s, whose intelligence was measured at the ages of 7, 9 and 11, and who were followed into adulthood. Statistically, those with a lower IQ had a higher risk of future cardiovascular problems. However, the link between lower childhood intelligence and cardiovascular risk virtually disappeared when men and women stayed mentally active as adults.

The study strongly suggests that keeping your brain agile in adulthood has a greater effect on your cardiovascular health than anything in your background and is a further key to avoiding heart attacks and strokes. If you've always wanted to get a few more qualifications, learn a language or take an Open University degree, now you have an extra reason to give it a go.

Keeping your brain agile by giving it plenty to do could help to stave off cardiovascular and cerebrovascular disease.

# sleep well

The average amount of sleep that we get each night has fallen by around 2 hours over the past 40 years – a development that is bad for our cardiovascular system. Adequate sleep is an important insurance against a range of risk factors, including obesity, metabolic syndrome, diabetes and high blood pressure, and people who don't get enough sleep are more likely to develop atherosclerosis. In one study, scans showed calcified arteries – a measure of atherosclerosis – in almost one in three people who slept less than 5 hours per night, whereas getting just 1 more hour lowered the number of people affected to one in ten.

## DON'T SKIMP ON SLEEP

Blood pressure and heart rate are typically at their lowest during sleep, and people who sleep less tend to have higher blood pressure.

Women who lose sleep are particularly at risk, says Francesco Cappuccio, professor of cardiovascular medicine and epidemiology at Warwick Medical School. 'Women who sleep 5 hours or less a night are twice as likely to suffer from hypertension as women who sleep 7 hours or more.' Research findings from a Warwick study of the sleep patterns of some 10,000 Britons showed that those who habitually slept 5 hours a night or less doubled their risk of dying from cardiovascular disease when compared with those who slept for 7 hours or more. Simply stated, people who sleep well live longer.

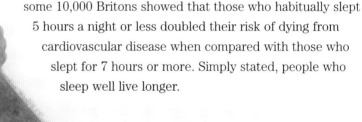

## THE MIDDLE WAY

In fact, sleeping too little and sleeping too much are both bad for the health of your cardiovascular system. Sleeping for 5 hours or less or for 9 hours or more are both linked with a higher death rate from cardiovascular disease compared with sleeping for around 7 hours a night. The results are so marked that, according to current scientific opinion, how long people sleep may be a key predictor of their heart-disease risk. The explanation may lie in the increased risks of diabetes and high blood pressure among people with very short or very long sleep-duration patterns.

Some people don't stay in bed for long enough to get a decent night's sleep. For others, however, insomnia prevents them from getting the sleep they wish they could have. There are several patterns of sleeping difficulties:

- Not being able to fall asleep – perhaps because you are too alert or worried, cold or hungry at bedtime.
- Being disturbed in the night – for example, by pain, noise or the need to go to the bathroom.
- Waking up too early in the morning and being unable to get back to sleep. This may be a symptom of depression, so if it happens frequently it is worth mentioning to your doctor.

## DAYTIME DOZE

Sleep disruption is particularly hazardous since it increases the levels of several blood-clotting factors and so raises the risk of blood clots. And if your sleep is regularly disturbed, the chances are that you will feel sleepy during the day. According to a large study of risk factors for cardiovascular

### SNORING

Often more than just a localised problem of the nose or throat, snoring may be linked to cardiovascular disease. If you snore, you are at risk of a condition called obstructive sleep apnoea, in which the throat narrows to the point where you stop breathing. Typically, you give a loud snort, wake up and then start breathing again. This may happen repeatedly throughout the night, though sufferers are often unaware of it.

Both snoring and sleep apnoea are more common in people who are overweight – and this is a double-edged sword, since you are more likely to gain weight if your sleep is disturbed. Sleep apnoea has also been linked with inflammation, insulin resistance (see page 30), abdominal fat and metabolic syndrome. It puts you at risk of cardiovascular disease and increases your chances of high blood pressure.

The good news is that measures to reduce metabolic syndrome – eating a healthier diet and taking more exercise, for example – also help to ease night-time breathing disturbances. In severe cases, the snorer may be advised to wear a special mask in bed that keeps the airway open by gently pumping through a flow of air.

If you have sleep apnoea, consult your GP, who will be able to advise on treatment and discuss referral to a sleep centre. He or she will also check your cardiovascular risk. And don't forget that, if you don't snore but you share a bed with someone who does, you may be at greater risk of disturbed sleep than your partner (see page 198).

disease, daytime sleepiness was associated with a 35 per cent increased risk of cardiovascular disease in men and a 66 per cent increase in women. It also increased the risk of heart failure by 49 per cent among men and more than 50 per cent in women. So it's worth taking time to find out the cause of your disturbed nights, especially if you are a woman.

## SNOOZE ALERT

Nodding off when you sit down to read a newspaper or watch television could be a sign that you are at risk of a stroke. According to one study of 2,000 people, those who reported snoozing during the day when they didn't intend to fall asleep were more than twice as likely to have a stroke over the next two years as those who did not – and those who said this happened often had a risk four and a half times higher than normal. So if you have developed a habit of unintentional daytime dozing, ask your doctor for a check-up.

Snooze alert ... If you've developed a habit of unintentional daytime dozing, ask your doctor for a check-up.

## SLEEP SOLUTIONS

When you are lying awake exhausted but too alert to sleep, it can seem that insomnia is an insurmountable problem. In fact, for many people it is easily resolved – and without a prescription. You just need to pay attention to what the experts call 'sleep hygiene'. Here are their recommendations for ensuring that you sleep soundly:

- Make sure your bedroom is dark, quiet and sufficiently warm, but not too warm – slightly cooler than your other living areas is ideal.
- Reserve your bedroom for sleep (and sex). Don't watch television or work in bed.
- Step up your daytime activity. Regular exercise, preferably in the fresh air, promotes night-time sleep. If you are tired during the day or having trouble dropping off at night, try exercise in the late afternoon. About 5 or 6 hours after exercising, there is typically a slight fall in body temperature, which helps to promote sleep. Don't exercise in the 2 or 3 hours before bedtime though, or you may be too alert to drift off.
- Go to bed at the same time each night and get up at the same time each morning.
- Establish a consistent winding-down routine in the evenings so that you are properly relaxed by bedtime. Avoid stimulating television or films and boisterous activities for at least 2 hours before bedtime.
- Avoid caffeine-containing drinks such tea and coffee in the evenings. Don't smoke (nicotine is a stimulant), and limit your alcohol intake.
- Don't eat a huge meal late at night.
- Shortly before you go to bed, have a small snack of a food rich in tryptophan. This amino acid (a protein building-block) is believed to boost brain levels of serotonin, a natural feel-good chemical that can also counter insomnia. Good sources include turkey, chicken, fish, pheasant, bananas, wheatgerm, avocados, eggs and cheese.
- Try herbal remedies to promote sleep, such as chamomile tea or valerian.

# moving forwards

The nine steps completed so far cover everything from knowledge and risk to diet, exercise and mental wellbeing, giving you most of the defences you need to avoid heart attacks and strokes – and to live more energetically and contentedly into the bargain. But there is one more step to follow, since key to the overall plan is to keep all your self-defence strategies going so that they become a life-long blueprint for health and happiness.

# self-defence plan

## STEP 10

ONCE YOU HAVE BEGUN TO DEVELOP YOUR PERSONAL PROTECTION PLAN AGAINST HEART DISEASE AND STROKE, YOU SHOULD SOON START TO EXPERIENCE SOME BENEFIT. BUT, TO BE EFFECTIVE IN THE LONG TERM, ANY LIFESTYLE CHANGES MUST BE SUSTAINED. HERE ARE SOME TACTICS THAT WILL HELP YOU TO REMAIN ACTIVE AND HEALTHY IN THE FUTURE.

# Make your plan
# life-long

If you have come this far in your quest to fend off heart disease and stroke, you will have absorbed a great deal of information. If you have also applied your discoveries to your own life, you should be feeling less stressed, more active and energetic, and generally happier.

It is important to take pleasure in your new healthy lifestyle – but it is equally important not to become complacent. Indeed, it is all too easy in the first few weeks and months to let goals slip as your willpower weakens. Step 10 describes the tools you need to keep your plan going and to build in new, positive strategies for life-long protection.

As you start to experience the benefits of cleaner arteries, reduced cholesterol and lower blood pressure, you will realise that they are a direct result of the well-informed choices you are making every day.

## stay motivated

Keeping your goals and rewards at the forefront of your mind will help you to stay motivated. So remind yourself repeatedly of the benefits of your new lifestyle: you will continue to feel re-energised, fitter and stronger – and you will almost certainly live longer, too.

Make positive, specific and detailed plans about how you can achieve your aims. If you change one element of a carefully thought-out regime, make sure to substitute it with something else that provides equal benefits and is just as easy to organise. For example, if your local swimming pool closes, switch your regular Tuesday afternoon swim with friends to the pool at the nearest health club – or resolve to go bowling or skating with the same group instead. Don't put this off. Make sure that you have something of equal 'value' to do the very next week. And enlist the help of like-minded people to help you to stay on course.

## MAKING PROGRESS

Motivation also relies on the ability to keep moving forwards. Although you may have made some progress since starting to read this book, it is unlikely that you will have achieved all your goals to your total satisfaction. Perhaps you've lost 10lb (4.5kg) but you'd really like to lose another 10lb. Or perhaps your resting pulse rate is still a few beats short of your target rate, or you could still afford to lose a few centimetres from your waist measurement. Keep going by breaking down larger goals into smaller ones. If you want to lose 10lb (4.5kg ), start by aiming to be 1lb (500g) lighter by the end of the week or 3lb (1.5kg) lighter by the end of the month.

And you can always add new ingredients to the mix: new ways to cook healthily, new sports to keep you interested, new activities to pursue, and new friends to make. That's all part of treating your plan as a life-long recipe for health and enjoyment, a pursuit that never ends.

## TACTICAL SUPPORTERS

Remember also some of the useful tactics that make it easier to fulfil your aims: using the stairs rather than taking the lift, eating breakfast, enjoying the sunshine ... music, olive oil, a glass of wine, yoga, laughter, chocolate, sleep, friendships. The sheer scope of this list shows that opportunities for boosting your health are everywhere. It may help to make a list of the tactics that you've found most helpful, or most fun, and put it up on the fridge or anywhere else where you will see it regularly. Don't forget to add to it. Part of the enjoyment of your plan is to make it a living, dynamic thing, so always be open to new ideas that could help you on the way.

Friends, laughter, sunshine, chocolate, music and many other elements of daily life can provide tactical support.

# mind over matter

**B**elieving in yourself will make it easier to maintain your new healthy lifestyle. The more confidence you have in your ability to exercise regularly, the more likely you are to enjoy it and the less likely you are to give up, say Canadian public health researchers who surveyed more than 5,000 people. The other key factor for success is motivation – or the extent to which you intend to exercise. If you stay confident and motivated, the chances are that you will stay physically active.

# take control of your destiny

As revealed in Step 9, optimists are less likely than pessimists to develop cardiovascular disease – and optimists generally feel more in control of their lives. If you think you need to develop a more positive mental approach, concentrate on the things you do well. The vital aspects are:

- **Focus** Try to keep your thoughts directed towards what you want, not what you don't want. Visualise yourself in elegant evening attire or in the jeans you've always wanted to wear; or on a beach with the sort of body you've always yearned for. Block out the reflection of the overweight person you spotted yesterday in a shop window. The sooner you focus on a positive goal, the sooner you can plan how to achieve it.
- **Self-confidence** Keep your mind on moving closer to your goals rather than indulging in negative thinking. Dwell on what you have accomplished. Take time to note down your successes, however small. You've reached Step 10 of this book, for a start, which means you probably know a great deal more about heart attacks and strokes, and how to prevent them, than many of your friends and neighbours.
- **Attention to detail** To achieve any long-term goal, you need to work on the detail. Breaking down big tasks into small steps makes them more manageable and allows you to follow a predetermined sequence – helping to avoid the procrastination that derails so many good plans.

## DEALING WITH SETBACKS

Staying positive is even more crucial if you fail to achieve your immediate goals as soon as you had hoped. In many cases, people embark on a new health regime with the best of intentions, succeed for a while, then slip back into less healthy habits. This can often make the original problems even worse. Remember the warnings in Step 5 about yo-yo dieting?

Remind yourself that you are only human. By being aware that you are likely to encounter setbacks, and by anticipating the bad spells, you can plan ahead for those times when you are most vulnerable.

If you find yourself falling back into old habits, the first thing to do is to think about your original motivation and assess whether it is still valid, and whether it can be strengthened and made more relevant.

Then, analyse your strategy to see whether the goals you have set yourself are as clear and specific as they should be. A vague desire to lose weight is not enough. You need well-defined goals, preferably written down. For example: eat just one chocolate bar this week; have an extra portion of vegetables instead of potatoes with dinner on three nights of the week; go for a swim after work on Wednesday; take the children for a bike ride on Saturday afternoon.

## STOP AND THINK

Before you open that packet of chocolate-chip cookies or light up another cigarette with gay abandon, stop and ask yourself why you are doing it. All too frequently, the underlying trigger that derails our good intentions is related in some way to stress. It may have been your clear intention to have pieces of fruit rather than other, less healthy snacks all week, but you're under pressure at work and had a row with your partner when you got home. The temptation is to think 'Forget it!' and tuck into those chocolates or down a double whisky.

### Feeling low or under pressure? Use a stress-buster – ring a friend.

## STRESS-BUSTERS

It is important to have some stress-beating tactics lined up to help you to survive the times when you are most likely to give way to temptation. Decide in advance on a few actions you can take when you are feeling low or under pressure – for example, put on your coat and go for a short walk, dig the garden, take a hot shower, or have a self-indulgent soak in the bath. Ring a close friend and have a good chat. You will find that your mood will lift and the craving for oral gratification will subside. See Step 9 (page 210) for more advice on getting through the difficult times. Finally, if you do fall off the wagon, don't berate yourself. Remind yourself that you are making progress – you are a success. Give yourself encouragement, get back on to the programme you have devised for yourself and focus on moving forward.

## GET TO KNOW YOUR BODY

Maintaining commitment to your goals is easier if you understand, and can visualise, how your body will benefit from a healthier lifestyle – which is why each individual step in this book has been designed to contribute to that overall picture. For example, Step 5 explains that our bodies respond best to certain types of food, and Step 7 that, just like our hunter-gatherer forebears, we are meant to be active; simply sitting down for too long makes blood fats collect in our arteries, causing plaque to build up over time (see page 146).

(see page 146)

### SECRETweapon

#### SET SMART GOALS

There is a formula used by business people for setting out their aims that can help almost anyone to be more effective in achieving success. When defining your own goals, make sure they are **SMART**, as exemplified below:

**Specific** 'I shall go to the gym for an hour at 4pm every Thursday.' (not: 'I'm planning to get more exercise.')

**Measurable** 'I shall substitute one portion of fruit for a chocolate bar every day this week.' (not: 'I shall eat more fruit from now on.') To find out if your goal is measurable, ask questions such as 'How much?' 'How many?' 'How will I know when it is accomplished?'

**Achievable** 'I've decided to cut out fatty meats, burgers, fried foods and takeaways.' (not: 'I'm going to avoid all saturated fat.')

**Realistic** 'I shall take a deep breath whenever my partner irritates me.' (not: 'I'm never going to argue again.')

**Timely** 'I'm starting a diet on Monday and aiming to lose a few centimetres from my waist by 1 May.' (not: 'I want a 66cm (26in) waist.')

## RED ALERTS

While you are making your body as fit as possible to minimise the risk of a heart attack or stroke, don't forget to take account of those trigger factors that were outlined in Step 1. Rather than the steady drip-drip of unhealthy factors that, over the long-term, can lead to plaque, atherosclerosis and cardiovascular disease, triggers act in the short-term to promote a heart attack or stroke in someone who is already susceptible.

In the context of a life-long plan for a healthier lifestyle, you need to remind yourself repeatedly where the danger points lie so that you can work out how to avoid or counteract them:

● Acute stress caused by, for example, a failing business or a highly challenging work deadline.

● Uncontrolled anger.

● A fat-laden, heavy meal.

- Extreme cold.
- Early mornings (especially Mondays).
- Commuting.
- Excessively loud noises.
- Unaccustomed heavy exertion.
- Air pollution.
- Severe emotional upset.
- Death of a loved one.
- Binge drinking.
- Flu and other serious respiratory infections.

## MORE COMPLEX THAN IT SEEMS

While the basic principles of avoiding cardiovascular disease are pretty straightforward – eat healthily, sleep well, avoid stress, take some regular exercise and keep your weight within normal limits – the mechanics of

## inside information
# understanding risk

**W**hen considering potential health risks, it is easy to get things out of perspective. Let's say, for example, that you are worried about having a heart attack during intercourse. You read a newspaper story that says, 'Heart attack risk for a healthy man doubles within 2 hours of having sex.' That sounds like a big extra risk – newspapers tend to play on our fears. But the actual baseline risk is tiny. The odds of a man having a heart attack in any particular hour are about one in a million. Even if this figure is increased to two in a million, it is still not very high – in fact, the risk of an average man having a heart attack during sex is about the same as it would be if he were walking at 2 to 4 miles per hour. So, if you can walk to the post box, you probably have no need to worry about sustaining a heart attack through sexual intercourse.

But are you much more vulnerable than average to a heart attack if you have had a previous attack? In that case, your baseline risk – or, in this case, what is called headline risk – increases ten-fold, and that too is doubled during or after sex. But that makes the odds a mere ten in a million without sex and 20 in a million with sex – so the risk is still negligible.

And the more exercise you take (which includes sex), the less likely it becomes that you will have a heart attack at all, because your overall risk will go down as you get fitter.

This is just one example of why doctors distinguish absolute risk – the one (or ten) in a million – from relative risk – the two-fold (or ten-fold) increase. Relative risks make good newspaper headlines, but, as explained above, even a ten-fold increase in risk may still represent a very small absolute risk. So, whenever you come across risk statistics, ask yourself whether the number in question refers to relative or absolute risk.

just how to achieve this are rather more complex. This book has set out to disentangle the complexity and to put forward an enormous variety of different suggestions for helping you to achieve your aims in ways that are most suitable for you.

In reading *Conquering heart attack & stroke*, you will also have gained much information about 'hidden' factors that can make a difference to your risk of both events – everything from the danger of gum disease or living next to a main road to the protective effect of friendship or watching comedy films.

## KNOWING YOURSELF

You will by now be aware of which topics covered in this book are most relevant in your case – whether these be health factors that you need to deal with or tactics for protecting yourself. It is worth making a note of these items now, and refreshing the list in the months and years to come, because neither you nor your life circumstances will remain static.

## HELPING OTHERS

If someone close to you is unfortunate enough to have a heart attack or a stroke, after reading this book you should be equipped with the knowledge to spot the signs and to act decisively and quickly.

It is worth refreshing your memory from time to time about the crucial symptoms of heart attack and stroke (see Step 2, pages 40–45). And, if you can, sign up for a short first-aid course, so that you will know what to do if you ever need to resuscitate someone. Information about training courses is included in the Resources section (page 240).

# social networks

Finally, never underestimate the important part that relationships with family, friends and even neighbours can play in helping to fend off cardiovascular disease. We are, after all, social animals – and supportive friendships have a much more crucial role in maintaining good health than most people acknowledge.

Take stress, for example. Many studies have demonstrated that chronic stress can take a serious physical toll, contributing to heart problems by raising blood pressure and increasing the blood's tendency to clot. Having a few close friends – the kind to whom you can talk about anything – can relieve stress and mitigate its harmful effects on your body. It is also worth recalling the research showing that happiness can spread among groups of friends (see page 217). Among the many remarkable findings from those studies, several particularly startling results stand out. One is that emotions, like happiness, are more closely influenced by our friends than by our partners or siblings.

## OUR INFLUENCE ON OTHERS

The researchers also found that states of mind and behaviours can spread through social networks almost like an infection. The explanation for this is not simply that individuals tend to make friends with people who have similar characteristics to themselves; rather, that certain character traits rub off on others with whom people come into contact. And the effects can be transmitted through three degrees of separation – your friend is most likely to influence you, but your friend's friend has some effect, and even your friend's friend's friend can play a small role, too.

The conclusions that have been drawn from the happiness study include the contention that the same phenomenon can be applied to smoking behaviour. The researchers suggest that there may even be a 'three degrees of influence rule' that could apply to depression, anxiety, loneliness, drinking, eating, exercise, and other emotional states and health behaviours.

## GETTING INVOLVED

Our bodies are responsive to a wide range of social relationships – even our interaction with our neighbours, who can exert a surprising influence on our happiness. The reason for this could be that, if we see our neighbours virtually every day, they contribute to our sense of belonging and support in the local community – and this has a big impact on our sense of satisfaction with life.

So remember the benefits to your cardiovascular system of just being 'involved'. Widen your social circle, talk to your neighbours, get involved in your community, volunteer with local groups, take up new hobbies, and get together regularly with other people.

You can also enlist others in your efforts to adopt a healthier lifestyle. Tell people if you're trying to stop smoking; get their support when you want to lose weight; get a friend to join a fitness club with you – or go swimming, cycling or walking together.

# relax in **heart-healthy style**

**H**ere are some additional ideas derived from recent research studies about how to improve the health of your cardiovascular system.

- **Choose joyful music.** Ultrasound scans of the blood vessels of people listening to various types of music showed that light music and love songs produced, on average, a 26 per cent widening of the arteries compared with silence. Heavy-metal rock music had the opposite effect and made the participants anxious; such arterial narrowing could encourage atherosclerosis.

- **Listen to calming CDs.** A small study of people living in retirement homes showed that listening to a CD designed to promote relaxation – a calming voice with ocean waves in the background – produced a 6.4 per cent drop in blood pressure after four months using the 12-minute CD three times a week. In comparison, playing a Mozart sonata for the same period yielded a fall of just under 5 per cent.

- **Try a Wii games console.** This involves holding a wireless remote control and swinging it like a golf club or tennis racket while an onscreen computer-generated character carries out the movements. The Wii Fit – designed to strengthen muscles and develop posture, flexibility and aerobic capacity – comes with its own balance board which has sensors that detect your body's movements. Exercises encompass yoga, aerobics (running, stepping and hula-hooping), muscle toning (sit-ups and lunges) and improving balance (simulating ski slaloms and walking on a tightrope). Playing on a Wii is a highly sociable activity; family and friends can join in. A study in the *BMJ* found that regular users of Wii sports could burn up to 1,830kcal a week and lose 2st (12.25kg) a year.

Listen to a calming CD.

# keep **going**

There is no point regarding your new lifestyle as a quick fix – you need to keep it going. Celebrate your triumphs, sustain the successful changes you've made, modify those that aren't working, and keep making small alterations and adaptations. Your plan shouldn't dominate your life, but neither should it disappear from it once you've finished this book; it should become a part of your daily routine, a continuing source of rejuvenation and enjoyment. So keep this book to hand, refresh your memory from time to time, and determine to sustain your plan for as long as you live.

# conclusions

You've seen throughout this book how simple lifestyle changes can slash your risk of cardiovascular disease and thus reduce your chances of succumbing to a heart attack or a stroke. In fact, what *you* do can make as much difference to your risk as medical interventions – and often more.

So, while your doctor can give you tablets to treat high blood pressure, losing a little weight and cutting down the amount of salt you eat may be sufficient. You may think it's easier to pop a pill, but it's important to remember that all medications can have side effects. Eating more healthily has multiple benefits and can't harm you.

Similarly, the miracle of statin drugs is revolutionising prospects for people with high cholesterol – but why not avoid the problem altogether in the first place? Eating less saturated fat helps to prevent plaque from ever building up in your arteries. And while technological developments can often save you if you suffer a heart attack or a stroke – why take the risk, when there are so many easy ways to avoid these hazards?

## THE MULTIPLE BENEFITS OF LIVING WELL

This plan is not all about self-denial. A healthy life is also a full, enjoyable, interesting life. There are many ingredients in this plan that are positively self-indulgent, such as chocolate, comedy and companionship.

And that's a crucial factor about protective lifestyle measures which is often overlooked: unlike drugs, they rarely have isolated actions. While scientists can pinpoint individual chemicals with specific effects, such as resveratrol in red wine (see page 111), all natural foods are made up of a host of different ingredients that together can have effects far greater than the sum of their parts. Similarly, red wine is often enjoyed in a supportive, social setting, along with friends and good conversation.

So, while each step outlined here is important, for optimal results make all of them a permanent part of your life. Don't allow yourself to become impossibly stressed at work; learn to relax, or you risk undoing, for instance, the good effects of a healthy diet or losing excess weight.

## THE SECRETS OF 'HEALTHIER' NATIONS

What becomes very clear when looking at cultures around the world where 'diseases of civilisation' like cardiovascular disease have taken less of a hold is that while they often have a healthier diet, there are usually other protective 'ingredients' in their lifestyle as well.

For example, green tea contains chemicals known as catechins and theanine that have been shown to have various positive effects. But the simple act of making the tea may be as beneficial. In one study of more than three thousand women aged 50 and over, those who regularly practised the Japanese tea ceremony – an elaborate ritual for brewing and drinking green tea – lived longer than women who did not. It appears that the calming and relaxing effect of the ritual itself bestows benefits.

## MORE THAN JUST FOOD

Often protection cannot be nailed down to a single factor, like food. No one knows if it was just the Palaeolithic diet that protected our ancestors from cardiovascular disease or also the activity that hunting and survival entailed. How much did tracking and chasing wild animals, or seeking and picking fruit and other produce contribute?

Similarly, you've heard how the Mediterranean diet reduces people's risk of heart attacks and strokes (see pages 108-109). And you've seen that multiple ingredients of the typical Mediterranean diet – such as olive oil, fish, fruit, vegetables and red wine – all individually have protective effects. But the Mediterranean 'package' also includes home-cooked food, leisurely meals with friends and family, laughter, siestas and sunshine.

Food in these countries is both important in itself and intimately interwoven with the joy of living, pleasant surroundings and good company. Contrast that with a hurried lunchtime sandwich out of a plastic wrapper, fast food and takeaway meals laden with salt and fat, or snatched ready meals in front of the television.

## THE WHOLE PACKAGE

So while it's good to find out just what works, and by how much, science can only provide a limited number of answers. What's really important is the whole package, because it represents a lifestyle, your lifestyle … and that's the ultimate message of *Conquering heart attack and stroke*.

Because, as you've seen, safeguarding yourself against heart attacks and strokes involves many diverse aspects, and there are so many different things that you can do to reduce your risk. The more that you can blend the ingredients together, the more likely you are to protect yourself not only from cardiovascular disease but also from all the other damaging effects of 'diseases of civilisation'. And the really great news is that alongside being physically fit, you are likely to live not just a longer and healthier life, but a happier and more fulfilled one too.

# resources

**British Dental Health Foundation**  For information/leaflets on oral health and all aspects of dental care visit www.dentalhealth.org.uk or call the National Dental Helpline on Tel: 0845 063 1188 (9am-5pm Monday to Friday)

**British Heart Foundation**  Greater London House, 180 Hampstead Road, London, NW1 7AW  Tel: 020 7554 0000  www.bhf.org.uk

**BHF Heart HelpLine**  Tel: 0300 330 3311 (9am-6pm Monday to Friday) or email: hearthelponline@bhf.org.uk  Cardiac nurses and information officers on the confidential Heart HelpLine can provide information and support on any heart health-related question.

**British Snoring and Sleep Apnoea Association**  Castle Court, 41 London Road, Reigate, RH2 9RJ  Tel: 01737 245638  email: info@britishsnoring.co.uk www.britishsnoring.co.uk  Also supply ear plugs specially designed to filter out snoring.

**Cardiac Rehabilitation**  To find your nearest cardiac rehab group visit www.cardiac-rehabilitation.net or call the BHF HelpLine on 0300 330 3311

**Diabetes UK**  Diabetes UK Central Office, Macleod House, 10 Parkway, London, NW1 7AA Tel: 020 7424 1000  email: info@diabetes.org.uk  www. diabetes.org.uk

**Freecycle**  (for all that unwanted exercise equipment)  www.uk.freecycle.org

**Genetic Information Service** launched by the British Heart Foundation to provide information and support for people with inherited heart conditions Tel: 0300 456 8383

**Heart Support Groups**  BHF affiliated support groups for people living with heart disease run across the UK. Some offer regular exercise sessions, walking groups, newsletters, social outings, others monthly meetings and a friendly atmosphere. To find your nearest group telephone the BHF HelpLine on 0300 330 3311.

**International Stress Management Association**  ISMA UK, PO Box 491, Bradley Stoke, Bristol, BS34 9AH, England  Tel: 0117 969 7284  www.isma.org.uk

**Laughter Yoga International**  A-001, Denzil Apartment, 3rd Cross Road, Lokhandwala Complex, Andheri (West), Mumbai – 400053, India  Tel: +91-22-40109840 email: raj@laughteryoga.org  www.laughteryoga.org/

**National Obesity Forum**  First Floor, 6a Gordon Road, Nottingham, NG2 5LN Tel: 0115 846 2109  email: info@nof.uk.com  www.nationalobesityforum.org.uk/

**NHS weight loss help**  www.nhs.uk/LiveWell/loseweight/Pages/Loseweighthome.aspx

**Nordic walking**  Tel: 0845 260 9339  email: info@nordicwalking.co.uk www.nordicwalking.co.uk

**Online cardiovascular risk calculators**
http://qr2.dyndns.org/
http://hp2010.nhlbihin.net/atpiii/calculator.asp

**Relate** Relationship and family mediation and counselling throughout England, Wales, Northern Ireland. To find your local Relate call 0300 100 1234 Or visit  www.relate.org.uk

**Relationships Scotland**  Counselling, mediation and family support, 18 York Place, Edinburgh, EH1 3EP  Tel: 0845 119 2020  www.relationships-scotland.org.uk

**Stroke Association**  Stroke House, 240 City Road, London, EC1V 2PR Tel: 020 7566 0300  www.stroke.org.uk

**Stroke Helpline**  Tel: 0845 3033 100 (9am to 5pm weekdays)
Staff on the Helpline can answer any questions you may have, listen to your concerns and help to reassure you. The helpline provides information about stroke in general, local services and stroke clubs in your area and advice on how to get help at home. In many areas, the Stroke Association's Family and Carer Support team can make home visits.

**Tai Chi Union for Great Britain**  Secretary: Peter Ballam, 5 Corunna Drive, Horsham, West Sussex, RH13 5HG  Tel: 01403 257918  www.taichiunion.com/

**The Sleep Apnoea Trust**  12a Bakers Piece, Kingston Blount, Oxon, OX39 4SW  Tel: 0845 606 0685  www.sleep-apnoea-trust.org/

**The Sleep Council**  For advice, free leaflets, helpful related links, visit www.sleepcouncil.com or telephone: 0845 058 4595

## First aid and resuscitation

**British Red Cross**  44 Moorfields, London, EC2Y 9AL  Tel: 0844 871 11 11 www.redcross.org.uk

**Heartstart UK**  Find details of your nearest course offering free emergency life support training by calling the British Heart Foundation Heart HelpLine on 0300 330 3311 or email  hearthelponline@bhf.org.uk  Alternatively browse for schemes by searching 'In Your Area' on Heartstart UK page of the BHF website  www.bhf.org.uk

**Resuscitation Council**  For detailed instructions on CPR, visit the Resuscitation Council website at www.resus.org.uk/siteIndx.htm

**St John Ambulance**  27 St John's Lane, London, EC1M 4BU  Tel: 020 7324 4000 www.sja.org.uk
Community first responder scheme  www.sja.org.uk/sja/what-we-do/neighbourhood-first-responder.aspx

## Alcohol

**Alcohol Concern**  64 Leman Street, London, E1 8EU
Tel: 020 7264 0510  email: contact@alcoholconcern.org.uk  www.alcoholconcern.org.uk

**Alcoholics Anonymous**  PO Box 10 Toft Green, York, YO1 7NJ
Tel: 01904 644 026  Helpline 0845 769 7555  www.alcoholics-anonymous.org.uk

**Drinkline**  Help and advice from the Department of Health for people worried about their own or someone else's drinking problems.  Free 24hr helpline 0800 917 8282 www.drinkaware.co.uk

**NHS Alcohol support**  The NHS has developed a free and confidential online 'Down Your Drink' programme. It tells drinkers what they need to know to become a 'thinking drinker'. www.drinkaware.co.uk/

## Stopping smoking

**ASH** (Action on Smoking and Health)  Tel: 020 7739 5902  www.ash.org.uk

**BHF Smoking Helpline**  Tel: 0800 169 1900  BHF's Giving Up Smoking microsite

**NHS Stop Smoking Helpline**  Tel: 0800 022 4 332 (7 days a week, 7am-11pm)
For detailed information about free NHS support services, including support at home or to chat to an adviser online visit  www.smokefree.nhs.uk

**Quit**  4th floor, 63 St Mary Axe, London, EC3A 8AA  Quitline 0800 00 22 00 www.quit.org.uk

# glossary

**aerobic exercise** the type that uses up oxygen, so makes you breathe faster. Aerobic exercise boosts cardiovascular fitness

**aneurysm** a ballooning out of an artery, due to weakness in its wall

**angina** chest pain due to coronary artery disease

**angiogram** an X-ray taken after injection of a special dye, to enable blood vessels to be seen

**angioplasty** widening a narrowed artery by threading a thin tube up from the groin and inflating a balloon at its tip

**arteries** the network of tubes carrying blood to supply oxygen and nutrients to body tissues

**atherosclerosis** the underlying process by which plaque is laid down in arteries in cardiovascular disease

**BMI** body mass index, a measure of body fat based on a person's height and weight

**cardiac arrest** the heart stops beating and cannot pump blood. Without urgent treatment, the person will die

**cerebrovascular disease** cardiovascular disease affecting the arteries supplying the brain

**cholesterol** an important component of cell membranes and hormones; too much accumulating in the blood can lead to plaque formation

**clotting** blood coagulation important in wound healing but also dangerous if it blocks an artery to cause a heart attack or stroke

**coronary artery bypass graft** replacing a diseased segment of coronary artery with a healthy blood vessel taken from elsewhere in the body

**coronary artery disease** cardiovascular disease affecting the arteries supplying the heart muscle

**cortisol** a hormone produced in the body at an increased level when someone is under physical or emotional stress

**CPR** cardipulmonary resuscitation - attempts to restart the heart after a cardiac arrest

**decibel** a measure of loudness; an increase of 10 on the decibel scale means that a sound is 10 *times* as loud

**diabetes** a disorder of insulin and blood sugar control

**diastolic blood pressure** the force on artery walls when the heart rests between beats

**ECG** electrocardiogram, a test of the electrical activity of the heart, often used to diagnose a heart attack

**embolus (pl emboli)** a clump of some abnormal substance travelling around the bloodstream, such as a clot, a globule of fat or an air bubble

**endorphins** chemicals produced in the body that have pain-killing and mood-enhancing effects

**fibrinogen** a protein involved in the blood's clotting response

**gangrene** death of part of the body, such as the cells of a toe

**glucose** the type of sugar produced from digestion of foods and used by the body for energy

**gum disease** infection and inflammation around the gums

**haemorrhagic stroke** stroke due to a bleed in an artery supplying the brain

**HDL cholesterol** high density lipoprotein cholesterol, the 'good' fat that mops up LDL cholesterol from the bloodstream

**heart attack** blockage of one of the arteries supplying the heart muscle by a *clot* or *plaque*

**hypertension** medical term for high blood pressure

**inflammation** response of body tissues to injury, irritation or infection

**insulin** a hormone produced by the pancreas and important in the regulation of blood sugar

**insulin resistance** lowered ability of body cells to respond to insulin and so metabolise blood sugar properly

**ischaemia** reduced blood flow to a part of the body, resulting in damage to the tissues

**ischaemic stroke** stroke due to a blood clot in an artery supplying the brain

**LDL cholesterol** low density lipoprotein cholesterol, the 'bad' fat that may accumulate in the bloodstream to promote plaque formation

**lipids** fats in the blood

**metabolic syndrome** a cluster of risk factors including abnormal blood fats, abdominal obesity, high blood pressure and disturbances in blood sugar control

**myocardial infarction** medical term for a heart attack

**omega 3 fatty acids** essential fatty acids found in oily fish and some plants

**omega 6 fatty acids** essential fatty acids found in processed vegetable oils

**pedometer** a device for counting how many steps someone takes

**periodontal disease** medical term for gum disease

**peripheral vascular disease** atherosclerosis affecting the arteries in the legs, causing a cramping pain on walking

**placebo** a pill or other treatment that has no active ingredient

**plaque** the fatty deposits laid down in arterial walls that are responsible for cardiovascular disease

**platelets** cells involved in the blood's clotting response

**potassium** chemical in the blood that balances the effect of sodium (salt)

**refined carbohydrates** starchy foods that have been heavily processed and are thus nutrient poor, for example white flour, white bread, white rice and pasta

**saturated fats** the type found in animal products, typically solid at room temperature

**sedentary lifestyle** one involving minimal activity, such as sitting at a desk all day

**sleep apnoea** episodes of interrupted breathing during sleep, often associated with heavy snoring

**sodium** part of a salt molecule (sodium chloride), may be used on labels to indicate the salt content

**statins** a type of cholesterol-lowering drug

**stent** a tiny tube left inside an artery to hold it open, often used to relieve coronary artery disease

**systolic blood pressure** the force on artery walls when the heart contracts to pump blood

**thrombolytic therapy** treatment with clot-busting drugs to try to relieve a heart attack or stroke

**trans fats** artificial, processed fats that behave like saturated fats in the body

**transient ischaemic attack (TIA)** temporary interruption of blood supply to a part of the brain, a 'mini-stroke'

**unsaturated fats** the type found in fish and plants, typically liquid at room temperature

**unstable angina** severe angina symptoms not relieved by rest that may be mistaken for a heart attack

# index

# G

gangrene 20

gardening 79, 221

garlic 111, 115

garlic supplements 191

gastric banding 123

gender gap 219

Genetic Information Service 81

getting up in the morning 42

ghrelin 133

gingivitis 177

glucose 30, 144

  *see also* blood sugar

glucose intolerance 30, 31, 134

glucose metabolism 145

glycogen 163

GPs 58, 63, 91

  health checks 81

  help with weigh control 122-123

grapeseed extract 111

green tea 111, 121, 239

gum disease 14, 29, 68, 79, 84, 176-177

  dental hygiene 29, 68, 176, 177

  warning signs 177

gyms 151, 152, 157, 164, 165-166

# H

haemorrhagic stroke 24, 44, 55, 56, 204

hand washing 190

happiness 34, 79, 216-219, 236

  questionnaire 77

heart 13, 15, 37, 145

  arrhythmias 25, 37, 43, 53, 175, 198

  blood supply, interruption of 38, 40

heart attack

  causes 19-20, 22, 26, 40

diagnosis 52

diet and 105, 106, 107, 111

emergency action 37, 41, 47, 48-51

first-time heart attacks 17

hospital treatment 43, 52-54

medications 57

myths 38

peak times for 42, 187, 188, 206, 207

recovery and rehabilitation 40, 57-58

risk factors 13, 17, 18, 22, 23, 26, 27, 32, 58, 59, 64, 68, 175, 176, 192, 203, 205, 207, 208, 212

stress and 205, 207, 208

symptoms 41

triggers 24-25

heart rate 145, 157, 211

Heartstart UK 50

Heart Support groups 59

heatstroke 194-195

heavy metal toxicity 200

heparin 53

high blood pressure 13, 14, 17, 19, 26, 64, 204

  and aneurysm 20

  benefits of exercise 28, 42, 145

  cardiovascular risk 64

  and diabetes 30

  and heart disease 26

  lowering 97, 98, 105, 110, 111, 145, 170, 174, 193

  medications 57

  and memory impairment 24

  sleep deprivation and 224

  stress and 204

  and stroke 24, 26, 58

  toxic chemicals and 200

homocysteine 32, 34, 106, 107, 108

# Q,R

risk factor for heart attack and stroke 13, 17, 27, 64, 203, 204, 205, 207, 235-236

stress-busters 232-233

stress-relief techniques 207

symptoms 208

work-related 58, 73, 87, 204-205, 206, 233

stress hormones 24, 42, 198, 203, 216

stroke

alcohol and 59, 175

benefits of exercise 28, 143

causes 24, 26

diagnostic tests 55

diet and 105, 107, 108, 110

emergency action 37, 45, 47

FAST test 45, 46

haemorrhagic stroke 24, 44, 55, 56, 204

hospital treatment 47, 54-56

ischaemic stroke 23, 24, 44, 55, 56

medications 57

myths 38

peak times for 42, 187, 206, 207

prevention 38

recovery and rehabilitation 38, 56-57, 58

risk factors 13, 17, 23, 25, 26, 27, 32, 38, 58, 59, 64, 67, 68, 105, 175, 176, 178, 203, 204, 207, 212, 226

symptoms 45, 46

transient ischaemic attack (TIA) 25, 39-40, 56

treatment 38, 39-40, 44

triggers 24-25

subarachnoid haemorrhage 215

Sudden Arrhythmic Death Syndrome (SADS) 81

sulphoraphane 111

sunscreen 194

sunshine 192, 194

support groups 59

surgery

angioplasty 29, 53

coronary artery bypass graft surgery 29, 53, 57

gastric banding 123

stomach stapling 123

sweating 41, 137

swimming 152, 153, 154, 164, 169

systemic circulation 15

# T

tai chi 153, 170

tea 111, 121

telemedicine 54

television watching 79, 134, 147, 163

tenecteplase 69

testosterone 42

tests

angiography 29, 53, 55

blood tests 52

computed tomography (CT) 19, 29, 55

echocardiogram 60

electrocardiogram (ECG) 28-29

electron beam computed tomography (EBCT) 82

electrophysiological (EPS) test 81

magnetic resonance imaging (MRI) 29

myocardial perfusion imaging (MPI) 29

radionuclide scans 29

theanine 239

thrombocytosis 20

thrombolytic drugs 38, 47, 53-54, 55-56, 69

thrombosis *see* blood clots

toxic chemicals 200-201

traffic noise 198, 199

transient ischaemic attack (TIA) 25, 30-40, 56

TrekDesk 146

trigger factors 24-25, 233-234

triglycerides 23, 30, 100-101, 105, 121

troponin 52

tryptophan 227

# V

veins 15

viral infections 19

visualisation 126, 213, 231, 233

vitamin C 21, 23, 108, 109

vitamin D 192-194

vitamin E 109, 121

# W

waist measurement 67, 81, 118, 120, 139, 201

waist-to-hip ratio (WHR) 67, 118, 120, 179

walking 65, 125, 143, 149, 152, 153, 154, 164-165, 171, 191

dog walking 169, 217

Nordic walking 153, 169

walking clubs 149, 168-169

warfarin 56

warm, keeping 187

weight gain

after quitting smoking 186

benefits of exercise 19, 34

*see also* obesity

weight, losing 116-139

crash diets 124, 126

exercise 134-135, 139, 153, 156

food diary 124, 130

goal setting 34, 90, 127, 139, 232

GP's help, enlisting 122-123

healthy eating plan 128-129

meals

savouring 132-133

scheduling 130

medication aids 122-123

motivation 119, 120

portion sizes 130, 131, 132

relaxation techniques, using 126

surgical means 123

sustaining weight loss 129, 139

top tips 125, 132

weighing yourself 138-139

willpower 129, 130

yo-yo dieting 126

white blood cells 22

whole grain foods 96, 100, 101, 128

Wii games console 237

women, and heart disease 38, 40, 41, 64, 67, 101, 107

World Health Organization 8

# X, Y, Z

Xenical 122-123

yoga 126, 170, 211

zinc deficiency 200

Zyban 181

**Reader's Digest Project Team**

**Editor** Rachel Warren Chadd

**Assistant editors** Tricia Mallett, Henrietta Heald

**Art editors** Jane McKenna, Simon Webb

**Proofreader** Ron Pankhurst

**Indexer** Marie Lorimer

**Reader's Digest General Books**

**Editorial director** Julian Browne

**Art director** Anne-Marie Bulat

**Head of book development** Sarah Bloxham

**Managing editor** Nina Hathway

**Picture resource manager** Sarah Stewart-Richardson

**Pre-press account manager** Dean Russell

**Product production manager** Claudette Bramble

**Production controller** Katherine Tibbals

**Colour origination** FMG
**Printed and bound in China**

**Conquering Heart Attack & Stroke** is published by
The Reader's Digest Association Limited,
11 Westferry Circus, Canary Wharf, London E14 4HE

Copyright © 2010 The Reader's Digest Association
Limited
Copyright © 2010 Reader's Digest Association
Far East Limited.
Philippines Copyright © 2010 Reader's Digest
Association Far East Limited
Copyright © 2010 Reader's Digest (Australia) Pty
Limited
Copyright © 2010 Reader's Digest India Pvt Limited
Copyright © 2010 Reader's Digest Asia Pvt Limited

We are committed both to the quality of our products
and the service we provide to our customers.
We value your comments, so please do contact us on
**08705 113366** or via our website at
**www.readersdigest.co.uk**

If you have any comments or suggestions about the
content of our books, email us at
**gbeditorial@readersdigest.co.uk**

ISBN 978 0 276 44546 0
Concept code UK2538/IC
Book code 400-429 UP0000-1
Oracle code 250013728H.00.24